THE NATIONAL TRUST GUIDE TO
Late Medieval and Renaissance Britain

THE NATIONAL TRUST GUIDE TO

Late Medieval and Renaissance Britain

From the Black Death to the Civil War

COLIN PLATT

George Philip/The National Trust
The National Trust for Scotland

British Library Cataloguing in Publication Data

Platt, Colin
    The National Trust guide to late medieval and
    Renaissance Britain; from the Black Death to the Civil
    War. 1. Great Britain——History——14th century 2.
    Great Britain——History——Lancaster and York,
    1399–1485 3. Great Britain——History——Tudor,
    1485–1603 4. Great Britain——History——early Stuarts,
    1603–1649. I. Title
    941   DA130

ISBN 0-540-01108-8

© Colin Platt 1986

Published by George Philip, 27A Floral Street, London
WC2E 9DP, in association with The National Trust and
The National Trust for Scotland.

Printed in Great Britain by
Butler & Tanner Ltd, Frome, Somerset

Illustration Sources and Acknowledgements

Aerofilms Ltd pp. 11, 22–3, 28, 39, 58–9, 112–13, 117, 123, 124–5, 148–9, 151, 152, 183, 184–5; J. Allan Cash pp. 20, 44, 46, 82, 84, 136–7, 155 (right), 179; John Bethell pp. 156 (below), 159 (above); J. and C. Bord pp. 66–7, 103, 111, 126, 200–1; British Tourist Authority pp. 78, 79, 89; Bruce Coleman pp. 154–5 (left), 158 (above); Committee for Aerial Photography, University of Cambridge pp. 144–5; Crown Copyright: Historic Buildings and Monuments, Scotland pp. 140, 174, 189; John Kelly p. 170; A. F. Kersting pp. 1, 2, 15, 24, 26, 34–5, 36, 38, 40, 42, 45, 48, 52–3, 56, 63, 64–5, 70, 73, 77, 90, 91, 94–5, 106, 108–9, 114, 115, 120–1, 122, 134, 135, 143, 165, 197, 204; Jorge Lewinski pp. 51, 74–5, 97, 104, 150, 166, 168; The National Trust pp. 14, 68, 81, 83, 85, 86, 87, 88, 96, 130, 133, 156 (above), 157, 158 (below), 159 (below), 160, 175, 177, 178, 182, 198, 199, 205; The National Trust for Scotland pp. 17, 153, 192–3, 194; Royal Commission on Ancient Monuments, Scotland pp. 18, 146–7, 190–1, 195; Edwin Smith pp. 8, 32, 37, 54, 72, 92–3, 98–9, 123, 128, 132, 138–9, 162, 172, 180, 186; Derek Widdicombe pp. 100, 171, 176.

Half-title illustration
LITTLE MORETON HALL (Cheshire)

Title-page illustration
IGHTHAM MOTE (Kent)

Contents

Preface

This book is what it says it is. I have taken the properties of the National Trust and of the National Trust for Scotland as my base. And I have used them to tell a story of social change: of shifting beliefs and of rising expectations, as precipitate and irreversible as our own. This is not another social and economic history of Britain. If it mentions monarchs and political events, it does so solely because they touch and illuminate my theme. That theme is the end of one way of thinking and the beginning, in architecture as in so much else, of quite another. The division between Medieval and Renaissance Britain is no artificial demarcation line, established for the convenience of historians. In buildings, at any rate, it works.

Of course, social change is never the product of a moment. Even in the eventful sixteenth century, progress could be hesitant and might, on occasion, be reversed. One reaction to Renaissance classicism was a creative nostalgia for the past, often described as 'Spenserian'. To the challenge of the Reformation in Northern Europe, the Counter-Reformation was the southerners' response. But the changes we have seen in our own times, distancing us so completely from the Victorians, were not unlike those of the so-called Ages of Discovery and of European Expansion, both occurring within the span of this book. We have walked on the Moon. They trod a New World on the shadowed side of their globe, shedding chivalry and the old religion in their passage.

I have begun with the old beliefs: with chivalry and with the faith. And I have shown how even these, in the generations touched by the catastrophes of plague, were already in their own state of flux. It is my case, argued with the help of National Trust properties among others, that the building, as an historical indicator, is as sensitive to social change as any document. Yet let us be clear from the start about objectives. If the debate is to be concerned with change in history, then the search must be for the new. It is this emphasis above all, and not in any way the description (except incidentally) of individual buildings, that has given direction to my text.

In architectural history – at least as much, let it be said, as in daily life – the temptation to drop names (in this case of buildings) may be irresistible. I have not always avoided it myself. But there has been a purpose, I would argue, in such self-indulgence. This book is intended as a springboard and guide to regions any reader might explore. The properties of the National Trust and of the National Trust for Scotland, though wide-ranging, are not comprehensive. Few churches, in particular, are held by the Trusts, and there are other gaps – though none quite as obvious – in their coverage. By all means use Trust properties, as I have done, to give structure to your travels. In almost every case, they are regularly accessible, well researched, and outstandingly intelligently displayed. Through all the travels that supported this book, I only once encountered a grumpy guardian, and that could have been just his bad day. But consider also how much else there is to be seen in the vicinity. Every name dropped in my book, except in the very few cases of buildings of which nothing remains, features again in my maps and gazetteer. Almost all these buildings are open to visitors; if private, they can often be studied from the road. No description or illustration can ever be the match, I have found, of personal experience of a monument. Do go and see what you can. And then, if the mood takes you, look it up in the index and consider how I have used the site myself.

Every book is a personal testament. The emphasis and the choice of materials are mine, as of course is the responsibility for any errors. Nevertheless, I have been assisted along the way by many friendly souls, not least by the owners and custodians of Britain's cherished monuments, to whom I offer it now as some return. The dedication is to Valerie – my love.

[1]

High Chivalry

The Black Death of 1348–9 is often seen as a turning-point. Rightly so, for its legacy of disease kept a clamp on growth for a century and more in Western Europe. Everywhere, transfers of wealth and social turmoil characterized the Late Middle Ages. Markets shrank in line with population. Rents fell and wages rose with the shortage of tenants and labour. Amongst survivors, a revolution of expectations occurred, one of its earlier manifestations being the widespread Peasants' Revolt of 1381. Yet the incidence of plague was uneven. In Ireland, the pestilence which was 'so great and hideous among the English lieges', fell less heavily on the thinly-populated Gaelic provinces. Similarly, Scotland, almost entirely rural at this date, escaped the high mortalities of the overcrowded south, which in some areas reached 50 per cent. Plague was not the only generator of change.

Another undoubtedly was nationalism. Both Ireland and Scotland, by the fifteenth century, were more than usually free of the English. With few and unimportant exceptions, the English presence in Ireland had been narrowed to the Pale – the counties in the vicinity of Dublin. Beyond this, in the native Irish lands, something of a Gaelic Renaissance occurred. Yet, as the poet sang, 'a man's inheritance will get no recognition except he has strength to fight'. And the price of self-rule was disorder. In Scotland also, the blood feud and kinship justice continued to operate as alternative laws. But they worked to better purpose in a nation which had lately discovered itself in the Wars of Independence (1297–1346), fully establishing the leadership of the Crown. Neville's

Cross, in 1346, was a Scottish defeat. Nevertheless, after that date, English armies came to Scotland only, as it were, by invitation. It was mounting Scottish self-awareness rather than English greed that provoked the remaining confrontations before the Union (1603).

Important in this new identity was the Continental role increasingly taken for granted by Scottish monarchs. The 'auld alliance' between Scotland and France originated in the Hundred Years War: that prolonged and bloody squabble between the English and French kings which had been launched already by 1337, a decade before the Black Death. The war, fought almost entirely on French soil or at sea, was a training ground for international chivalry. It promoted castle-building on both sides of the Channel and, as one magnate after another spent his working life in France, encouraged the migration of French culture. This was as true of Scotland as of England, the two aristocracies competing at home, as they had on the battlefield on opposing sides, to live up to the image of their class. In a very real sense, they needed the wars to restore (by pillage, ransom, and office under the Crown) the income they had lost on the land. They were short in numbers, eroded by mortalities in plague and battle, and always liable to a failure of heirs. After the Black Death, as never before, they feared the hostility of the mob. High Chivalry, even amongst enemies, promoted a reassuring solidarity: a community of tastes and interests that was everywhere the response of an embattled ruling class to what it recognized as assault from all quarters

LAYER MARNEY (Essex) The huge prodigy gatehouse of Henry Lord Marney's brick and terracotta mansion, left incomplete on his death in 1523, commanding fine views from its upper chambers and parapeted platforms across the Essex countryside.

Imagine an antique jigsaw puzzle of which the National Trust properties are the pieces. Many are missing, but enough remain to suggest the overall form of the picture while filling in few of its details. This is a picture, it becomes plain, of the changing aspirations of Man as reflected principally in his buildings. But because there are no distinctions of time in the picture, and because it is anyway incomplete, much will have to be done to recover its entire meaning. We may recognize the fortresses of Bodiam, Scotney, and Tattershall among others. But what is their significance in this context? How was it that such castles were ever built? How do they relate, moreover, to the churches and manor-houses, the abbeys, barns, guildhalls and cottages which are identifiable also in the puzzle?

One thing is immediately obvious. The three castles mentioned, all now cared for by the National Trust, resemble neither the great professional fortresses of a few generations earlier – known to us most familiarly in Edward I's castles in Wales – nor the artillery works that would immediately succeed them. They are residences first, castles second. While presenting a bold front to the world, their internal planning behind that facade belongs rather to the manor-house or lesser palace. In the Edwardian castles of North Wales, designed to keep a hold on conquered territory, the emphasis had once been very different. Even Caernarvon, most palatial of these, locks its accommodation gloomily behind defensive wall-passages. Yet Caernarvon was the king's residence, the birthplace of his son. Here, if it were to happen anywhere in Wales, new standards might have been expected to intrude.

Indeed, at Caernarvon and in Edward its builder we have more than one clue to what would become the common practice of later years. Caernarvon was a symbol. Its Eagle Tower, the tallest of those punctuating the walls, recalled former imperial dignity: the eagles of Rome. The decorative horizontal banding of Caernarvon's outer walls was a quotation from the defences of Constantinople. Such echoes were the meat and drink of contemporary chivalry. In addition, their political purpose was very clear. Prematurely in the event, Edward I held a 'Round Table' tournament at Nefyn in 1284 to celebrate his conquest of North Wales. In 1306, his Feast of the Swans, commemorating the knighting of his son Edward of Caernarvon, would be made the occasion for a renewed commitment on the part of his knights to the current campaign against the Scots. Chivalry, like the honours system of today, was a joke only

among those who took no part in it. To insiders, it was the very stuff of life.

By the later fourteenth century, when Scotney and Bodiam were built, the chivalric life-style had come to be understood very precisely. Artificial and pretentious in many of its particulars, it had much also to recommend it in human terms. High on the list of a nobleman's priorities was his obligation to be generous and to keep an open house. To maintain his dignity and the welcome of his table, he would have to be the unstinting employer of local labour. Riding abroad, he required to be attended by other gentlemen. All these together determined what he would need in his house. Scotney, begun on an over-ambitious scale in the late 1370s, was probably never completed. Only one of its four angle towers survives to this day, and scarcely more than the site of its hall is now known. Bodiam, on the other hand, though roofless is entire. It is, as we shall see – in defence, display, and accommodation alike – the epitome of the architecture of High Chivalry.

For our purposes, Bodiam has many advantages. It was a single period building, put up for the most part between 1386 and 1388. It was the work, furthermore, of an experienced soldier thoroughly versed in the latest military engineering as practised in its principal laboratory in contemporary France. Yet Sir Edward Dalyngrigge, by the time he built Bodiam, had retired from the wars. Although certainly intended to play its part in deterring French raids on the Sussex coast, and given sanction by the king on that understanding, Bodiam's role was primarily residential. Dalyngrigge began by determining the accommodation he needed; then wrapped it in the clothing of defence.

The result is as close a guide as we are likely to get to 'state of the art' fortress-building in the 1380s, about midway through the Hundred Years War. Like its many companion buildings in France, Bodiam combines a contemporary ideal of the life of luxury with the military posture that was still believed to be chivalry's essential justification. Thus everybody in Dalyngrigge's company was to be appropriately housed. The servants had their common hall and separate kitchen in the west range of the central court. In the northwest corner, the

BODIAM CASTLE (East Sussex) The most perfect and unspoilt of the Hundred Years War castles, built in the late 1380s by a retired soldier, Sir Edward Dalyngrigge, as a contribution to the defence of the south coast.

garrison was placed next to the great gate. On the far side from the gate, where traditionally any courtyard mansion would have placed them, were the hall, its service rooms (buttery and pantry) and kitchen. To the east, with private access to the hall on the south and the chapel on the north, were the personal chambers of Dalyngrigge himself and of his wife, Elizabeth, the Wardeux heiress who had brought him the lands of Bodiam on their marriage.

Dalyngrigge's household was a large one. At one time or another, it would have included many gentlemen of standing, whether as clients of the old knight, as estate officials, or as guests. In providing for their housing, Bodiam reveals what is perhaps the most characteristic innovation of the late medieval lordly residence, the addition of separate suites for the gentlemen of the affinity, individually heated and provided with private lavatories, like modern lodgings or a studio flat. At Bodiam, these lodgings were packed, one on top of the other, into the gatehouses and mural towers of Dalyngrigge's fortress. In the country mansions of the time, among them the Archbishop of Canterbury's rural palace at Knole, another major property of the National Trust, they would have been found space in the ranges of the courts. What is certain is that they would always have been present in some form.

Having put together the ingredients of an appropriate life-style, in the close company of his family and his friends, Sir Edward Dalyngrigge had next to meet the obligations of defence. Once again Bodiam is entirely typical of its period. It is surrounded, as were many of the French fortresses on which Dalyngrigge modelled his own, by a broad water-filled moat, serving the double purpose of making access difficult while reflecting and exaggerating the castle's strength. As in France, defence is concentrated on the fighting platforms of the towers and along the tops of the walls. With effective siege artillery still barely known, there is no attempt at Bodiam to lower the profile of the castle, the emphasis being rather on its height. All this was deliberate and was common enough at most major defensive buildings of the period. Where Dalyngrigge displayed his expertise at Bodiam was in the systematic protection of its main entrance. Facing north towards the rising land on the castle's most vulnerable quarter, Bodiam's gate could be approached only along the length of a dog-legged causeway overseen by the great gatehouse and northwest tower. There was a barbican and three drawbridges; there were gunports, in the latest fashion, commanding the

third drawbridge; behind them, three gates and three portcullises closed off the gate passage, which had murder-holes pierced in its vault.

Picturesque though it is, beloved by photographers and unfailingly successful with school parties, Bodiam is not thus just another textbook castle. It represents little further development on the defensive capability of an Edwardian castle, and indeed can be seen as a retreat. Yet as a document of its times, Bodiam is without peer. In its bulk and ostentation, in its comforts and in its bold display of coats of arms, Bodiam makes a statement about contemporary values fully in accord with everything we know about its period. Sir Edward Dalyngrigge had fought in France under Sir Robert Knollys, one of the most successful of the English war captains of his day. Like Knollys, to whom he paid personal tribute in the heraldic bearings over the south gate at Bodiam, Dalyngrigge had made a fortune in booty and in ransoms. He spent it on the kind of building that would help establish his social rank, just as Roger Ashburnham built Scotney not very far to the north, as John Lord Cobham put up Cooling (the precise contemporary of Bodiam), as Richard le Scrope built Bolton, John de la Mare Nunney, Richard Abberbury Donnington, or John Lord Lovel his extraordinary French-influenced polygonal tower-house at Old Wardour. These buildings, still the most ostentatious reminder of a lengthy war conducted almost exclusively on French soil, are as individual as the suburban villas of a modern 'millionaires' row', and they say much the same thing (even to the progressive elaboration of security devices) about their builders.

But why should men like Dalyngrigge have taken up this position? And what was it overall that they wanted? Certainly, these were not especially easy times for noblemen, or for landowners anywhere as a class. The Black Death of 1348–9, although not the watershed it was once thought to be universally by social historians, had begun a long process of attrition for the employer as labour became less available and more expensive. Judgements differ about when the crisis was fully recognized by most landowners. However, it is clear that the plague, once come to Britain, was there to stay. The soft times of high farm prices and cheap labour were recognizably on the way out by the 1370s when the monks of Westminster, never the quickest to sense a change in the wind, began the systematic leasing of their estates. Just a decade later, they were to be joined by their rich brethren at Christ Church, Canterbury, reversing the long tradition of home farming on their manors in which only lately they had been conspicuously successful.

In charting such changes, historians are accustomed to use the monastic evidence for the very good reason that the monks kept better accounts than their lay neighbours. But the problems were identical on all estates. Under especially good management, the trend could be reversed, as it was indeed for the monks of Canterbury under the direction of their remarkable Prior Chillenden (1390–1411). Nevertheless, the most common experience was of declining land revenues at just that time when, as the accommodation at Bodiam has shown, standards of personal comfort were on the ascent. What took men like Sir Edward Dalyngrigge to campaign in France was the opportunity it gave them to recover their fortunes, practising the skills they knew best. In addition they might marry money – and Dalyngrigge took that path also – or they could look for a reward in the royal service. What was denied to them was an adequate return on their estates.

Not unnaturally, these men's residences reflected their former interests. Bodiam, certainly, is a veteran's toy, and so (although we know less of the circumstances of its building) must be Roger Ashburnham's water-girt fortress at Scotney, hidden away on the floor of a steep-sided valley, out of sight and out of mind of the French. But there were good reasons too, in this generation more than most, for keeping private property secure. Heavy plague mortalities, the common lot of both peasant and townsman since the onset of the Black Death in the mid century, had given labour for the first time a scarcity value, inducing a revolution of expectations. Employers and landlords fought back as best they could. They imposed wage controls and used the political muscle given them by their wealth to throttle the demands of the poor. Nevertheless in 1381, in an explosion of resentment also seen on the Continent but which seems to have passed Scotland by, the peasants rose in revolt. Joined and often led by discontented townsmen, they murdered their oppressors. They burnt castles, manor-houses and churches, experiencing for the first time the adrenalin of common action, and savouring the bile of revenge.

Within a short space of time, the authorities had regained control. But the Peasants' Revolt of 1381, like the Black Death itself, was no more than an opening salvo. In the towns, from this time forward, riots and other civil disturbances commonly accompanied the more provocative public occasions such as mayor-makings. In the country-side, few large estates escaped rent strikes, incendiarism and deliberate dilapidations, or could keep a labour force intact against its will. Social divisions, far from being eased by the more general distribution of wealth, were driven deeper. The privileged world of the aristocracy, more introverted by the day, floated off ever further on its own. Behind it the gentry, with their tenants at their heels, had to struggle still harder to climb aboard.

Some of the consequences of the aristocracy's increasing isolation are clear in the buildings of the Late Middle Ages. A magnate and great aristocrat like Thomas Beauchamp, Earl of Warwick, hero of English victories at Crecy and at Poitiers and veteran campaigner in France, inevitably felt the pressure to remodel his own castle in the current French fashion, furnishing it with a spectacular new entrance front. Here, one of the great towers was to be called 'Caesar's Tower', the other 'Guy's Tower' after Guy of Warwick, legendary local hero of chivalry. And there would be closely comparable works of very much the same date at the Douglas fortresses at Bothwell and Tantallon, meeting the needs of Scottish magnates who, in a different cause, had fought on the French side in the same battles. But skip a century or so and the identical motivation stands revealed again in the bristling north facade of the National Trust's Compton Castle, a chivalric re-clothing of John Gilbert's domestic manor-house, scarcely earlier in date than the 1520s. In between lies a whole galaxy of pseudo fortresses.

Prominent among them is Tattershall Castle, in the flat lands of southern Lincolnshire, the imposing brick tower-house of Ralph Lord Cromwell, a former companion-at-arms of Henry V and subsequently Treasurer of England. Like Bodiam, Tattershall owes its present excellent state of preservation to Lord Curzon, statesman, scholar and amateur architect, who subsequently bequeathed both buildings to the National Trust. But Tattershall is a fragment, albeit a significant one. It has lost most of the elements of the complex defences that once protected its approaches, as at Bodiam. What remains is the bulk of Ralph Cromwell's huge tower, illustrating as does no other English building of comparable date the importance in chivalric symbolism of great height.

Of course, flat country is natural territory for tower-builders. Just to the southwest of Tattershall, Sir Gilbert de Umfravilles' four-storeyed tower-house at South Kyme is half a century earlier in date. To the southeast is the astonishing

COMPTON CASTLE (Devon) John Gilbert's show-front of *c.* 1520 is the fiercely military facade of an otherwise lightly defended manor-house.

upward-pointed finger of Boston's 'Stump', one of the great prodigy towers of the Late Middle Ages. In such company and at this time, Ralph Cromwell's tower could well be dismissed as a pardonable local extravagance. But a larger context is needed for it than southern Lincolnshire. Cromwell himself built another 'High Tower', very differently situated, at his manor-house at South Wingfield, in Derbyshire. Moreover, Tattershall's true parallels are not at home. The tower is of brick, a newly fashionable material for which English travellers had acquired a taste recently in Flanders. In other respects, the form of the tower is very French. As on the one surviving angle tower at Scotney, much decorative play is made at Tattershall with the prominent overhang of machicolations at the wall-head. They support a fighting gallery, continuous at wall-head level, which had come to be a characteristic of French defensive systems as developed at castle-palaces like Pierrefonds.

Tattershall was built in the 1430s and 1440s, at just that time when Ralph Cromwell for a full decade was Treasurer of England (1433–43), enjoying the profits of high office. He recorded the fact by using the purse of the Treasurer as a decorative motif, and he clearly derived, as anybody would, a good deal of satisfaction from his success. In his case, again not exceptionally, this satisfaction required to be expressed in lavish building. And if we take Cromwell's tower as a guide to the scale of the remainder of his castle, Tattershall must indeed have been spectacular.

The ostentation was well calculated and quite deliberate. Ralph Cromwell, as the third Baron Cromwell of his line, did not need to make the difficult first ascent into the aristocracy. Certainly, he was not as sensitive in this regard as Richard

TATTERSHALL CASTLE (Lincolnshire) The great brick tower at Tattershall housed the personal quarters of Ralph Lord Cromwell (d.1456), a former Treasurer of England; under the battlements, the machicolated fighting gallery is of French inspiration, as were many other details of English castle architecture following the campaigns of the Hundred Years War.

Lord Scrope, an earlier Treasurer and son of a chief justice, who had built his great fortress at Bolton in North Yorkshire at least in part to compensate for what were recognizably non-noble origins. Yet there is no limit to the ambition of the successful. While living, Tattershall would continue to publish Cromwell's rank; after death, it would serve as his memorial. Either way, the castle put his fortune to good purpose.

It was a purpose little served by false modesty. The tower-house at Tattershall, although already larger than most manor-houses of its period, housed the private lodgings of the Treasurer himself in much the same way as the east range at Bodiam was exclusive to Sir Edward Dalyngrigge and his lady. Over a vaulted basement, there were four great chambers, each of them occupying an entire level. On the ground floor was the parlour, with a hall on the first floor and audience chamber above it, the whole surmounted by the Treasurer's personal bedchamber at third-floor level, below the flat fighting platform of the roof. The tower was an addition to existing buildings, no doubt modified by Lord Cromwell but already including a great hall of some kind, nothing of which now survives above ground. Adjoining the hall and encircling the inner court would have been the lodgings, now gone, of Cromwell's household – of the great company of armed gentlemen that a man of his rank could scarcely have afforded to be without.

Almost everything about Tattershall is significant. Of the collegiate church and bedehouse, completed by Cromwell's executors long after his death, there will be more to say in the next chapter. At the castle itself, the tower is rather an emblem of chivalry than a tower-house of the conventional kind. Yet in its fashionable new brickwork, its insistent heraldry and highly individual internal planning, Tattershall opens a window on the past. At South Wingfield, the Treasurer's Derbyshire manor, the planning by comparison was routine. Wingfield, simultaneously under construction in the 1440s, was laid out conventionally as a double courtyard mansion, with few of the French echoes of the great *donjon* (tower keep) at Tattershall and little to distinguish it from contemporary country mansions like Ralph Boteler's Sudeley, the work of Cromwell's successor at the Treasury.

Yet Wingfield, as we have seen, and Sudeley also, were each to have strong towers of their own. And it is the tower especially, descendant of the *bergfried*, or fighting-tower, of the castle's remote Germanic origins, that remains the *leitmotif* of the architecture of chivalry. By the mid fifteenth century, at major English country houses like Wingfield, Sudeley or Archbishop Bourchier's Knole, the tower was less a defensive device than a strong-box for the goods of a rich and nervous owner. Topped by flags, it made a point of some importance about status. Lacking a tower, a great house of the period would undoubtedly have appeared incomplete. But we would certainly make less of the tower's significance in English domestic architecture of the Late Middle Ages were we not acquainted with its cousins in northern Britain. There the tower was to swallow up the house.

One of the earliest complete tower-houses to have survived intact in Britain is the National Trust for Scotland's Tower of Drum. Opinions differ on the date of Drum Castle. The tower could be as early as 1286 or as late as the mid 1320s. Nevertheless, there is a rugged simplicity and lack of refinement about Drum which mark it out, however the argument may be resolved, as a pioneering building of its class. Drum is a great rectangular stone tower, rounded at the angles, originally divided horizontally by three vaults. Over a vaulted basement kitchen with no access from outside, there was a big common hall (now the library) at entrance level. A newel stair linked the common hall with the next unit in the tower, being a third vaulted space (incorporating two stages) under the fighting-platform of the roof. It was below this third vault that the laird had his apartments, with bedchamber above and private hall, floored over, underneath.

There was nothing original about the internal arrangements of the Great Tower of Drum. The three-part division between kitchen at base, common hall at centre, and private apartments above had been familiar since the beginning of tower-keeps right back in the twelfth century and perhaps earlier. It was a practical separation that continued to work adequately until the final dying-out of the tower-house tradition in such extravaganzas as the early seventeenth-century Craigievar. But convenient and economical though the tower-house might be, well-suited to a society of minor noblemen and lairds, it was seldom these qualities on their own that recommended it. From Drum at one end of the Scottish tradition to Craigievar or Castle Fraser at the other, the merit of the tower was what it said so unequivocally about its owner. At each of these castles, now jewels in the crown of the National Trust for Scotland, a man had stood up to be counted.

Tower-houses are spread thickly through Scotland and northern England. In Ireland, again, they

DRUM CASTLE (Grampian) The Tower of Drum (*c.* 1300) is one of Scotland's earliest tower-houses, dominating the adjoining Jacobean mansion; the great hall (entered at first-floor level) had two further stages of chambers above, with a basement kitchen (having no external access) below.

are the characteristic castle of the Late Middle Ages. Many of them, of course, were very simple in plan, being the vertical equivalent (in kitchen, hall and chamber) of the horizontal undefended manor-house of the same period. Towers like these answered the needs of the laird of moderate means who had only his immediate family and household servants to protect. As such, they were widely (and deservedly) popular with the gentry, with pro-minent churchmen and even with the more prosperous burgesses of the threatened regions, and we shall be returning to them again in due course. For the magnate, rating a brave show above defence, the tower never lost its attraction. Thus the highly professional Edwardian gatehouse of Thomas of Lancaster's Northumbrian fortress at Dunstanburgh was to be converted in the 1380s, within two generations of its first building, into a tower-house for John of Gaunt and his suite. A new lesser gate (barbican protected) was built to the west; the former gatehouse, its entrance passage walled off, became the spacious tower-keep of a small private courtyard, or bawn.

At Dunstanburgh, a great though incomplete fortress of the finest early fourteenth-century tradition was to take on fresh life before the end of the same century as a tower-house. And there were to be parallel developments at other castles of the North, similarly exposed to the new fashions. Dirleton, just east of Edinburgh, and Bothwell, south of Glasgow, were both sophisticated fortresses of the later thirteenth century. The long peace of the Alexanders had brought prosperity to the Lowlands, and Scottish castles such as these were no less cleverly engineered than their contemporaries south of the Border. What happened in later years was again closely comparable. Damaged but not destroyed in the Wars of Independence, both castles were rebuilt by subsequent generations in a style that was primarily residential. The Halyburton range at Dirleton, squared off at the angles like any country house, sat astride and ignored the foundations of the drum towers which had characterized the castle of the de Vaux. At Bothwell again, the Douglas refurbishing of Walter of Moravia's pioneering French-style fortress neglected the great bulk of the defensive refinements which had made it so

DOUNE CASTLE (Central) Albany's high office as Regent of Scotland required pomp and display to support his position; at Doune, two great tower-houses are linked by a large common hall, and further accommodation was intended in the walled court before Albany's death in 1420 brought the extension of the castle to a halt.

remarkable in its day. Merely patching Walter's circular keep and abandoning the kite-shaped courtyard he had projected, the Douglas earls spent their money instead on a scaled-down rectangular enclosure, equipping it, however, with a big first-floor hall, with an impressive chapel and with an adjoining range of lodgings, protected by massive towers on the east. The work was expensive and the towers, only one of which survives to full height, were fearsomely machicolated at parapet level. But whereas the earlier castle had put security first, the later gave priority to display. A major change of attitudes had occurred.

Dirleton and Bothwell are both remodellings. While providing useful evidence of the introduction of new priorities, they may be less certain guides to contemporary taste than single-date castles of the same period. Bodiam was just such a castle in the South. In Scotland, Bodiam's equivalents include Threave and Tantallon, Hermitage and Doune. Of these, the first three, like Bothwell, were Douglas castles. The fourth, scarcely altered in its arrangements since the late fourteenth century, was the work of Robert Stewart, the Regent Albany.

Each of these castles is very different. Both Threave and Hermitage were large tower-houses. Tantallon was a major headland fortress protected by a lofty towered curtain. Doune, double-towered, was a more conventional castle with a walled court. Yet all share that characteristic most recognizably of their time: an overwhelming emphasis on undisguised bulk, the better to impress and to dismay. Threave, in about 1450 shortly before it was besieged, was refortified for artillery, being equipped at that time with a low pierced curtain and circular gun towers. In 1455, when James II determined to break the Douglas power, he used a great siege gun (a 'bombard') in Threave's reduction. But the truth about these castles, when originally devised in the late fourteenth century, is that their builders were well aware of the little they had to fear from artillery. Even much later, James II's huge bombard was a public instrument of terror, hardly more. The king was fond of gunnery and would plan a castle for his queen, at Ravenscraig opposite Edinburgh on the Firth of Forth, that was remarkably innovative, being among the first purpose-built artillery fortresses of the North. But enthusiasm ran ahead of the gun's effectiveness. For a long time yet, men could still feel safe in building high.

Following existing precedents like the Great Tower of Drum, by far the most economical method of achieving such an effect was to stack the essential elements of lordly accommodation in a single pile. Thus the Douglas tower at Threave, built by Archibald 'the Grim' in the 1370s and 1380s, began at ground level with a huge vaulted space, itself divided horizontally into kitchen above, cellarage and prison below, and lit only by the narrowest of defensive loops. Over these, a great hall ran the full length of the building, with fine windows at this level overlooking the River Dee, with a big fireplace and corridor-like latrine in the wall thickness. Next above again were the two principal bedchambers, sharing a garderobe but each with its own fireplace and handsome windows. On the top floor, a large undivided multi-windowed space was probably intended to double as quarters, in time of siege, of the castle's garrison.

More sophisticated internally, and these days very difficult to unpick, was that other near contemporary Douglas tower-house at Hermitage, in Liddesdale immediately north of the Border. Hermitage was a former English fortified manor-house, almost entirely rebuilt by the Douglas earls at the turn of the fourteenth and fifteenth centuries. The Douglases re-used little except the walls of the original building's central courtyard, retaining them at the core of the big rectangular tower which was itself the first element of their reconstruction. Next they built corner-towers against the rectangle, the last of these (on the southwest) being much bigger than the others, better described as a wing. Today, the unusual flying arches joining the corner-towers on Hermitage's east and west fronts can make the castle appear, from these quarters especially, a single gigantic almost featureless block, bleakly exposed on the moor. Yet within Hermitage are all the features of a great nobleman's dwelling: the kitchen and associated serving rooms, the earl's hall and chambers, and the numerous independent lodgings of his suite.

One of the closer parallels to Hermitage, even to the flying arches which link its towers, is the great Irish tower-house at Bunratty (Co. Clare), built in the mid fifteenth century by the McNamara chiefs of the Clan of Cullein and later improved by the earls of Thomond. At Blarney (Co. Cork), the MacCarthys' huge tower, contemporary with Bunratty and as sophisticated internally, was similarly to become the home of an earl. However, a tower-house of any kind, even on the scale of Threave or Hermitage, Blarney or Bunratty, could only rarely have lived up to the accommodation needs of a magnate of the social standing of an earl. In practice, what more usually resulted was a

clustering of tower-houses, whether linked, as at Doune, by a big domestic range, or joined by a defensive curtain as at the Douglases' Tantallon or at Cahir, the great fortress of the earls of Ormond in Tipperary.

The visual effect of such clustering is intensely and appropriately dramatic. Cahir, round the block of its surviving Norman keep, groups a series of late medieval residential tower-houses to create the characteristic profile of a fortress of chivalry. At Tantallon, the line-up of central gatehouse and flanking corner-towers recalls the same arrangement on the Beauchamp show-front at Warwick, and both clearly aim to dazzle the beholder by the sheer bulk of what they bring together in one place. High chivalry, in dramatic building works of just this kind, has never been better illustrated than at such castles, nor has the contrast with what came later been made more clearly. During the sixteenth century, the refortification of Tantallon for artillery included the construction of a new gun-carrying forework against the lofty central gate-tower. Later, a low-profile triangular ravelin was to be laid down well in advance of Tantallon's fourteenth-century inner curtain as further reinforcement of the castle's existing outer moat. Gunners, before the end of the century, had learnt to recognize the advantages of the cushioning earthwork and of the defensive system which hugged, rather than rejected, the ground. Priorities in fortress-building had been reversed.

Tantallon's entrance front is the castle's sole major survival. While preserving a fine pit-prison in the southwest tower under six storeys of former single lodgings, Tantallon otherwise largely lacks that domestic accommodation which remains such a feature, for example, of Doune, a magnate fortress of comparable date. Doune today, although certainly over-restored in the 1880s, is still substantially as it was left in 1420 on the death of its builder, Robert Stewart, Duke of Albany. Militarily unsophisticated even by the undemanding standards of its time, Doune's main elements were its two tower-houses linked by a range which, at first-floor level, accommodated the castle's common hall. To the south, a modest courtyard was enclosed by a tall angled curtain, commanded along its length by bartisans. The greater of the

towers, holding the duke's private lodgings, doubled throughout its life as a gatehouse.

To the military engineers of Edwardian Britain, Walter of Hereford or James of St George, Doune's plan would have seemed lamentably inadequate. Yet in its own day, there was much to recommend it. Robert Stewart, even before his long regency during the captivity of James I, was a man of great influence in the kingdom. From 1373 he had been governor of the royal fortress at Stirling, just down the road from Doune. He was a notable commander, the leader of successful raids into England, and he could call up powerful forces at will. Doune, accordingly, was less in need of sophisticated defences than a Welsh castle of the Edwardian conquest period or its equivalent Scottish fortress of the Wars of Independence after 1297, when military engineering had indeed attained its peak. Doune's fortifications, while not without purpose in such restless times, were nevertheless largely for show.

Within the castle, there were other characteristic elements of display. Doune had two halls: the vaulted lord's hall at first-floor level over the gate passage of Albany's tower, and the still grander retainers' hall, a third again as long, open to the rafters of the roof. Although adjoining each other, the halls were not linked, and other precautions had clearly been taken to separate the lord's quarters from the rest. Controlling the entrance passage, Albany could block off his apartments in the northeast tower if threatened at any time by a riot among his servants or his guests. More important, he might enjoy the same privacy, rare enough in his day in the turmoil of castle life, as did a wealthy knight like Dalyngrigge at Bodiam. Albany was a nobleman who swapped stories with princes, the first ever in his native Scotland to be created duke. His quarters had appropriate touches of magnificence. At the high-table end of his hall, the unusual double fireplace may be Albany's own version of the huge triple chimney-piece of Jean de Berri's hall at Poitiers, the principal state apartment of a French royal duke, soon to be repeated at the palace of Linlithgow. Above the hall, a fine solar had an oratory, or small chapel, against its south wall, and there were well-lit bedchambers at the next level under the roof, supplementing the private chambers in the big northeast turret, the whole equipped with garderobes in the wall thickness.

With its separate hall, its spacious solar, its bedchambers, its control of the gate passage and its well exclusive to the lord, Albany's tower-house, as an individual unit, was complete. Nevertheless a

BUNRATTY CASTLE (Co. Clare) A major tower-house built in the mid fifteenth century for the Gaelic McNamara chiefs and modified internally a century later for the Anglicized earls of Thomond.

magnate of Albany's quality was expected to keep a large company, and it is in the duke's provision for his retainers and his more important guests at Doune that the internal arrangements of his castle tell us most. To the southwest of the common hall, joined to it by a vestibule of irregular plan, was Doune's vaulted kitchen, its equipment including a large arched fireplace, big serving hatches, a slop-drain, and ample provision of wall-cupboards. Then over the kitchen, warmed by its huge chimney, was a guest suite made up of solar, or 'presence chamber', and two bedrooms. It was here that successive queens of Scotland are thought to have lodged when Doune Castle came their way as a dower house.

Substantial windows still preserved in the south curtain wall suggest that another range of lodgings was intended (though perhaps never built) on this quarter. However, even without such an addition, what Doune in its present state allows us to examine is a representative private fortress of the later Middle Ages, commissioned and built within a short space of years to meet a variety of identifiable needs. Certainly, Albany required his new castle to make a brave show, and so indeed it still does to this day. But his rank asked more of him. Behind the aggressive facade of a castle like Doune had to be that other essential prop of the chivalric life-style: full equipment for the practice of conspicuous hospitality and for an unstinting display of largesse.

Most important in this equipment was the great common hall, of which Knole alone, among National Trust properties, preserves a major specimen, dating back to the first building period under Archbishop Bourchier (d.1486). Here the hall, even so, was largely rebuilt during Sackville's modernization of Knole in 1603–8. It acquired a ceiling at the time, a full set of panelling, and a fabulous oak screen, to emerge from this remodelling as a domestic apartment with little hint of the stark and lofty dignity of its predecessor. Yet the life of Knole's great company, in Bourchier's day, had centred on the hall, as had been the case at other late medieval castles and fortified manor-houses like Bodiam and Scotney, Tattershall,

KNOLE (Kent) Begun by Archbishop Thomas Bourchier of Canterbury (1454–86), whose contribution included the inner Stone Court (centre). Henry VIII, in the 1540s, added the larger Green Court (front) for additional household lodgings. The Dutch gables, together with much high-quality interior work, date to a remodelling of 1603–8 for Thomas Sackville, Earl of Dorset.

Dunster and Croft, Grey's Court, Boarstall and Oxburgh, each of them now held by the Trust. To understand these buildings, we shall have to look elsewhere for our models.

In point of fact, there are abundant halls of chivalry to choose from, and here again the emphasis, significant in such a context, was to be on height at least as much as on floor area. Consider, for example, the hall at Minster Lovell, built in the 1430s for William Lord Lovell as the centre-piece of his fine new Oxfordshire mansion next to the parish church. It is short but disproportionately high. Lovell had returned, like Dalyngrigge of Bodiam and Cromwell of Tattershall, from the wars in France, and his work at Minster Lovell can reasonably be expected to have been as up-to-date as any of his period. Fashions in chivalry, though, were slow in changing. Almost a century earlier, Sir John de Pulteney's great hall at Penshurst, much grander in every way, had been remarkable already for its height. Pulteney was a wealthy draper, four times mayor of London. Like others of his kind, he aspired to the nobility to which he believed success entitled him, and he would have known very precisely what he wanted. In plan, Pulteney's custom-built manor-house at Penshurst was traditional. Put up in the 1340s during the last decade of the financier's life, it had the familiar private chamber over undercroft at one end of the building, with kitchen and associated service rooms at the other. What was exceptional was the hall in the middle. Rising 18 metres (60 feet) into the roof, Penshurst's hall was very nearly as high as it was long. Such height, of course, had no practical function, its purpose being merely display. Just before the Black Death, in the deep country at Penshurst, an expensive new manor-house had been used by a rich Londoner to make a point about his ability, his good fortune, and his rank. Very similar was to be the message of many individual castles of chivalry, the accolades of superannuated war captains.

Sir John de Pulteney, who died in 1349, is believed to have been a victim of the plague. And it might perhaps be thought that the long-term recession experienced on many great estates after the Black Death would have prevented further building on that scale. In point of fact, the driving

PENSHURST PLACE (Kent) The great hall at Penshurst, one of the loftiest of its kind, built in the 1340s for Sir John de Pulteney, a wealthy Londoner with ambitions to penetrate the aristocracy.

force of chivalry continued to be such that in halls, as in towers, each extravagance inspired another to surpass it. Many took their cue from the king. Edward III's Windsor, at which a major remodelling began in 1350 within a few months of the retreat of the Black Death, became over the next two decades one of the greatest fortresses of contemporary Europe. With its Garter associations, its grand collegiate church, its deliberately heightened central tower and mighty Hall of St George, Windsor (when complete) was to be every bit the equal of the ambitious Valois castle-palace, formerly a hunting-lodge, at Vincennes near Paris. It would itself provide the model for a rebuilding, among others, of the royal castle at Edinburgh, on which work had begun already by the 1360s.

Nothing above foundation level is left of David II's Edinburgh, and precious little of Edward III's Windsor is visible through the over-zealous restorations of later years. Nevertheless, it is easy to appreciate, on grounds of scale alone, the impact of such programmes on contemporaries. Richard II's reconstruction of Westminster Hall, to be furnished with a fine roof that remains to this day the greatest glory of late medieval English carpentry, was only the grandest of many such enterprises. At Dartington, John de Holand's impressive hall was closely modelled on the Westminster works of Richard II, his royal patron. John of Gaunt, Richard's uncle, likewise spared nothing in a lavish reconstruction of the existing hall at Kenilworth, his great castle in the Midlands. As transformed by the Duke of Lancaster, son of one king and father of another, Kenilworth became as much a fortress in the grand chivalric manner as the Beauchamps' Warwick, just down the road, or as those mighty French exemplars of English castles of their kind: the great ducal fortresses of Jean de Berri at Mehun-sur-Yèvre, or of Louis d'Orléans at Pierrefonds.

John of Gaunt's hall at Kenilworth had all the trappings appropriate to ducal rank and to the quality of Gaunt's household and affinity. Set imposingly over a low vaulted undercroft, it was originally equipped with a noble porch approached up a wide flight of steps. At the other end of the hall, the high table was lit by a big polygonal oriel. Fine stone panelling survives on the window jambs, and there are remains of expensive moulding on the opposing fireplaces, centrally placed in the side walls of the apartment. In the 1380s, to which the hall at Kenilworth belongs, equipment of this kind had become standard form, so that we shall see it repeated, in descending degrees of quality and opulence, right down into the manor-houses of the lesser gentry.

Amongst the magnate classes, display at such a level was obligatory. Take, for example, the great fifteenth-century chivalric hall of the earls of Desmond at Askeaton, their principal seat and fortress in County Limerick. Of course, the earls had their own fine tower-house on the adjacent castle mound, reserved for their immediate family and close friends. Nevertheless, it was at Askeaton's hall, in the court below, that the Desmond affinity would have gathered on all major occasions. Appropriately, the hall was of large size, placed over an earlier vaulted undercroft and approached, as at Kenilworth, by an imposing stair. There were fine big windows, especially grand at the high-table end of the hall, where there was good-quality blind arcading, behind the principal diners, on the south wall. Askeaton's tall gables, still the most obvious and memorable feature of the building, must have supported a timbered roof of suitable magnificence.

Certainly, for those of the rank of duke, count or earl – John of Gaunt at Kenilworth, the Beauchamp earls at Warwick, the Desmonds at Askeaton – the building of a large hall and the hospitality it implied were inescapable obligations of their position. A king could hardly have settled for less. At the Scottish royal palace of Linlithgow, so little has changed since the fifteenth century that we can now see exactly what this meant. Linlithgow today is geometric and severe; seen from the air, it looks as if it has been put together out of children's building blocks, too precise in its alignments to be authentic. Yet when laid down by James I in 1425, and then pressed forward with exceptional vigour over the next decade, Linlithgow was a royal palace in the very latest mode, as closely matched to the individual needs of James I and of his young English queen as had been Pulteney's Penshurst, Dalyngrigge's Bodiam, or the late Regent Albany's Doune.

James I, who had returned to Scotland only the previous year, had spent almost the whole of his youth in captivity. He had been imprisoned in England (at Windsor among other places) and,

DARTINGTON HALL (Devon) Though subject to considerable later rebuilding, John de Holand's great house of the late fourteenth century has kept its grand tower-porch, with great hall (right) and kitchen (left), together with a long terrace of retainers' lodgings of which the southernmost unit shows on the extreme right of the photograph.

while still in his impressionable twenties, had been to France with Henry V during the English king's final victorious campaigns. His recent bride, Jane Beaufort, daughter of the Earl of Somerset, had been brought up similarly in a court society that ranked among the most cultivated of its day. Both James and his queen took a deep and informed interest in Linlithgow. Indeed, the palace was to become Queen Jane's favourite residence, purpose-built for the life-style formerly known to her at Windsor, where she and her future husband had first met.

Not all Linlithgow, as we see it now, is of James I's original building period. The south range (completing the quadrangle) is an addition of the late fifteenth century. It holds a big hall, probably intended as a guardroom, together with the splendid palace chapel, both the work of that great builder, James IV. The north range, also, is a much later rebuilding, following an early seventeenth-century collapse. It would have contained the queen's personal quarters, separated from the king's bedchamber by a shared oratory of which the fine fifteenth-century oriel, projecting on the north front, is still intact. All the main apartments of the palace were on the first floor, a true *piano nobile* in the Italian manner, over stores and huge wine-cellars at basement level, out of reach of the pervasive rising damp. They included a big royal suite in the west range, with James I's bedchamber to the north, a generous personal hall to the south, and a smaller business room (or presence chamber) in between.

To the east, taking up the better part of the range, was the great common hall, undoubtedly the show-piece of James I's new palace. Sited over what was then the main gate of the palace, the hall was distinguished externally by big ornamental panels: royal heraldry facing outwards where it might greet all arrivals, a composition symbolizing the division of society into Three Estates towards the courtyard. Called the 'Lyon Chamber' and certainly among the major such gathering-places of fifteenth-century chivalry, Linlithgow's hall carried originally, like Westminster or Dartington, a big hammerbeam roof, with a stone vault – a sort of 'canopy of honour' – over the king's table and its adjoining end-wall chimney-piece. As at Doune,

LINLITHGOW PALACE (Lothian) A rare example of a complete late medieval palace which, despite later rebuildings, still has the courtyard plan established by James I in 1425; the great hall is the long apartment at first-floor level in the east range (nearest the camera).

albeit on a much grander scale, the big triple fireplace of the hall at Linlithgow was made a deliberate feature of the apartment. Another such was the large window next to the high table, lighting and (like the vault above) helping to distinguish an area of royal private space.

Linlithgow's hall is already grand enough. It can stand comparison with Edward IV's great hall at Eltham Palace, built some forty years later in the 1470s, and was both bigger and better fitted than the equivalent apartments at the majority of the great houses of its day. Characteristically, though, neither Linlithgow nor its hall were to match up to the ambitions of James IV. True, James added to his palace at Linlithgow, where he was responsible, as we have seen, for the south range. But it was for Stirling Castle, more securely placed on its great rocky eminence, that James IV reserved his major effort. What he built there was truly extraordinary.

Unlike his great-grandfather, James IV spent little time away from his own kingdom. His taste, in consequence, might well have had cause to be more conservative than that of James I. Certainly, the old-fashioned inner facade of the south range at Linlithgow might suggest as much, while the pleasure James obtained from the ceremonial of chivalry, in particular from the increasingly out-moded tournament, could again imply a similarly backward-looking temperament. Yet such an emphasis would surely be misleading. The Renaissance, introduced for the first time whole-heartedly to Scotland by James V in the later 1530s, and received there with such instant and uncritical enthusiasm, was still remote in Northern Europe in 1500, when James IV was actively engaged in rebuilding the Upper Square of his palace at Stirling. Nor was James – patron of learning, musician, astrologer, surgeon, artilleryman, and correspondent of princes – much behind the times in other ways. It was not that James IV deliberately rejected the Renaissance, but that he had little reason, in his own generation, to make much of it. His great hall at Stirling, the sole surviving element of his Upper Square, while undoubtedly last among the products of a long tradition, belonged to what was still a living, even flourishing, culture.

James IV saw himself (and was seen) as a patron of chivalry, characteristically prone to invite the favours of fair and noble ladies, and by temperament something of a knight errant. It was said of James at the time that he had a working knowledge of all the major European languages. But whether or not this was the case, the Scottish king assuredly spoke the language of international chivalry, counting the kings of England, of France, and of Denmark among his friends, and negotiating on equal terms with both the Pope and the Holy Roman Emperor. Attracting noblemen of similar chivalric tastes to his court, and the frequent host there of glittering foreign envoys, James IV inevitably felt the need for a great common hall: a concourse for state occasions of every kind.

Stirling's hall, on the scale on which James IV required it, was to have few uses for later generations. Subsequently broken up and subdivided, the hall lost many of its original features, including the grand hammerbeam roof that once added dignity to its huge space. Nevertheless, what is left of the hall is still impressive. It had five great fireplaces, one on the south wall behind the high table, the others in facing pairs along the hall's length. Lighting the king's end were two full-height bays to east and west. A balcony about midway along the eastern wall allowed onlookers to view the feasting and other entertainments below. At the north end, above the screens passage usual at all major apartments of this kind, was a loft intended for musicians.

Time has stripped the decor from the walls at Stirling, and we cannot now be certain of the devices chosen by the king to remind his guests of their place in the lengthy roll-call of chivalry. James was addicted to the Arthurian romances, had instituted an order of chivalry modelled on Arthur's knights, and had held at least one major tournament of the Round Table. Very likely, the paintings and wall-hangings of the grandest hall in his realm would have reflected this particular enthusiasm. In any event, heraldry undoubtedly played its part at Stirling. If we are curious to know just what heraldry it was, we can obtain some idea of it at St Machar's Cathedral in Old Aberdeen, on the great painted ceiling of the nave.

Aberdeen had come to prominence during the fruitful episcopate of Bishop William Elphinstone (d.1514), a close advisor and confidant of James IV with whom he founded Aberdeen University. Elphinstone was a much travelled man. He was a lawyer with interests that went beyond the law into fields like printing, which he helped introduce into Scotland, and medicine, of which his new university was to be a pioneer. The heraldic ceiling at Aberdeen was not his work, being commissioned by a successor, Bishop Gavin Dunbar, and executed no earlier than 1520. Nevertheless, the supervisor of Bishop Dunbar's works was the same Alexander Galloway who had once been the friend of William Elphinstone and had similarly looked

after his building enterprises. The great bishop's influence survived his death, while the ceiling at Aberdeen records what were effectively the alliances of Elphinstone's patron, James IV, lately slaughtered with his chivalry at Flodden (1513).

The glory of the ceiling is its carved and painted heraldic bosses, forty-eight in all, each taking its part in a single decorative scheme readily intelligible to the learned and ecclesiastical society of Aberdeen. Thus the central row, as we would expect of a building of this purpose, was headed by the escutcheon of Pope Leo X (1513–21), followed by the archbishops of St Andrews and Glasgow and then by the remaining eleven bishops of Scotland and its Isles, with the Prior of St Andrews (senior Scottish religious house) and the new university of Aberdeen at their foot. Leading the south row, to the right, was the reigning king, James V, with Margaret of Scotland (the devout queen of Malcolm III) in close support. Next after St Margaret was the Duke of Albany, succeeded by the earls of March and Moray, Douglas, Angus and Mar, Sutherland, Crawford and Huntly, Argyll and Errol, the Earl Marischal and the Earl of Bothwell, and rounded off to the west by the three castles of the royal burgh of Aberdeen. Less predictably, the third row (north of the bishops) was dedicated to contemporary diplomacy. James IV's overseas alliances, many soon to be revived by his son on attaining his majority, were there laid out in appropriate sequence behind the familiar double-headed eagle of the Holy Roman Empire. Immediately after the Emperor (Charles V) was the King of France (Francis I), with the King of Spain (Charles V again) just behind him. Grudgingly, Henry VIII of England was then given his place, allowed his English leopards but stripped of the fleurs-de-lys by which traditionally he and his predecessors had asserted the claims of their line to French lordship. After England came the lesser kings, at least as far as Scotland was concerned: the kings of Denmark and Hungary, Portugal, Aragon and Cyprus, Navarre, Sicily, Poland and Bohemia, with the premier dukes of Bourbon and of Gueldres, all in the curious company of the proud citizenry of Old Aberdeen, identified by their pot of lilies and fret of salmon.

There was nothing unusual in the employment of heraldry for didactic display: at best a 'reminder to all of the lessons of good conduct', at worst a crass exhibition of naked power. At James IV's court, such display was inescapable. Among James IV's undertakings at Stirling was the building of a great defensive forework, with a noble gatehouse at the centre and big towers at each end, precisely contemporary with his huge hall. Although so different in execution, the two projects shared an important common purpose. Each was to play its part in publishing abroad the strength and the dignity of the Scottish monarchy. Like the Aberdeen ceiling with its subtle stress on the independent nationhood of Scotland, the gate-front of Stirling (now sadly stripped down) conveyed its own message of dynastic and national pride. Behind it, plain for all to see, rose the tall gables of the king's mighty hall, unequalled anywhere in the North.

Stirling's gate would at one time have mounted its own proud heraldic display, much as the entrance-front at Hylton, south of Newcastle, still carries its escutcheons, as Warkworth Castle, in Northumbria, displays the Percy lion on its north facade, or as Huntly, nearer home, remains embellished with the complex heraldry of George Gordon, sixth earl and first marquess of that name. Gordon's self-commendatory decoration of Huntly in the 1600s had a double purpose. It commemorated his elevation to a new higher rank and complimented James VI, his current patron and former enemy, not least in the advanced Renaissance detail of its execution. Heraldry still had its role.

The same message was usually made less subtly. When James IV had wanted to refortify the ancient castle of Rothesay, on the Isle of Bute, what he did was to supply it with a bold new forework, projecting aggressively northwards into the moat. His son, James V, who continued the work at Rothesay, was himself the builder of an ostentatious gatehouse, very French in style, at Falkland Palace, among his favourite residences, now cared for by the National Trust for Scotland. Other Trust properties exhibit the same emphasis. We have noted it already at Bodiam Castle in Dalyngrigge's obsessional care for his gatehouses. At Compton, that cardboard castle in its hidden fold of Devon, John Gilbert's entire defensive effort was to be concentrated on a spine-chilling facade. Much earlier, shortly before the Black Death, the comparatively modest Buckingham-shire manor at Boarstall had been equipped with a handsome gatehouse, to be given an appropriately military face-lift in the seventeenth century in a not untypical perpetuation of the same tradition.

Still, when Dunster Castle got its gatehouse in 1420, there might have been serious military purpose in such works. Sir Hugh Luttrell, the first of his long line to take up residence at this Somerset

fortress, was an experienced soldier who had held important appointments in the English cause in France, being familiar with the trappings of war. His new gatehouse, barbican-protected, undoubtedly heightened his own security on a coastal site at which such precautions continued to make very good sense. Yet even at Dunster, defence was not the sole reason for such expenditure. Luttrell had fought an expensive legal battle for his estate. His victory in the courts, as in war, required to be followed up by an energetic reinforcement of his position. Prestige in the locality was important to him, and the gatehouse at Dunster, as a fine new work very prominently placed, had its value in proclaiming Luttrell's dignity. A parallel enterprise at the castle, similarly calculated, was the refurbishing of Luttrell's private quarters and his hall. Through the last decade of his life, in peaceful enjoyment of a considerable estate, another old soldier could keep the fine table that his contemporaries had come to expect of him.

Gatehouses, presenting a noble frontispiece, were an obvious target for display. Everywhere they were the common currency of aristocratic building in late medieval Britain, as ubiquitous as the great hall and the private tower. Luttrell's gatehouse at Dunster has direct parallels, among others, in the Courtenay castles at Bickleigh, Tiverton and Powderham (Devon), in Sir Richard Abberbury's Donnington (Berkshire), in John Lord Cobham's Cooling (Kent), in Michael de la Pole's Wingfield (Suffolk), in the Marmion Tower at West Tanfield (Yorkshire), in the Nevills' Raby (Co. Durham), and in the great Percy castles at Alnwick and Warkworth (Northumberland).

Contemporaneously, an archbishop of Canterbury, William Courtenay (d.1396), was himself to engage in such building. Courtenay was the fourth son of Hugh de Courtenay, Earl of Devon; through his mother, Margaret de Bohun, he was related to a still more venerable aristocratic line, the de Bohun earls of Hereford. Accordingly, his noble residential gatehouse at Saltwood, in coastal Kent, although having its role as a deterrent, is unlikely, even in a period of repeated French raids, to have been designed exclusively for such a purpose. When, a couple of generations later, another aristocratic archbishop, Thomas Bourchier (1454–86), built Knole in the same county, defence was no longer a serious consideration, although some of its manifestations were retained. Bourchier was a generous host. He kept a fine table for his gentle friends, and was a noted patron of letters and of the arts. Knole's common hall and its provision for

private lodgings were both, in the circumstances, exceptional. Yet it was not these that gave character to Bourchier's palace. Central to the facade was a mighty gatehouse. There were strong towers at the angles and crenellations everywhere along the parapets. Knole, even under the layers of its later disguises, retains the formal habiliments of a fortress.

In the Late Middle Ages, as would remain the case at all but the most advanced new buildings of the sixteenth century, such styling would have been difficult to avoid. Take the grand but not untypical facade of Oxburgh Hall, a Norfolk moated manor-house now owned by the National Trust and first built by Sir Edmund Bedingfeld in the early 1480s. Oxburgh in many respects was a strikingly modern building. Its construction was adventurous, for brick used so exclusively was still a relatively new and expensive building material. With its stepped Flemish-style gables, topped by tall chimneys, Oxburgh had the relaxed domesticity appropriate to the life-style of a notably successful royal servant, everybody's friend, as much at home among Lancastrians as among Yorkists. Nevertheless, even at Oxburgh, a great entrance tower, disproportionately lofty and decoratively pierced to the top with serried gunports, was to remain the central feature of the entrance facade, turning a brave face to the road. These indeed were the characteristics of a full-dress building as Bedingfeld and his associates understood them.

Other country-house builders of the same generation – Baron Herbert at Raglan or William Lord Hastings at the unfinished Kirby Muxloe – had more reason to fear for their personal safety. The stakes they were playing for were very much higher, and each, in the event, lost his life in their pursuit. Not surprisingly, Raglan Castle, with its great anachronistic tower keep (the 'Yellow Tower of Gwent'), and Kirby Muxloe, conscientiously equipped for artillery, continued fortresses in more than mere name. In contrast, defended manor-houses like Oxburgh and its close Norfolk cousin at Baconsthorpe Castle, while re-using the motifs of military architecture, neglected to apply any of them systematically. Such mansions' broad water-filled moats and tall residential gatehouses may associate them superficially with the Donningtons and the Wingfields, the Coolings and West Tanfields of the past. In truth they looked forward to another future altogether, in which the gatehouse served exclusively for display.

The new mood was not long in arriving. Most remarkable among early examples of the fresh tradition is the surviving central gatehouse of Coughton Court, built by Sir George Throckmorton in the 1510s and happily preserved as the formal centre-piece of an otherwise Gothicized mansion. Throckmorton was a prominent Warwickshire landowner, a neighbour of Thomas Cromwell and one of the very few men known ever to have got the better of Henry VIII's masterful Secretary. Well established in court circles, it was Throckmorton's intimate knowledge of contemporary fashions that put him among the pioneers of English building. Even while the instinctively conservative Edward, Duke of Buckingham, notably unwelcome at Henry's court, was furnishing his own Thornbury Castle with a defendable gatehouse still very much in the traditional style, Throckmorton's gatehouse, in striking contrast, was to be all glass. Over its entrance, a fine two-storeyed oriel was equipped with side-lights entirely filling the space between turrets similarly glazed. Vestigial battlements finished off the roof-line; they had nothing to do with armed men.

Both Henry VII and Henry VIII were obsessive builders. Inevitably, those most intimate at court picked up the enthusiasm of their patrons. One of these, Henry Lord Marney, Captain of the Bodyguard and Keeper of the Privy Seal, died in 1523: too early to complete his ambitious new mansion but not before he had finished the huge brick tower which he had obviously intended as its centre-piece. Layer Marney Tower, although a degree more severe on its northern outer front than on its court and garden side to the south, could never have been seriously defendable. It had windows at ground-floor as at every other level; its machicolations were false and its battlements a charade; its gate passage was broad and hospitable. As a gatehouse pure and simple, Layer Marney had

FALKLAND PALACE (Fife) A section of James V's Renaissance courtyard facade, built in 1537–9 with classical pilasters and portrait medallions in the style of contemporary France.

Overleaf OXBURGH HALL (Norfolk) A central gatehouse with viewpoint turrets dominates the northern show-front of Sir Edmund Bedingfeld's castellated manor-house of the 1480s, fully moated but otherwise with only token defences.

Above LAYER MARNEY (Essex) Detail of the moulded terracotta ornament of a window at Henry Lord Marney's house, with characteristic Early Renaissance motifs favoured among fellow courtiers of Marney's day but still little known beyond that circle.

Left COUGHTON COURT (Warwickshire) Between Gothick wings of 1780, Sir George Throckmorton's prodigy gatehouse, conspicuously turreted and well-windowed, is the principal survival of a typical courtier's residence of the 1510s, still very traditional in its planning.

less to offer than many of the formal entrances it predated, among them those of Sir William Fitzwilliam's Cowdray or Thomas Wriothesley's Titchfield, both of the later 1530s and each the work of a favourite courtier more successful than Marney himself. In compensation, it looked beyond such buildings to the tall prospect towers, already foreshadowed in its gazebo-like turrets, which were to become so popular in the next generation: to Lord D'Arcy's St Osyth (before 1558) and to Sir Richard Baker's Sissinghurst (in the 1560s), each with its viewing-platform where the owner and his guests might assemble.

Fashions indeed had changed by that time, but the old emphasis on hospitality remained central.

Left SISSINGHURST CASTLE (Kent) Built in the 1560s, Sir Richard Baker's inner gatehouse at Sissinghurst was always more a viewpoint tower than a fortification, intended as a noble centre-piece for the main facade of his courtyard mansion, now almost wholly demolished.

Below MAXSTOKE CASTLE (Warwickshire) Built for William de Clinton following his elevation to the earldom of Huntingdon in 1337, and equipped at that time with everything, including multiple lodgings for the earl's extended household, that was considered appropriate to the rank.

Queen Elizabeth, a good judge of lodgings, is known to have spent three nights at Sissinghurst in 1573. She would have climbed the tower with others of her party to admire the view east across the Weald. In the court below, she must have anticipated quarters of at least adequate standard or she would not have come to Sissinghurst at all. Only fragments of these still remain. However, enough survives to recall, even at Sissinghurst, that other prerequisite of magnate housing, the purpose-built lodging – sometimes of one chamber but frequently of two, and almost always with private lavatory and other necessaries. Less spectacular than the tower, less colourful than the gatehouse, and less immediately evocative than the hall, the massed individual lodging was nevertheless as much a part of the chivalric life-style, where every great man, whether at home or abroad, was expected to surround himself with a fine company.

Bodiam, the quintessential castle of chivalry, has already given us an example of this practice. But, of course, such preconceptions were very widely shared, and had been so for many decades. When Edward III, conscious of the late 'serious decline in names, honours and ranks of dignity', determined to increase the number of his magnates, one of the close associates he chose to promote from his household in 1337 was William de Clinton, newly

created Earl of Huntingdon in the deliberate revival of an antique title. Accompanying the promotion went a fresh royal endowment of the earldom, and it was an understood requirement of Earl William's elevation that he should build himself a castle in proportion. Maxstoke was the product of that effort.

Although conservatively sited on the family estates, Maxstoke Castle was an entirely new building. It had the broad moat, the bold projecting gatehouse and polygonal flanking towers of its time. At the northwest angle, the earl's tower rose above the others, and there was ample provision for a great hall. But most obvious at Maxstoke, and most significant of its new purpose, was the clearly communal quality of its arrangements. A magnate of Earl William's rank could not expect at any time to be alone. Like the later Bodiam, as at a rather earlier magnate fortress like

Aymer de Valence's Goodrich with which it had much to compare, Maxstoke was crowded with private lodgings. They packed the towers and hugged the curtain walls, providing quarters for the earl's family and his guests, for the gentlemen of his household and the officials of his estates, for his servants and the soldiers of his garrison. When William de Clinton was at home, Maxstoke must have throbbed like a beehive.

Similar swarms settled at the great squarely-built castles of late fourteenth-century England: apartment blocks at least as much as fortresses.

BOLTON CASTLE (North Yorkshire) The west range and angle towers of Richard le Scrope's late fourteenth-century fortified mansion, providing accommodation for his large household and a safe repository for the goods he had accumulated as Treasurer.

The National Trust's Croft Castle was one of these, high on its hill in remote Herefordshire. But Croft, like the Trust's Coughton Court, has been destructively Gothicized. To appreciate what it offered, we must go instead to such roofless shells as William Strickland's Penrith or Ralph Nevill's Sheriff Hutton, with Bolton Castle (Richard le Scrope's pride and joy of the 1390s) as the best-preserved example of the plan. Each of these castles, albeit impressive in bulk, placed defence a poor second after accommodation. Their big square angle towers gave convenient space for private lodgings, stacked like the trays of a dumb-waiter. Between the towers, straight-sided ranges carried the public rooms – hall, great chamber and chapel – around a central court. Other lodgings filled every available slot, with the kitchens and stores down below.

Bolton supplies vertically what the typical country mansion of the same period, in a less threatened location, might have laid out horizontally in a great courtyard. When John de Holand, first Duke of Exeter, built Dartington Hall, he was secure in the favour of Richard II. He had less to fear from casual raiders than Lord Scrope at Bolton, and was more confident in the protection of his patron. Reflecting that sense of ease, Dartington still preserves a remarkable set of two-storeyed lodgings, the upper approached by outside stairs, formerly the north range of an outer court. Exactly the same dispositions, similarly collegiate in style

and on a still grander scale, would have characterized Thornbury Castle, over a century later, had the Duke of Buckingham survived the malice of Henry VIII long enough to complete his outer courtyard as planned. Furthermore, when Henry VIII himself added another court (the so-called 'Green Court') to the front of Bourchier's former palace at Knole, it was for lodgings essentially that he built it. The archbishop, in his time, had lived surrounded by a great company. The king travelled with still more.

John de Holand, Duke of Exeter, Edward Stafford, Duke of Buckingham, Thomas Bourchier, Archbishop of Canterbury, and Henry Tudor, King of England – each practised a life-style seldom unrelated to political purpose and usually performed on open stage. Not surprisingly, the backcloth was dramatic and the props were splendid: they could hardly have been anything else. Like Suryavarman II's Angkor Wat or the Sun King's more accessible Versailles, the architecture of high chivalry had nothing to gain by concealment. Forget military considerations when you view these buildings, and try to see them instead through the eyes of the men who made use of them. 'Is it not passing brave', Marlowe asks, 'to be a King, and ride in triumph through Persepolis?' The king in question was Tamerlane of Samarkand, 'Scourge of God'. But he might just as easily, in such bold display, have been Richard II, his contemporary.

[2]

A Ghostly Bargain

For every Christian believer in the Late Middle Ages, there was at least the prospect of the 'purchase of Paradise'. Since 1274 (and in practice before), official Church doctrine had defined Purgatory as a condition in which the departed soul, cleansed by suffering, might be prepared for eternal life. Pain after death was unavoidable. But the Church also taught that intercession on Earth might soften that pain, introducing the elements of a bargain. Who might profit by that bargain had as yet to be decided. But one thing, at least, was certain. The older monastic orders, even before the onset of plague in 1348–9, had ceased to hold the frontiers of the faith. Set in their routines, identified with the ruling classes, rigid in doctrine and relaxed in morals, the monks had lost the credibility they had once possessed as intermediaries between Man and his God.

Most favoured of the alternatives was the privately endowed chantry, at one time itself given over to monks but increasingly entrusted to others. Such chantries might be established at any level – shared altar, chapel, or aristocratic college – by individuals or co-operatively through a guild. But essentially their purpose remained the same in the repetition of memorial masses. That purpose was reinforced by endemic plague and by the perception, common to disease-ridden societies, of Death's premature and arbitrary sweep. Thus the sculptures at Rosslyn, most 'sumptuous' of the aristocratic collegiate chantries of mid fifteenth-century Scotland, included a rendering of the Dance of Death accompanied by another favourite legend, The Three Living and Three Dead, evergreen reminders of mortality. With shocking disregard for youth, rank or wealth, the Pestilence led all away in the Dance.

Other pressures sharpened the faith. From 1309, the popes had been held 'captive' at Avignon. Then, when eventually they returned to Rome, there was the appalling continuing scandal of the Great Schism (1378–1417), when different popes competed for recognition. In times like those, it was hardly surprising that energetic monarchs like Henry V of England and James I of Scotland should each have taken the initiative in reform. In the 1420s, they were to accuse the long-established Benedictine communities of 'somnolence and sloth', urging them (unsuccessfully) to set their houses in order, and placing before them the example of the reclusive Carthusians, favoured by both kings with new foundations. Others took the line of continuing support for the Mendicant friars, whose hell-fire preaching and pastoral care still gave them a clear role in the community. In Gaelic Ireland especially, Mendicant houses of the stricter observance multiplied during the later Middle Ages. By the 1460s, Observant Franciscans were in Scotland also, to penetrate England by 1497, introduced in each case by the Crown.

Patronage of the Observants, as against the more relaxed Conventuals, was one form of protest within the Church. Another was a retreat into solitary mysticism, as practised, among others, by the Carthusians. A third, of more general application, was self-help. Wherever they could afford it, parishioners united in the rebuilding of their churches, raising great monuments to their faith. When all else looked black in the economy, when houses tumbled and grass grew in the streets, the parish church underwent a degree of investment it had never seen before, or has seen since. The brothers and sisters of innumerable parish guilds entered their separate compact with the Lord.

THORNTON ABBEY GATEHOUSE (Humberside) The most remarkable of the great prodigy gatehouses of late medieval Britain, built in 1382 immediately after the suppression of the Peasants' Revolt, and lavishly furnished with arrow-loops.

If the architecture of chivalry needs to be seen in context, so too must contemporary church building. The National Trust is not rich in former ecclesiastical properties. Nevertheless, what it holds is both varied and significant. Late medieval Britain was the setting for profound changes in religious observance. Parish churches and colleges, the new priories and the old, are as faithful a reflection of contemporary values as the castles of the magnate and war captain.

Indeed, some of these values were the same. Included among the buildings now cared for by the National Trust is the mid fourteenth-century gatehouse of the Augustinian canons of Cartmel, in Cumbria. Cartmel was at no time a rich com-

munity. Yet its gatehouse was tall and imposing, placed well away from the priory church itself and the key to an extensive walled enceinte. The canons had powerful friends in the locality, and it was from these, inevitably, that they took their colour. Even today, the pride of their church is the magnificent tomb of John, first Lord Harrington (d.1347), a monument notable for the high quality of its sculptures and a work of considerable expense. Very probably, Harrington also financed the

Below CARTMEL PRIORY GATEHOUSE (Cumbria) The mid fourteenth-century gatehouse, with tall entrance passage and chamber above, of the Augustinian canons of Cartmel.

building of Cartmel's south chapel at this date, intending it as a chantry for himself. Chantry chapel, monument and gatehouse are contemporary. They recall a society in which much the same preoccupations were shared by priest and layman alike, with predictable consequences in architecture. Thus the east window of Lord Harrington's chapel picks up a theme – a Tree of Jesse – which to many must have seemed self-selecting. The Tree is a genealogy of the Christ Child, compiled as any nobleman would have done it. It traces His descent through the Jewish royal line from Jesse's son, David the King.

Cartmel Priory's gatehouse, although handsome and of fair size, was not among the more elaborate of its kind. Grander by far was the much later gatehouse of the Benedictines of Ramsey, similarly under the guardianship of the National Trust but today no more than a fragment. Too splendid to be left where it was, the bulk of Ramsey's gatehouse was removed, shortly after the Dissolution, to Hinchingbrooke where it has continued to do duty as the principal entrance of a mid sixteenth-century mansion, itself built on the remains of a former nunnery. What is left at Ramsey is one side only of the entrance passage. Yet even this, florid and ornate, picks up the mood of a rich and proud community which in 1500, at about the time that the gatehouse was built, was entering another century of its over-long existence, having survived for more than half a millennium.

Venerable antiquity may not be the monk's best friend. It can blunt the edge of a vocation. Ramsey Abbey was older and richer than most. However, there were few religious communities in late medieval England which, on the eve of their suppression, had not seen three centuries at least. Their age showed plainly on their faces. Gatehouses in particular, being the community's public front, had got more than their fair share of attention. Take a gatehouse like that of the wealthy Augustinians of Butley, built on a scale that would not have shamed a castle and similarly loaded with heraldic display. Butley's gatehouse, dating to the 1320s, is one of the earlier of its kind. But it is

45

already insensitively magnificent. On its outer facade, no fewer than five rows of escutcheons begin with the heraldry of the great European dynasties (as celebrated again two centuries later on Bishop Dunbar's painted ceiling at Aberdeen). Below are the arms of the principal officers of state and of the major aristocratic families. Under these again are the devices of the landowners and greater gentry of the counties of East Anglia, the natural allies of the community that thus recorded them.

The gatehouse at Butley had close cousins, similarly substantial and of much the same date, at the priories of Worksop and Bolton. Both (like Cartmel and like Butley itself) were Augustinian houses. But both again were the public fronts of communities of above average means, and it was wealth rather than religious allegiance that explained them. Bolton's riches were very quickly to come under threat. The crushing English defeat at Bannockburn in 1314 had left the northern counties dangerously exposed. Four years later, Scottish raiders penetrated as far south as Wharfedale. They were there again in 1319, and the community at Bolton, in the following year, had to suffer the indignity of dispersal. Attached to Bolton's gatehouse are the impressive remains of a massive stone precinct wall. They remind us that the monastic gatehouse, like the castles of chivalry and of the Hundred Years War, shared display with a second purpose, defence.

In the course of time, defence became less and less the object of such prodigy gatehouses as those of the Benedictine monks of Colchester Abbey or of their local rivals, the Augustinian canons of St Osyth's. By the late fifteenth century, when these were built, the English religious houses had little to fear, whether from outsiders or from the tenants to whom, as a general rule, they had leased out their estates on easy terms. Accordingly, the battlements at St Osyth's are for show alone. Both there and at Colchester, the real cost of such gatehouses lay in the decorative flint flushwork of their facades. However, the prospects had not always been as favourable. There had been riots at Bury St Edmunds in 1327, when, in the tumult of Edward II's deposition and murder, the monks had found themselves hostage to the mob. Building themselves a handsome new gatehouse almost im-

mediately afterwards, as part of a general programme of refortification of the abbey precinct, the abbot and convent of Bury took the precaution of hiding an array of arrow-loops behind the decorative statuary of its facade.

At Battle, in the same generation, no attempt was made to disguise the purpose of a great gatehouse, facing the market square, which was to be the key to the abbey's defensive system. Like their neighbours, the gentry castle-builders of Scotney and of Bodiam, or like the moat-digging canons of Michelham Priory within a few miles to the southwest, the Benedictines of Battle were reacting to pressures which included the threat of French invasion.

Each defensive system has to be considered in context, and motives, of course, continued to be mixed. Prior John Leem of Michelham, during his long term of office from 1376 to 1415, took an active part in organizing the defence of the south coast against the French. His own establishment, strongly moated, still bears the marks of this concern. Nevertheless, even Michelham's fortifications are in part for show. Prior Leem's gatehouse, in its upper storeys, is equipped with comfortable well-windowed lodgings, one above the other, with individual garderobes draining into the moat. In its comfort and its display, as well as in the provision it makes for defence at ground level, Michelham's entrance is the more modest equivalent of another exceedingly grand Augustinian gatehouse at Thornton, in northern Lincolnshire (Humberside), unusually precisely datable to 1382, the year after the Peasants' Revolt. Thornton's isolation is still extreme. The perceived threat of further peasant uprisings in the region could well have been a major reason for fortification. Certainly the gatehouse, on both facades, was peppered with arrow-loops, serviced at the rear by a complex web of defensive passages. Yet the style of the whole was restlessly boastful, very obviously intended for display. Thornton's gatehouse, in the manner of its period, was a celebration of exceptional wealth. Beyond it, protected by the high stone wall of the abbey precinct, were buildings so splendid as to attract the interest of the king himself at the eventual suppression of the community. Much later, when all else was demolished, the gatehouse survived to make a bold, nostalgic front for the great Jacobean mansion intended behind it.

That mansion immediately collapsed, falling 'quite down to the bare ground, without any visible cause'. In the early seventeenth century, when the

BATTLE ABBEY GATEHOUSE (East Sussex) Built facing Battle's market-place in c. 1338, when the whole precinct of the abbey was fortified as a precaution against local disorders and coastal raids.

project aborted, there were still those in the region who might draw a moral lesson from the failure. They saw it as a form of retribution. If so, the spirits of the place were of exceptional malevolence, for Henry VIII's earlier scheme for the setting up of a new College of the Holy Trinity at Thornton, in place of the dissolved abbey, had been no luckier. In 1547, immediately following the king's death, Thornton was suppressed by the more radically Protestant Edwardian reformers. Yet Henry's initial choice of institution had been significant. Although considered conservative by the mid sixteenth century, collegiate chantries in the style of Thornton had once themselves been the front-runners of reform.

Long before the Dissolution, wealthy founders had begun to neglect the old-established and adequately endowed 'possessioner' houses, of which the abbey at Thornton was typical, in favour of communities of a more austere observance or in support of the secular Church. Thornton and other similar establishments, as we shall see, continued to live comfortably on their endowments right up to the point of their suppression. Indeed, some did outstandingly well. But a rich man of the Late Middle Ages, bargaining for his soul with his 'ghostly' Father, would not usually have chosen monks as his assistants. That 'solemn celebration of Masses' which, it was generally agreed, had most power to 'draw down the mercy of God', had come to be thought better entrusted to a new breed of clergy for whom such specialized obligations would be central. Inevitably, the four prebendaries and six minor canons, the schoolmaster, choir-master, and four 'singing men' of Henry VIII's short-lived college at Thornton, would have had a variety of duties to perform at the establishment. But one duty, certainly, would have overridden the rest, being the regular celebration of a founder's mass – the *De profundis* on behalf of the dead.

By common consent Purgatory, that state of temporal punishment between Death and admission to the Beatific Vision, was not a condition to look forward to. There, so the Church's teaching went, the smallest pain would be greater than any yet experienced on this Earth. But at least techniques had become available to alleviate it. When, at last, formal definition of the doctrine of Purgatory was reached at the Council of Lyons in

1274, the conditions of an oft-repeated bargain were laid down. Hereafter, relief from the pains of Purgatory could be purchased by pious works or through the endowment of memorial masses. For every man of property in Christian Europe, a way was now open, according to his means, for investment in the comfort of his soul.

Such insurance could take many forms, from the great collegiate chantry of Henry's luckless project at Thornton, to the humble candle or 'light' of the parishioner. But everywhere the purpose was essentially the same, bringing resources in new abundance to the Church. At the peak of their popularity, in the twelfth and thirteenth centuries, the monks and canons of the older enclosed orders might have expected to take their share of this bonanza. By the fifteenth century, their light was out. Others reaped the harvest they had sown.

Certainly, when Ralph Lord Cromwell, on 14 July 1439, was granted licence to found a new college next to the castle he was rebuilding at Tattershall, he put aside all thoughts of dealing with the monks. Some of this coolness he could conceivably have owed to his late master, Henry V, himself a noted hammer of the Benedictines. But few of Cromwell's generation, had they possessed the same resources, would have reacted any differently in such circumstances. In this respect, the Treasurer spoke generally for his class. Characteristically, too, he did so with an exhibition of maximum display, dedicating his college collectively to the Holy Trinity and the Virgin, to SS Peter, John the Baptist and John the Evangelist, all enlisted to do battle for his soul.

Tattershall was to be equipped with an almshouse for thirteen paupers, rebuilt in the seventeenth century but still used for the same function even today, immediately north of the church. However, the main purpose of the college was never charitable. Its huge church, built in accordance with Cromwell's instructions after his death, was everywhere decorated with the Treasurer's purse as an act of personal commemoration. After the fashion of a monastic church, the chancel (or choir) at Tattershall was especially spacious. It was shut off from the nave by a fine stone screen, and housed the stalls of the numerous collegiate body sustained by the former Treasurer's rich endowment. In its last decades, Tattershall became noted for its music: the nursery of the talent of John Taverner, one of England's most gifted pre-Reformation composers. Taverner, in his youth, had sharpened his skills on memorial masses. He was one of a fellowship of

MICHELHAM PRIORY GATEHOUSE (East Sussex) The big gatehouse, with lodgings on its two upper floors, of an Augustinian priory fortified against the French in *c.* 1400.

priests, clerks and choristers who repaid the generosity of Ralph Cromwell, their founder, with a perpetual *De profundis* in his name.

Among the known models for Tattershall was the slightly earlier Yorkist college at Fotheringhay, in Northamptonshire, where rebuilt castle and new collegiate church were similarly grouped together in an association increasingly characteristic of the period. Edmund of Langley, first Duke of York, was the founder of a powerful dynasty. He had acquired the castle at Fotheringhay in 1377 from his father, Edward III, and before his death in 1402 had made the first moves to establish a college there, subsequently completed by his son. Just a couple of generations before, and in marked contrast, the response of William de Clinton to his own promotion to an earldom in 1337 had been to upgrade an existing collegiate chantry at Maxstoke to the full status of a community of canons. Yet before the end of the same century, these priorities had been completely overturned. Fotheringhay was to be (and to remain) a college of secular priests. As at Tattershall, Fotheringhay's community would possess a charitable function in the care of the old, but its purpose overwhelmingly was memorial. Every day, according to the statutes of their house, the twelve chaplains, eight clerks and thirteen choristers of Fotheringhay's rich community were to gather after compline at the tomb of their principal founder, Edward (second duke), to sing him to rest with a *De profundis*. Among others they remembered regularly were Duke Edward's father (Edmund of Langley), his uncle (John of Gaunt), his cousins (Henry IV and Henry V), with that whole imposing gallery of departed royal persons, the quarrelsome brood (at one remove or more) of Edward III Plantagenet.

Certainly nobody at Fotheringhay, from the lowest servant to the Dean himself, would have been allowed to forget his founding family. Nothing now survives of the domestic ranges which, in the fifteenth century, filled the fields to the south of Fotheringhay's church. Like those of Tattershall, similarly lost, they await systematic excavation. However, we know them to have included a cloister and great hall, and we have a record also of the glazing of these quarters, as replete with heraldry as that of any castle and as concerned to establish a clear pedigree. From Edmund of Langley to Richard III, the house of York and that of the allied Nevills touched the Fitzalans of Arundel, the Mortimers of March, the Mowbrays of Norfolk, the Percies of Northumberland, and the de Vere earls of Oxford among others.

Ralph Nevill, first Earl of Westmorland (d.1425), had had a total of twenty-two children, few of whom he failed to marry well. One of them, Cicely Nevill, married the factious Richard, third Duke of York (d.1460), to become the mother of two kings: Edward IV and Richard III. Cicely long outlived her husband, spending much time at Fotheringhay and contributing generously to its buildings. Another Nevill alliance brought the great Beauchamp inheritance to Richard Nevill, Earl of Salisbury (d.1471), himself featuring prominently in the Fotheringhay glass and better known to us as Warwick 'the Kingmaker'.

The Nevills, of course, had their own collegiate chantry, established almost exactly contemporaneously at Staindrop (Co. Durham), next to their principal fortress at Raby. There, reassembled at the southwest corner of the nave, are some Nevill monuments, among them the tomb of Ralph Nevill himself, lying in effigy between the two wives (one a Stafford, the second a daughter of John of Gaunt) who had brought him new estates and who had given him his numerous progeny. The Earl of Westmorland's monument is a fine piece of extravagance in the Burgundian taste, as developed at the dukes' tomb-church at Champmol (Dijon), with great display of fashionable dress and with elaborate architectural ornament against the tomb-chest. But handsome though it is, it has nothing of the quality of Richard Beauchamp's tomb, best known of the aristocratic memorials of fifteenth-century England and itself the centrepiece of a purpose-built chantry chapel in the parish church close to Warwick Castle.

By a chance documentary survival, we are exceptionally well informed about the testamentary arrangements of Richard, fifth Earl of Warwick in the Beauchamp line and a noted captain of the

Right TATTERSHALL CHURCH (Lincolnshire) The church of Ralph Lord Cromwell's collegiate chantry, sited immediately east of his castle and completed at great cost in the 1480s, almost a generation after the former Treasurer's death (1456); the huge south transept window (centre) gives a good indication of the scale and expense of an enterprise entirely dedicated to the health of Cromwell's soul.

Overleaf FOTHERINGHAY CHURCH (Northamptonshire) The former college buildings (under the field in the foreground) have now been lost, as has the entire chancel (right) of the medieval church; but Fotheringhay is still an impressive fragment of the great family chantry of the fifteenth-century dukes of York, sited within hailing distance of their castle.

Hundred Years War. Earl Richard, before his death in 1439, had established a trust to settle the disposal of estates not already assigned to his heirs and to provide for the future comfort of his soul. The second objective was the more important of the two, and it constituted a first charge on his estate. No fewer than 5000 masses, according to the terms of Richard's will of 1437, were to be said for the earl's soul after death. In addition, Richard provided, there was to be a 'Chapel of our Lady, well, fair, and goodly built, within the middle of which Chapel I will that my Tomb be made'. Both chapel and tomb remain intact to this day in precisely the form he would have wished to view them. At the family's collegiate church of St Mary's (Warwick), the Beauchamp Chapel, as it is now known, lies to the south of the grand vaulted choir already appropriated for his burial place by Richard's grandfather Earl Thomas (d.1369), hero of the English victories at Crecy and at Poitiers, and a founding member of Edward III's Order of the Garter.

Today, Earl Richard's chapel at Warwick is one of the greater legacies of English chivalry. Costing nearly £4000 to build, in a programme extending through the better part of two decades from 1442 to 1457, it provided an appropriately magnificent setting for the founder's tomb-chest and effigy, themselves adding another £700 to the bill. No expense was spared by Richard's executors. The chest of his monument was to be of 'as good and fine marble, as well coloured as may be had in England'. Against it, there were to be fourteen gilded images in 'the finest latten' (brass) of 'lords and ladies in diverse vestures, called weepers'. They included Warwick the Kingmaker in miniature. Above, the earl's life-size effigy was to be of 'a man armed, of fine latten garnished with certain ornaments, viz. – with sword and dagger; with a garter; with a helm and crest under his head, and at his feet a bear muzzled, and a griffin'.

Three chaplains, separately endowed for the purpose, were to celebrate daily soul-masses in perpetuity for Earl Richard. And it was precisely this unambiguous definition of benefit and cost that attracted lay founders in such numbers to the

WARWICK CHURCH (Warwickshire) Richard Beauchamp, Earl of Warwick (d.1439), still lies in the fine chapel for which he had left instructions before his death; his tomb-chest and effigy (centre) are of the highest quality, as is every detail of this remarkable building, not finished until 1457.

institution of the chantry, against which traditional monasticism could offer little. Archibald the Grim's suppression in 1389 of Scotland's only Benedictine nunnery, re-using the same site for the fine buildings of his new college at Lincluden, was indeed scarcely typical. Nevertheless, it showed clearly enough the current direction of the wind, being an early example of that rash of late medieval collegiate foundations – Rosslyn and Dunglass, Seton and Crichton among them – for which the Scottish aristocracy would soon take enthusiastic responsibility. In England, similarly, magnate colleges like Warwick, Fotheringhay and Tattershall inspired many imitations throughout the country. Thus, in Shropshire, the Vernons were to make Tong Church their family memorial, furnishing it appropriately with collegiate-style choir-stalls and cramming it with the monuments of their line. In Cheshire, there was to be Sir Hugh Calveley's Bunbury; in Surrey, Sir Reginald Cobham's Lingfield; in Somerset, Lady Elizabeth Botreaux's North Cadbury; and many more. At each, the founder's tomb took centre-stage.

Towards the beginning of this tradition, not so very long after the doctrine of Purgatory had been given the formal blessing of the Church, another family of Beauchamps – the Beauchamps of Hatch – established their own collegiate chantry in modest buildings at Stoke-sub-Hamdon, now among the lesser-known properties of the National Trust. As lords of this Somerset manor, the Beauchamps already held the patronage of Stoke's parish church. In addition, they had a private chapel, dedicated to St Nicholas, in the court of the manor-house they had recently rebuilt, and it was there that John de Beauchamp in 1304 established a college of five full-time chaplains, one with the title of Provost. This little community, although not without its troubles, survived until the general suppression of the colleges in 1548, outlasting Henry VIII's much grander Thornton College by several months. But Stoke had never been rich, and what survives there now is a knocked-about range of buildings of small size but great charm, the long-term residence of impoverished chaplains, adapted slowly to their needs over time.

Under the relaxed Rule of St Augustine, a well-loved harbour for many small communities of this kind, each chaplain at Stoke was required to make his professions of chastity, stability and obedience. After this, his duties were light but unambiguous. He must offer soul-masses for Edward I, king at the date of the college's foundation, and for Walter Haselshaw, then Bishop of Bath and Wells, whose sanctioning of the appropriation of Stoke-sub-Hamdon Church had guaranteed the new college its chief revenues. Heading the list of others to be remembered in perpetuity was the founder, John de Beauchamp, with his parents, his children and his wife, with his brother and two sisters, and with all the faithful departed.

The Chapel of St Nicholas, burial-place of the Beauchamps, was demolished shortly after the suppression. But the collegiate buildings in the village at Stoke had been restored only recently, in the mid fifteenth century, following a period of dilapidation and mismanagement, and other uses were to be found for them without difficulty. Today, they are still entered through a big arched gateway from the street, next to which is a blocked pedestrians' postern. Within the court, there are the two barns and dovecot of the chaplains' late

medieval farmstead. A comfortable residential range, mainly of the fifteenth century but probably incorporating earlier work, fronts the village street on the southeast; at right angles to it, the surviving common hall has its porch and screens passage at the eastern end, beyond which (to the east again) was the original first-floor chamber and adjoining chapel; on the same level, but at the other end of the hall, another smaller chapel in a projecting southwest annexe may once have been part of further domestic buildings in that quarter.

Almost everything at Stoke-sub-Hamdon is of the fifteenth century. It witnesses to the unassuming domesticity of a small clerical community of the Late Middle Ages, for which there is other closely comparable evidence in the local records. At Bridport, due south of Stoke-sub-Hamdon on the Dorset coast, John Munden's Chantry was a foundation of 1361. Supporting two chaplains at St Michael's Chapel, with the founder's former town house as their residence, it had been entrusted to the supervision of the rector, bailiffs and commonalty of Bridport, who thus obtained an interest in its muniments. Of course, the records of Munden's Chantry, like all such occasional private archives for which the purpose of preservation was

BEAUCHAMP CHANTRY, STOKE-SUB-HAMDON (Somerset) The porch and hall range of the chantry priests' quarters of this small college, founded in the early fourteenth century, originally for four chaplains under the direction of a provost; the surviving buildings are mainly of the fifteenth century, though they incorporate earlier work.

quickly lost, are incomplete. Nevertheless, they include a unique account book of the mid fifteenth century, prepared by William Savernak, so-called 'Warden' of Munden's Chantry, to cover the seven years (from 1453) of his administration. Savernak laid out small sums repeatedly in the repair of the Chantry House (now vanished) and of the other properties (for the most part put out to rent) of the foundation. But he bought little in the way of household goods – just a few cups and pots, with some kitchen equipment and a new pantry cupboard – and most of what he spent was on service and food, keeping his small establishment clean and fed. The chaplains had only one servant, hiring in occasional labour for work in the garden, and finding part-time employment on a more regular basis for a laundress. They drank a lot of ale, but usually only of the second quality. Their diet, although certainly adequate and of perhaps surprising variety, seldom – only once in Savernak's stewardship – rose to such luxuries as a goose.

The unhurried last years of two aged chantry priests of Bridport, of William Savernak and of John Trewen his companion, are no model of late medieval piety. Savernak and Trewen kept their founder's name in remembrance and little more. Yet such tranquillity of spirit, in other contexts, was to bring out the best in the Church. In contemporary lay circles, a great lady of renowned devoutness was that same Dame Cicely who, eventually laid to rest at Fotheringhay in 1495 next to her husband Duke Richard, had done so much in her long lifetime to help the college. Dame Cicely's domestic routine allowed her plentiful opportunities for contemplation and reading; she liked, even while eating, to listen to devotional works. What she chose to read or to hear on such occasions is very important. Dame Cicely and her ladies were all potential benefactors. They belonged to a class which, because of its continuing financial muscle, largely determined new directions in the Church.

Among the works known to have been read at Cicely's table was a popular treatise by Walter Hilton, the English mystic, on the contrasting merits of the active and the contemplative life. The treatise was much beloved by the Carthusians, a contemplative order practising silence and seclusion. And it was one of their number, Prior Love of Mount Grace, who had himself prepared a vernacular version of another work familiar to Dame Cicely and her household, the *Life of Christ* attributed to St Bonaventure (the Franciscan), which he rendered as *The Mirrour of the Blessed*

Lyf of Jesu Christ. The duchess, we know, was a benefactor of the Carthusians. She also had a special interest in the Bridgettines of Syon, naming (as godmother) one of her grandchildren after their founder, St Bridget of Sweden, as well as keeping a copy of the widely-read *Revelations of St Bridget* in her personal library, and leaving it on her death to another grandchild, Anne de la Pole, by then herself Prioress of Syon. Both grandchildren, Bridget and Anne, had chosen to practise their vocation in houses highly fashionable in their period. Bridget joined the austere sisters of Dartford, the only English nunnery of the Dominican allegiance. At Syon, Anne similarly was one of a sisterhood well known for the strictness of its interpretation of the Rule and much influenced by the writings of contemporary mystics. In each case, the community survived in good condition until and beyond the Dissolution, retaining the loyalty of its banished members even in the years of their diaspora.

What Dartford, Mount Grace and Syon all had in common was unimpeachable sincerity and unquestionable devotion to the Rule. They were late foundations – Dartford of 1346, Mount Grace of 1398, Syon of 1415 – and they continued to stand out as islands of hope in a sea of monasticism otherwise characterized by disillusion. Dartford has left few visible remains. At Syon, little more than the plan of the original cloister was retained in the central court of an ambitious post-suppression mansion. Yet Mount Grace, even today, lives up to its name and reputation. Owned by the National Trust and under the guardianship of the Historic Buildings and Monuments Commission, Mount Grace Priory is a choice example, happily preserved, of the finest product of fifteenth-century spirituality. Its North Yorkshire setting is remote and hauntingly beautiful, damaged but not spoilt by the modern trunk road immediately to the west. Its church is small, never much in use by the monks. But round its great cloister still are the substantial remains of the individual cells and private gardens of a community of recluses: of hermit monks who came together only for special occasions, finding their greatest comfort in silent communion with their Maker, not in a crowd but by themselves.

Few could emulate the taxing self-discipline of the Carthusians. But there were many, nevertheless, who respected the Carthusian ideal, and the comparisons it suggested with the busy routines of a Benedictine ('black monk') community were almost invariably unfavourable to the latter. It was a Carthusian, Prior Layton of Mount Grace, who stood at Henry V's side in 1421 as the principal accuser of the Benedictines. And although the reforms agreed at Westminster came to nothing, it was already obvious who the victims would be if it came to a competition between the orders. Henry himself, earlier in his reign, had overseen the formal suppression of the 'alien priories', those cells and other offshoots of French religious houses (usually Benedictine) which – so their detractors claimed – had sheltered spies in the recent wars, syphoning off the national wealth.

The argument was xenophobic and unfair. Yet its consequences were hugely profitable to Mount Grace and its fellows, bringing them their share of the confiscated estates in the post-1414 re-distributions. First to benefit was Henry V's own Carthusian foundation at Sheen, established that same year next to his palace. Sheen was planned for a community of forty monks. It became richer than any other English house of the order. Similarly favoured were the Bridgettine nuns of Syon, just across the River Thames from Sheen. It was to Syon Abbey that Henry V allotted the valuable alien priory of St Michael's Mount, off the Cornish coast, until then a dependency of Mont St Michel, one of the wealthiest Norman 'black monk' abbeys. St Michael's Mount has been much enlarged and rebuilt. It is now almost wholly Victorian. Yet it preserves the original chapel and refectory of its small community of Norman French exiles, subsequently re-used (until the suppression of Syon itself in 1539) by a trio of chaplains, and now cared for by the National Trust.

The endowment of Sheen and Syon out of the spoils of the dissolved alien priories might have been seen – as indeed it was in some quarters – as a deliberate affront to the older 'possessioner' houses. In the king's view, forcibly expressed in 1421, the Benedictines had failed to keep their side of the bargain with their founders. Neglecting their vows, they had lost the ear of God. This was not the case with the austere communities Henry V himself favoured. In the prayers of the exceptionally devout, intercession could still be effective; for those who had kept their faith with God might expect Him to listen in his turn. In point of fact,

MOUNT GRACE PRIORY (North Yorkshire) Carthusian monks maintained a hermit-like privacy in their individual cells round the great cloister (left); their church (centre) was used only on feast days.

there were rather more of such people, even in the monastic Church, than Henry's own austere predilections might have suggested. Henry himself, towards the beginning of his reign before the revival of the French war put a stop to it, had contemplated bringing a community of Celestines (strict reformed Benedictines) to England. Others in his circle looked more familiarly to the Mendicant orders: to the Franciscans and the Dominicans, the Carmelites and the Austin friars, among whom the 'grey friars' (Franciscans) led the field.

One great patroness of Syon, Dame Cicely of York, shared her largesse with the Dominicans of Dartford among others. Such preferences, by her date, had become routine. The great Mendicant colonization of Britain had occurred as far back as the thirteenth century. But the friars, unlike the monks and canons, never lost the favour of their benefactors. Their practice of corporate poverty, reinforced by frequent renewals, kept them in touch with the lay community, upon whose daily charity they depended. Offering care and salvation to the bereft and the poor, they were as appealing, as an ideal, to the rich. Dartford, founded in 1346 for the well-born sisterhood of whom Bridget, Cicely's grandchild, was representative, was itself an offshoot of Edward II's outsize Dominican community, the source of his confessors, next to his country palace at King's Langley. Contemporaneously, the Franciscan nuns of Waterbeach were to find their own wealthy benefactor in Mary de St Pol, Countess of Pembroke and widow of Aymer de Valence (d.1324). Like Dame Cicely, similarly widowed and rich, Mary de St Pol dedicated her long life to good works. Before her death in 1377, she had uprooted the sisters at Waterbeach, to re-establish them more grandly at Denny Abbey, the site until 1312 of a Templar hospital which had itself taken the place of a former dependency of Ely Priory. Dame Mary, though never a nun, is thought to have become a Franciscan Tertiary, living by the Rule but in the world. She kept private apartments at Denny, carving them out of the existing Templar chapel to which she added another larger church to the east. It was in this second church, before the high altar, that she ordered her bones laid to rest.

The Templars' suppression in 1312, political rather than religious in inspiration, had nothing to do with monastic reform. Yet even at Denny, the failure of this former Ely Priory estate to revert to Benedictine ownership is itself suggestive of altering priorities, while there are other signs –

King's Langley and Dartford among them – of an irrevocable sideways move in founders' preferences. When Elizabeth de Clare, the Gloucester heiress, brought Franciscans to Walsingham in 1347, she brushed aside impatiently the objections of Augustinians, custodians of the famous shrine next to their own priory church, who had reason to fear the friars' rivalry. For Dame Elizabeth, as for Denny's Countess of Pembroke, what the Franciscans promised was the ear of God, denied to the soft company of canons. Characteristically, both ladies took other precautions. Each founded a college – Clare and Pembroke – with a purpose as much commemorative as educational. At Cambridge today, their piety and names are still remembered, although perhaps not in the manner they might have chosen.

The pattern of charity, taking shape in this mould, persisted unchanged until the Reformation. For the older orders, the outlook was anything but promising. The collapse of the Augustinian Creake Abbey in 1506 was perhaps neither wholly predictable nor representative. More communities of its kind, at least as ill-endowed, held on by their fingernails than went under. Nevertheless, the impoverishment of the religious orders was very real by this period, nor were there fresh donors in the wings to deliver them. Creake itself, burnt out by a savage fire in the 1480s, found temporary assistance locally in the rebuilding programme which kept the canons busy through the next decades. But when a second catastrophe, the epidemic of 1506, carried off Creake's remaining community, there was nobody left to restore it.

The abbey's endowment, reverting to its patron Henry VII, was assigned by the king to Margaret Beaufort, his mother, to further the religious works that were her interest. Once, Dame Margaret herself had favoured the old-fashioned Benedictines of Westminster. It was to be in their church, in right royal company, that both she and her son would later rest. In her last years, however, on the advice of John Fisher, her scholar confessor, the king's mother had turned in a new direction altogether. The estates of Creake Abbey, far from remaining within the order, went instead to the endowment of Christ's College (Cambridge), one of the two colleges – St John's was the other – that Margaret Beaufort was promoting in the university. That model of piety of whom, it was said, 'all England for her death had cause of weeping', had snatched the bread of the Augustinians to cast it in the path of the reformers.

It was not for nothing that the Benedictines of Worcester, from soon after the friars' coming in the late 1220s, had lamented the arrival of the Franciscans in the strongest terms. At Worcester, their settlement had been one of the first in the kingdom. Yet in the 1480s, when the grey friars built the fine timber-framed guest-house now maintained by the National Trust, they were prospering there still in direct competition with the monks of the cathedral priory, their neighbours. Elsewhere, such rivalries were the common experience wherever the old orders and the new were both present. Thus, at fifteenth-century Oxford, the sluggish progress of the Cistercians in the building of their own St Bernard's College, contrasting so markedly with the current activity of the friars, was to occasion much ribald comment from passers-by. Again, late in that same century, the English Franciscans were to undergo a purge and renewal of their own. Under the personal patronage of Henry VII and at the urging initially of Margaret of Burgundy, sister of Edward IV, the austere Observants were introduced to England, to spread from bases next to the royal palaces at Greenwich and Richmond (Sheen). Too late in England to do much good, this reforming branch of the Franciscans, insisting on absolute poverty and on the literal observance of the Rule, had already found a welcome in other parts of Europe, not least of its triumphs being in Ireland.

There, to this day, the distinctions remain very striking. Against the poverty of many older houses, often much reduced (as at the Cistercian Monasteranenagh and Knockmoy) in the fifteenth century, and in obvious contrast to the monastic 'fortresses' of the embattled Cistercians of Bective, the Benedictines of Fore, or the Augustinians of Athassel and Kells, none of whom felt safe outside their walls, the friars flourished as never before. Take the fine sets of buildings, on their exposed estuarine sites, of the former Observant communities at neighbouring Moyne and Rosserk, in County Mayo. Or the almost equally isolated Ross Errilly (Co. Galway), at first a Conventual (unreformed) house of fourteenth-century foundation, becoming Observant as late as 1470. None of these houses, representative of many similar Mendicant communities in Ireland, were fortified. Yet all were fully and expensively equipped, and each could be walked into and resettled today, with only the roofs to restore.

The Irish took the friars to heart for reasons of race as well as class. Customarily excluded by the older orders, native-born Irishmen had found a welcome and a home amongst the friars. In England, the class dimension was especially important. Most English friaries, with only the very occasional exception like King's Langley, were urban-based. Since the thirteenth century, the friars had specialized in the cure of souls in the towns – in hearing confessions, in preaching, and in the remembrance and burial of the dead. Acknowledging these services and feeling a special kinship with the Mendicants as men with the same interests as themselves, the townspeople rewarded the friaries routinely in their wills.

The record of testamentary bequests is unequivocal. In late medieval London, it was the Mendicants who, increasingly, attracted the majority of donations to the regular clergy, leaving the older orders (the Possessioners) far behind. Notably, too, the Observants found rapid favour amongst Londoners, their reception being comparable to that of the Carthusians, also generously remembered by testators. The same preferences show up again in contemporary Norwich wills where, although individual donations are certainly present both to the Bridgettines of Syon and to the Carthusians of London and Mount Grace, the great bulk of bequests to the regular clergy went again to the four Norwich communities of Mendicants. Significantly, whereas legacies to Norwich Priory multiplied also at this time, they were directed not to the support of its Benedictine custodians but to the repair of the fabric of the cathedral church, an asset shared with the city. The cathedral, of course, survived the Dissolution. But so also, by a happy chance, did the Norwich Blackfriars, the great church of the Dominicans, or Friars Preachers. This huge building, only recently restored, provides two big halls, one in the long chancel of the former friary church, the other in its broad preaching nave. Extensively rebuilt in the fifteenth century, following the fire of 1413, the church was furnished at that time with armorial glass (now lost) recording the beneficence of local families, still patrons of the friars, over thirty of whom had been major contributors to its reconstruction.

Many of these families were of leading Norwich citizens, members of the mayoral class. But even more belonged to the lesser gentry of the region to whom the friars offered similar facilities, hearing their confessions and instructing them in the mysteries of the faith. Indeed, the endowment of sermons, at interments and other solemn occasions, had become common practice by the mid fifteenth century, enthusiastically taken up by the laity. And it was for this that the friars were peculiarly well equipped, being the best preachers available at precisely the period when the sermon had come into its own. Unsurprisingly, similar status testators elsewhere, as one recent study of the contemporary Yorkshire gentry has established, rarely forgot the friars in their wills. There was a scatter too, among the same Yorkshire will-making class, of donations to the local Carthusians at Mount Grace. But the mighty white monk (Cistercian) houses, so attractive to local benefactors in the twelfth and thirteenth centuries, had come to be regarded with indifference by fifteenth-century testators, as had those other great possessioner communities – the Gilbertines of Watton and Malton, the Augustinians of Bridlington, Guisborough and Nostell, or the Benedictines of Whitby, Selby and York – similarly the leaders within their own brotherhoods, yet low in the league of testators' preferences.

Of great significance also in the Yorkshire wills was the declared wish of the overwhelming majority of testators for local burial, not (as had once been the case) at the monastic house of the region, but at home amongst their kin in the parish church. The consequences of such a shift were important. In the fifteenth century, when they began to show up most obviously, prosperity was no more a characteristic of the late medieval rural gentry than of the contemporary upper echelons in the towns. Both had suffered from falling rent-rolls and from a shrinking market consequent on plague. Nevertheless, in town and country alike, parish churches thrust upwards in the Late Middle Ages – re-roofed, towered, and porched all anew, in a surge of commemorative activity.

One of the local churches undoubtedly known to the Yorkshire gentry was St Mary's, Thirsk, the focal point of an exceptionally large parish that included both country chapelries and market town. Thirsk Church is just a short way down the road from Mount Grace Priory, with which it has a building date in common. Yet the traditions represented by the two establishments are in complete contrast. As reconstructed from the ground in the mid-to-late fifteenth century, St Mary's, Thirsk, is all display. Particularly showy are the lavish openwork battlements, pinnacled at intervals along their length. In addition, Thirsk Church has those other characteristic embellishments of its period: the great west tower, the grand clerestory, the well-windowed aisles and big two-storeyed porch – all at their most elaborate on the southern show-front.

As with so many parallel building programmes all over the country, the impetus for the refashioning of St Mary's seems to have derived from the foundation of a personal chantry in the church, triggering off other donations. Robert Thirsk (d.1419), a wealthy civil servant, was the native son whose generous endowment of the Chantry of St Anne (mother of the Blessed Virgin Mary) gave the necessary confidence to his successors. At Wymington (Bedfordshire), the credit belongs to John Curteys (d.1391); at Chipping Campden (Gloucestershire), to William Grevel (d.1401); at Swaffham (Norfolk), to John Botright (d.1474); at Newbury (Berkshire), to John Smallwood (d.1519); at Lowick (Northamptonshire), to the Greene family; at Isleham (Cambridgeshire), to the Peytons; at Long Melford (Suffolk), to the Cloptons, in particular John Clopton (d.1497); and so on.

One of the most celebrated individual initiatives in the rebuilding of a parish church was at Fairford, in Gloucestershire, begun by a rich clothier, John Tame (d.1500), and finished by his son, Sir Edmund Tame (d.1534), who similarly lies buried in the chancel. Fairford was an investment. Its 'founder' expected to recoup his costs in the afterlife, and tells us as much on his tomb: 'For Jesus love pray for me / I may not pray, nowe pray ye / with a pater noster and an ave / that my paynys relessyd may be.' John Clopton, likewise 'founder' of the rebuilt parish church at Long Melford, took a less direct line – 'May Christ be my witness that I have not done these things in order to earn praise, but so that the Spirit should be remembered.' Both men, of course, meant the same. In each church, the founder's tomb occupies the place of honour, next to the high altar, where it might benefit most directly from the ritual. At each again, a personal chantry, supporting specially appointed chaplains, was intended to ensure continual intercession until the summoning of souls by the Last Trump.

Both churches were richly furnished and glazed – Long Melford by the Cloptons and other good men of the parish (Giles Dent and Roger Moryell, John Hill and Richard Loveday, John Keche and Richard Ellis, and many more); Fairford by Sir Edmund Tame, after his father's death. To this end at Fairford, Sir Edmund bought a full set of fourteen collegiate-style stalls. He may have obtained them ready-made at a bargain price, for they do not fit their present setting exactly. Fairford's famous glazing, too, is of exotic provenance, almost certainly made for elsewhere. Probably commissioned by Henry VII and

intended originally for a more central location like the king's personal chantry at Westminster Abbey, Fairford's glass is of exceptionally high quality. Its glory, until the storm of 1703 blew it in, was the great west window, catching the last rays of the westering sun in a Last Judgement of extraordinary size and splendour. In the Fairford window as it has since been restored, the chosen stand to the right of Christ the Judge, while the damned, pitchforked by demons, are flung into a Hell Mouth to his left. Sir Edmund Tame and his clothier father had done all they could to be numbered on that day with the former.

It is easy to imagine the Last Judgement window at Fairford incorporated in the homilies of visiting preachers. At many other churches, the same theme – appropriately called a Doom – was developed in full view of the seated congregation, over the chancel arch. The pious were quick to learn their lesson. If Purgatory's pains (as John Tame had asked) were indeed to be released, and if Judgement Day were to hold no further terrors, then something would have to be done, whether in private or co-operatively, to make a bid for effective intercession. For the very wealthy, a memorial college might serve this purpose; for the moderately rich, a personal chantry could be endowed in perpetuity or for a fixed term; lesser men settled for an obit (annual memorial mass at the parish church), or got together in the fellowship of a guild.

In late medieval England, the guild as co-operative benefit society was very fully developed, in the countryside hardly less so than in the towns. Many such associations were trade guilds also. But all shared an interest in the commemoration of former members and in the fitting interment of the dead. The movement had been given a strong boost by the Black Death. At King's Lynn, certainly, the Corpus Christi Guild (one of many of that allegiance all over the country) owed its origins directly to the pestilence. In the same town, the antique mercantile 'Great Guild' of Lynn, to which every trader belonged, was also known as the Trinity Guild and was similarly preoccupied with the funerals of its members, with obsequies and soul-masses for the departed. Of Lynn's more than sixty late medieval guilds, two of the largest – the Trinity Guild and St George's Guild – have left substantial buildings still intact. Next to Lynn's principal church, where the guildsmen would regularly have worshipped, the handsome fifteenth-century hall of the Trinity Guild remains in municipal use. St George's Hall, by Tuesday Market in the later northwards extension of the town, is of similar date and again of great size. Now adapted as a theatre and festival headquarters, it is owned by the National Trust.

Another property of the Trust, the Guildhall at Lavenham, is one of the latest of such halls to be built in England and, because of its associations with the Corpus Christi Guild, undoubtedly among the most interesting. Lavenham's Guildhall, prominently sited next to the Market Place, is an exceptionally handsome timber-framed building, thought to date to 1528–9 when the guild was granted a fresh charter. Very probably, the brotherhood at Lavenham had been constituted long before this time, and it had certainly become both rich and powerful by the 1520s. The feast of Corpus Christi (of the Blessed Sacrament or Body of Christ) had been introduced first to Britain in the 1320s. Observed on the Thursday after Trinity Sunday, it had quickly become the occasion for much civic pageantry and splendour, including a solemn procession of clergy and lay dignitaries to which the guilds might contribute 'pageants', or floats. In all this pomp, the Corpus Christi Guild was, of course, especially prominent, with a consequential effect on recruitment in the towns, seldom less than the majority of the citizenry.

Lavenham, in the days of the guild's glory, was a wealthy community. It had grown rich on the profits of the woollen cloth industry, generating (in the Spring family) a dynasty of entrepreneurial clothiers, and experiencing a rebuilding of both town and parish church, in which Thomas Spring III (d.1523), especially, was prominent. Contemporaneously, the men of Thaxted prospered co-operatively. A small borough, not far from

LAVENHAM GUILDHALL (Suffolk) Built for the rich Corpus Christi fraternity in 1528–9, shortly before the guild's suppression, Lavenham's Guildhall has had many uses since that time and has only recently been comprehensively restored.

Lavenham and close to the heart of the cloth-making region, Thaxted flourished on the allied trade of cutlery, particularly on the manufacture of shears. Its wealthy craftsmen poured money into Thaxted's noble parish church, of which the arcades date to just before the Black Death, but in which almost every other element of the building was to be replaced during the following century. In addition, just down the hill at the head of the market-place, the cutlers built themselves a fine new guildhall, jettied out on two stages for maximum display, in the most prominent position in their town.

Unlike the Corpus Christi hall at Lavenham, Thaxted's guildhall had a trading function, having an arcaded display and sales area on the ground floor. But its purpose was social as well. Just as the guildsmen of Lavenham would meet at their hall on Corpus Christi day, mustering for the procession and 'breakfasting' immoderately on their return, so Thaxted's cutlers and their wives gathered on 10 August every year to keep the feast of St Lawrence, their patron saint, co-dedicatee (with the Virgin and St John Baptist) of Thaxted parish church. When in 1508, as we know from their accounts, the brothers and sisters of St John Baptist (Swaffham) sat down to their own guild breakfast, they had a wide choice of meats, well sauced and spiced, with bread and cheese, and with as much ale as they could possibly consume. Including the fees of the cooks, and with minstrels and torch-bearers in attendance, the breakfast cost them between five and six pence a head, or as much individually as each had contributed to the common chest and pious rites of the guild.

These rites, of course, were chiefly memorial. Although conducted in common by the 'burial club' of the guild, and for many affordable only in such circumstances, they were essentially bids for individual salvation and for a personal contract with the Almighty. Before 1500, popular demand for such contracts would result in the goldsmiths of London complaining, with some reason, that fully one working day in twelve had come to be dedicated to the formal commemoration, by attendance at the obits or mind-days of the deceased, of late departed members of their fellowship. Indeed,

THAXTED GUILDHALL (Essex) An unusually complete fifteenth-century guildhall, built as a sales-point and meeting-place for the master cutlers of Thaxted, whose Guild of St Lawrence had also contributed substantially to the rebuilding of Thaxted parish church.

it was just this mounting burden of pious ceremonial and civic display that had helped empty many towns by the Late Middle Ages into the less demanding communities of the surrounding countryside.

Yet here too a personal religion, flowering with the plagues as had the Corpus Christi guilds, had begun to find expression in domestic building. Few manor-houses, from the fourteenth century, were to be without their private chapels or oratories. Licences to worship in the bosom of the family had never been so much in demand. Among the earlier of these private oratories is the fine first-floor chapel, lavishly fenestrated in the Decorated style,

IGHTHAM MOTE (Kent) The reconstruction of the north range at Ightham in the 1520s included the provision of this fine private chapel, with its contemporary furnishings still perfectly intact.

at the National Trust's Clevedon Court, near Bristol. Clevedon is of the early fourteenth century, and its chapel still, at the time that it was built, could reasonably have been justified in terms of convenience, for church and manor-house were sited far apart, at opposite ends of the same parish. By the fifteenth century, with private oratories everywhere the fashion, such excuses were neither necessary nor even relevant. William Lovell's considerable manor-house at Minster Lovell, an entirely fresh project of the 1430s, is immediately next door to the parish church in which Lovell himself lies buried. Yet a handsome chapel, on the first floor as at Clevedon, was nevertheless included as equipment of the new building. It had been put there by Lovell's architect as of right.

Minster Lovell was a 'great' house, more like Haddon Hall (with its own impressive chapel, very similar in date) than like Clevedon or other manor-houses of that class. However, there was nothing unusual about the provision at Minster Lovell for private worship. Take the case of such other manors, in most respects routine, as Lytes Cary (in Somerset) or Bradley (in south Devon), both now in the care of the National Trust. At Lytes Cary, the fourteenth-century chapel, originally free-standing, became very much a family facility, the home from 1343 of a personal chantry of the Lytes and afterwards continually in use. It is now chiefly remarkable for the fine furnishings installed there by Thomas Lyte as late as 1631, including a heraldic frieze of his descent. Equally personal to the family, which it celebrates similarly in the heraldic bosses of its roof, is the chapel built at Bradley when the better part of the house was reconstructed, in a programme datable to the 1420s. Licensed for worship on 7 February 1428, the new chapel's consecration coincided with that of the rebuilt parish church at neighbouring Highweek, to which the Yardes, owners of Bradley and lords of the manor, had again contributed generously, maintaining a family vault there in the north aisle.

Certainly the private chapel, once recognized as equipment appropriate to such a life-style, was slow thereafter to disappear from the manor-house, even when overtaken in the 1530s by the Reformation. Just before that upheaval, William Sandys's chapel at The Vyne (also National Trust) ranks undoubtedly among the grandest of such apartments. It has a full set of canopied stalls, rivalling those of a collegiate church, with high-quality glass (including an image of Sandys's royal patron, Henry VIII), and with expensive painted tiles from the Netherlands. At just the same time, Richard Clement, similarly a Tudor royal servant, extended and modernized the already handsome manor-house which he had bought in 1521 at Ightham Mote. One of his improvements to the mansion (recently acquired by the Trust) was the re-siting of the chapel, formerly next to the solar, which he rebuilt at first-floor level in the north range. What resulted was an exceptionally generous chamber, still furnished today with the stalls, screen and pulpit of Clement's time, and with a fine barrel vault obsequiously painted in Tudor livery. The royal badges on the ceiling, dating it to 1527 or before, include the pomegranate motif of Catherine of Aragon, whose divorce from Henry VIII, rejected by the Pope, visited such catastrophe on the Church.

Sudden and dramatic though the changes in public policy were to be, they took longer to work their way through into private homes. The Moretons of Cheshire were a conformist family, as ready to bend belief in obedience to the regime as were Sandys and Clement, lackeys of the first Tudor monarchs. Yet still, early in Elizabeth's reign, John Moreton was to add a new private chapel to the accommodation at his remarkable timber-framed manor-house at Little Moreton Hall, and this in turn would be extended, before the queen's death, into a chancel projecting to the east. At much the same time, in 1598, Edward Norris was making the additions to Speke Hall, just south of Liverpool, which completed the quadrangle with a new north range, and of which an element was a spacious family chapel. But the Norrises, unlike the Moretons, were recusants – upholders of the old faith. And the private chapel at Speke, with its accompanying priest-holes, was a luxury replete with danger for their kind.

In succeeding generations, the Norrises suffered for their beliefs, and so did others of their allegiance like the Whitgreaves of Moseley Old Hall, another National Trust property, now principally remembered for the part the house played in 1651 in Charles II's escape from the Parliamentarians. Charles came to Moseley from Boscobel, itself a recusant household (where he had hidden in an oak), after the Royalist defeat at Worcester. He was made welcome by Thomas Whitgreave and was attended by Whitgreave's chaplain, Father John Huddlestone, who showed him the oratory, under the eaves of the building, which is still on display there to visitors. It was then (we are told) that Huddlestone obtained the king's promise, which he was never able to keep, to restore the Catholic families to their full liberties. The clock was too far forward to be corrected. Family priests and private chapels, guilds and chantries, colleges and everything (both good and bad) about the monks – all had been swept away, or rendered treasonable, by the Reformation. There was no base on which to build for their return.

[3]

The Gentle Life

For two centuries before the Black Death, the great landowners had kept their best estates in hand, steadily improving their farming methods and drawing huge profits off the land. Benefiting directly from the population surplus, they had been favoured by high prices and good rents. Yet both prices and rents were to go into a decline after 1350, and options narrowed dramatically. To maintain the lavish life-style required by their condition, landowners commonly leased out their demesnes on increasingly generous terms, looking elsewhere for alternative support. Shortly, what had begun as a temporary retrenchment following the Pestilence of 1348–9, turned into a full-scale retreat. Even the most sluggish of landlords – and there were none more conservative than the monks – had abandoned demesne farming by the 1420s. Their successors were their neighbours and former dependents, the gentry and the yeomen, who had been waiting long enough in the wings.

This middling class of person, ranging from the big-time squire (or laird) to the comfortably-off small-holder, was ideally placed to profit from the crumbling of the great estates and well suited by the slowness of their failure. The Leghs of Adlington, for example, still in residence there today, can look back into the fourteenth century for their origins. Keeping their heads below the parapet and their fortunes immune, the Leghs survived and prospered where magnates and great churchmen, like comets in the firmament, made their swift and careless passage into oblivion. By 1500, the family's manor-house at Adlington, like that of the Heskeths at Rufford or the Lytes at Lytes Cary and many others, was comfortable and even passing grand. Such buildings headed a chain of housing – standardly equipped with kitchens, halls and chambers – which ran down and out through the bottom of the class into the compact terrace dwellings of the towns.

To the towns themselves, unless by some chance they were to profit from the cloth trade, the population retreat had been near-fatal. Expansion had ceased; plots were left vacant; burgesses, learning the danger of living at close quarters, took to their heels before the plague. Yet while the economy closed down, while the guilds established their grip on what trade was left, and while municipal government fell to the oligarchies, a good living could still be made by the few. In the cloth towns especially, burgess housing grew more sophisticated by the day. Paycocke's House, in Coggeshall, built in about 1500 for a family of 'millionaire' clothiers, had all the comforts of a manor-house like Adlington. However, wealth such as the Paycockes' was no longer the prerequisite of ease. Nobody could have seen the tower-houses of fifteenth-century Ireland as in any way ideal family homes. Their purpose, when the chips were down, was defence. Nevertheless, all the basic comforts of everyday life were to be found from the start in even the smallest of these towers, while their larger equivalents – in Scotland and the frontier zones of England also – developed a style of vertically-tiered accommodation as comprehensive as any on the flat.

Broadly, in any event, the quarrels of magnates in late medieval Britain – most oppressive in the prolonged dynastic contest of the Wars of the Roses (from 1455) – touched gentry and burgesses only tangentially. At worst, the enemy of the Anglo-Irish squire was the Gaelic cattle-rustler; in Scotland, the laird's assassin was his acknowledged opponent in the blood-feud. Elsewhere, left to himself in modest affluence, the middling man, both in town and country, fashioned a life-style more private than in the past, more closely resembling our own. Standards, except in plumbing, have hardly changed.

SMALLHYTHE PLACE (Kent) A comfortable small farmhouse of the early sixteenth century in which the central hall (left of the door) is still preserved, although floored over from the start to provide extra accommodation at first-floor level.

Private wealth and general, or corporate, poverty are old companions. Recessions are seldom universal. Short of catastrophe, the high expectations of one generation are only exceptionally abandoned by the next. Before the Black Death, domestic standards had already long been in the ascent. Nor would anything that followed change a style of life to which men of most conditions had grown accustomed. Indeed late medieval Britain, as we may now appreciate, had many points in common with our own era, not least in its insistence on excessive personal spending, placing special emphasis on the comforts of the home.

OLD SOAR, PLAXTOL (Kent) The spacious great chamber of a manor-house of *c.* 1290, illustrative of the tendency already evident by that date for the lord to retreat to his private apartments, away from the hubbub of the hall.

Such comforts were not unrecognized before the 1350s. The National Trust's manor-house at Old Soar, near Plaxtol (Kent), now in the guardianship of the State, preserves a representative chamber-block of the 1290s. It is a handsome two-storeyed building, with solar and chapel at first-floor level, and with its own private garderobe annexed. Already the functions of the great common hall, so much a part of the old tradition, were at risk. Old Soar's Colepepper lords could retreat, if they wished, to the ease and seclusion of their private apartments, leaving the bustle of the household behind. And while many might regret the passing companionship of the hall – life-breath of the feudal affinity – the will to preserve it was on the wane. Old Soar's great hall, since disguised by rebuildings, still had a purpose in the manor-house. Yet even as early as this, in the 1290s or before, what deserves emphasis rather is the privacy that everywhere, from castle to farmstead, was replacing the life lived in common. Individual apartments proliferated in the later Middle Ages. They might have done so, of course, for specialized purposes – as business chambers or for dining away from the crowd. But the common instinct all displayed was a need we still share: the desire for a room of one's own.

Strikingly, many houses that survive from the Late Middle Ages are comfortable even by today's standards, commanding a high price as family homes. Plainly, this is the case with the modest timber-framed town-houses of centres like Lavenham or Saffron Walden. It has also long been true of the country cousins of these, the much sought-after 'Wealden' houses of Kent and Sussex, now the resort of city stockbrokers. Both are currently favoured for their size. However, it is worth recalling too that even the larger manor-houses of late medieval England, as built to a common but grander formula by the fifteenth century, have only recently begun to outgrow their modern owners, to be turned over to the care of the Trust among others, while many yet remain in private hands. What was this formula, and why did it continue to be relevant? In National Trust properties like Cotehele and Great Chalfield, Baddesley Clinton, Ightham Mote and Lytes Cary, the answers become obvious enough.

The first thing to notice is their scale. Houses like these show little of that duplication of living units so characteristic of the greater fortresses of chivalry. They are family homes, and have been preserved as such because the family fitted into them so well. Take the Edgcumbes' Cotehele, for example, most complete of these houses and scarcely altered since the mid sixteenth century. Cotehele, like Baddesley Clinton, Ightham Mote and many others, is a courtyard house, entered through a small crenellated gatehouse on the south side of the court, with the hall in the opposing north range. The main surviving works at Cotehele are of the late fifteenth and early sixteenth centuries. And by this time, certainly, the domestic courtyard plan had settled down to include standard elements, all of which were to be repeated in the Edgcumbes' manor-house. As at the much earlier Old Soar, Cotehele's chamber block (subsequently extended to the north) adjoined one end of the common hall, with the service rooms and kitchen at the other. In the west range, next to the chamber, was a private chapel. Other lodgings and stores completed the court, while (exceptionally) a second court was later added to the west of the first, with a diminutive 'kitchen court' to the north.

Cotehele, with its so-called 'retainers' court' and other secondary extensions, was to spread out further across its plot than most manor-houses of comparable date. Nevertheless, Cotehele's proportions remained intimate and domestic, and it was on just such a scale that Baddesley Clinton was planned, or the only marginally grander Ightham Mote. Both are confined within water-filled moats which probably date to 1300 or before. And defence, certainly, was another consideration in

COTEHELE HOUSE (Cornwall) The hall range on the north side (opposite the gatehouse) of the main court at Cotehele, built by Sir Piers Edgcumbe shortly after he inherited the manor-house in 1489; to the left of the door, the big window lit the high table, with the private apartments to the left again, separating the hall from the chapel (far left), built by Piers' father, Sir Richard.

developing the formula plan. The modest but determined crenellated gatehouses of Baddesley Clinton and Ightham Mote precisely parallel Sir Richard Edgcumbe's late fifteenth-century entrance at Cotehele. Each, in its time, was to be tested by a later attack. And each gave admittance to a small court, or quadrangle, surrounded by ranges of which the principal elements were the great public hall, the private apartments of the family's solar block, and the kitchen with service rooms (pantry and buttery) attached.

Baddesley Clinton's great hall has now gone, nor is there much today of the fifteenth-century mansion later so thoroughly rebuilt by Henry Ferrers ('the Antiquary') in the 1580s. Ightham Mote has been luckier in what has survived. The hall, although re-glazed by Sir Richard Clement in the 1520s when he modernized the private apartments and built his chapel, is otherwise substantially of the mid fourteenth century. Moreover, already at that date Ightham's hall was clearly less a place of public assembly than a vehicle for family display. Clement, the Tudor courtier, would reinforce this purpose by introducing a brave show of armorial glass: the red rose of Lancaster and the white rose of York, the portcullis of Beaufort (Henry VIII's personal emblem), and the pomegranate of Catherine of Aragon. Yet it had been implicit all along in the frame of the apartment – in a height altogether disproportionate to its length – as well as in the quality of the fittings.

Ightham Mote's hall is almost exactly half the size of Sir John de Pulteney's contemporary great 'hall of chivalry' at Penshurst Place, a few miles away to the southwest. Yet a hall of adequate scale was clearly as obligatory for the Cawnes of Ightham, at their own level in society, as for Pulteney and his magnate successors. Indeed, regardless of what use might be made of it, no late medieval manor-house, rectory, or urban tenement of any size would be complete without a hall of appropriate substance. Plainly furnished (though spacious and lordly) halls have survived at the National Trust's manor-houses at Great Chalfield and Lytes Cary, both dating to the second half of the fifteenth century. At contemporary Rufford Old Hall, the Trust maintains one of the most

elaborate examples – complete with full apparatus of screen, roof and canopy – of the entire long-lasting tradition.

Sir Thomas Hesketh, probably the rebuilder of Rufford Old Hall in its present form, was a wealthy man. He had come into a fortune lately much increased, not least by himself, through a succession of well-judged marriages. Like his father, grandfather, and great-grandfather before him, Hesketh had married an heiress. He recorded his debt in the heraldry of the manor-house to which these accumulated riches had contributed. No expense was spared on his new buildings. As it stands today, Rufford's great hall is the sole survival of Hesketh's house; the chamber block (formerly to the west) has gone completely, while the kitchen wing (to the east) has since been very extensively rebuilt. Yet the hall itself is perfect and untouched, kept immune from later interference by its grandeur. Much of Rufford's display is in its fine hammerbeam roof, with shield-bearing angels against the hammers, like a church. At the lower (service) end, a movable screen, curiously carved, is the hall's most memorable furnishing. It is framed between panelled speres and backed by blind quatrefoils in a deliberately theatrical set-piece.

Easily lost in such dramatic total effects is the domestication of an apartment of this kind. At Rufford's upper (high table) end, a coved 'canopy of honour' lowered the ceiling over Hesketh and his guests, while next to them a tall bay window again served to delimit (as we have seen it do already in the much grander circumstances of Linlithgow and Stirling) an area of inviolable private space. The definition of such space was important. A couple of generations later, in the 1530s, it would cause the addition of a family parlour (now called the 'oriel') to the hall at Lytes Cary, developing on Rufford's bay window. However, there was to be no replacement as yet for the hall itself, still regarded as a badge of gentility. John Lyte's improvements to the private quarters at Lytes Cary did little to reduce the centrality of the existing hall to his manor-house. If anything, the addition of a new porch and annexed parlour enhanced its prominence, even as the family increasingly withdrew.

Previous page IGHTHAM MOTE (Kent) England's most picturesque moated manor-house, with accommodation ranging in date from the mid fourteenth to the early sixteenth centuries, the gatehouse (left) being a rebuilding of *c.* 1450.

Right RUFFORD OLD HALL (Lancashire) Sir Thomas Hesketh's mid fifteenth-century timber-built hall is one of the finest survivals of its kind, still containing the richly carved movable screen which helped shut off the activity at the lower (service) end.

Lytes Cary has its parallels in the stone-built Dorset halls at Milton and Athelhampton. Samlesbury (Lancashire) and Adlington (Cheshire) each share characteristics with Rufford. Of course, such halls could accommodate an entire household at a sitting, but what mattered increasingly was the gesture. Athelhampton, built in the late 1490s as the country retreat of a former city merchant, was furnished externally with a fine set of fairy-tale crenellations. It had the porch and full-height bay of the contemporary hall of chivalry, but while perfect in every detail and most expensively finished, was military in no other way. Furthermore, despite Sir William Martyn's considerable personal fortune – he had been Master of the Skinners' Company and Mayor of London before retiring to his family home in Dorset – he built only to accommodate his immediate household, the scale of the new manor-house being miniature. Compare Athelhampton, for example, with Gains-

Above ATHELHAMPTON (Dorset) The great bay window, fine porch and expensive crenellations of Athelhampton's hall (centre) are as Sir William Martyn (d.1504) left them, the west wing (left) being an extension of c.1540, greatly enlarging the private quarters.

Right GAINSBOROUGH OLD HALL (Lincolnshire) A remarkable late fifteenth-century timber-framed great hall to which, behind the end wall, a contemporary brick kitchen block is still attached.

borough Old Hall as rebuilt by Sir Thomas Burgh in the 1470s. Burgh's hall at Gainsborough was a very grand apartment, humbling the spectator by sheer space. In contrast, Sir William Martyn's hall, much smaller overall, achieved its effects rather through the deliberately contrived splendour of its elaborately cusped roof-beams and the expensive stone panelling of its bay. Burgh entertained the

king at Gainsborough in 1484. In Burgh's hall and kitchen, surviving in splendid partnership, the full demands of a large company could be met. Martyn's needs, a few years later, were quite different. Enjoying the fruits of his civic labours in rural retreat, Martyn quoted chivalry only to domesticate it. Athelhampton, unsurprisingly, remains a family home, while Gainsborough has been thoroughly municipalized.

What Martyn required from his hall at Athelhampton was characteristic of his class and his period. Nor was it confined to lay landowners of Martyn's standing. Related to Athelhampton in more than one detail was William Middleton's hall at Milton Abbey. Completed in 1498, the abbot's hall at Milton was not a large apartment, being intended only for Middleton's private lodgings. Nevertheless, its roof was finished with exceptional display, piling one effect insistently upon another. It was generously windowed, and there was much show of heraldry, with an elaborate carved screen, less exotic and more architectural than the screen at Rufford, but equally theatrical in effect.

Certainly, a sense of drama pervades these apartments. At Samlesbury, another huge movable screen, the closest direct parallel to Hesketh's screen at Rufford, is carved with oppressive exuberance. Similarly, the entire hall at Adlington is operatic in flavour, and while much of this is owed to seventeenth-century alterations which included the insertion of a fine organ over the former screen, dramatic emphasis was clearly present from the start. Thus Adlington's hall is a tall apartment, almost as high as it is long. It has the lofty hammerbeam roof, richly embattled and with angels on the hammers, found already at Rufford. A canopy of honour, no fewer than five tiers deep, has been painted since the sixteenth century with the heraldry of the Cheshire gentry, among whom the Leghs of Adlington and their relatives were prominent.

The prominence was long established by 1500 when Thomas Legh was remodelling his manor-house. The Leghs had been at Adlington since the early fourteenth century, frequently holding office in the county. They still keep their name on the land. But they have never risen above the rank of country gentry to join the aristocracy of the nation. And Adlington today, as it has always been, is no more than a gentleman's family home. This, of course, is its particular importance. Like Rufford or Lytes Cary, yet in a peculiarly evocative manner which it owes to its naïve seventeenth-century redecoration, the hall at Adlington models that

public space, furnished to a set formula of screen, roof and canopy, which was one major element of the 'gentle life' as Thomas Legh and his contemporaries understood it. A second element, the private space of the solar, or great chamber, is better illustrated at the National Trust's property at Great Chalfield.

Thomas Tropnell (d.1488), builder of Chalfield, was another country landowner, especially gifted in the law and owing much of his wealth to that skill. For fully thirty years before acquiring absolute ownership of the estate in 1467, Tropnell had coveted Great Chalfield. Consequently we might suppose that the manor-house he then built was the fruit of much forward planning. It was a courtyard house, considerably larger in Tropnell's day than at present, with additional domestic ranges to the south of his own quarters, and with a service wing and gatehouse to the northwest. What survives, essentially, is Tropnell's private range, in which a hall was central to two chamber blocks, each equipped with a stair of its own. The hall was spacious but traditional. It had bays, north and south, at the high-table end, with a big fireplace next to one of them in the north wall. There was an expensive panelled roof, a fine set of windows, and a porch and screens passage to the west. More original were the private chambers with which, for its day, Great Chalfield was exceptionally well endowed. What is now called the 'dining room', at the lower end of the hall, was probably always intended for that purpose. It was close to Tropnell's kitchen, and provides evidence already of a move to private eating, away from the cold spaces of the hall. Above it, a fine bedchamber was equipped with a polygonal oriel window only a degree less handsome than the semicircular oriel of Tropnell's own great chamber, at the opposite end of the same building. All the family chambers had fireplaces of their own, with adequate provision of individual garderobes.

Great Chalfield, in rural Wiltshire, was only lightly defended, owing what little formal protection it enjoyed to a pre-existing moat and curtain wall. In more threatened areas, builders of Tropnell's class had fewer choices in the layout of individual units of accommodation, although what they required of them overall was the same. Comparatively immune from later adaptation, the tower-houses of the North of England, of Scotland and of Ireland, again establish the uniformity of gentry tastes.

One of the more comprehensive transformations of a fourteenth-century tower-house has taken

SCOTNEY CASTLE (Kent) A surviving angle-tower at Roger
Ashburnham's water-girt fortress, built in the late 1370s as a
precaution against French coastal raids.

Left CAHIR CASTLE (Co. Tipperary)
Clustered tower-houses give a
characteristically Irish profile to this great
late medieval fortress of the earls of
Ormond.

Left MICHELHAM PRIORY GATEHOUSE (East
Sussex) Prior Leem's big gatehouse of
c. 1400 was the key to the defences of this
small Augustinian priory, moated as a
precaution against the coastal raids which
were a constant threat during the
Hundred Years War.

Right ST MICHAEL'S MOUNT (Cornwall)
Although much rebuilt, both the church
and former refectory of a Benedictine
priory have been preserved on the
Mount, strikingly situated away from the
shore like its Norman mother-house at
Mont St Michel.

Above FOTHERINGHAY CHURCH (Northamptonshire) Shorn of
its chancel (right) and lacking the college buildings that show
now only as grass humps in the foreground, the church at
Fotheringhay nevertheless gives a fair idea of the scale of a big
aristocratic collegiate chantry, richly endowed in the fifteenth
century by successive dukes of York.

Below left BEAUCHAMP CHAPEL, WARWICK CHURCH
(Warwickshire) The fine monument of Richard Beauchamp,
Earl of Warwick (d. 1439), is the centre-piece of the chapel
commissioned by his executors shortly after his death but not
finished until 1457.

Above right BADDESLEY CLINTON (West Midlands) Seen from the
north, Baddesley Clinton has lost the hall range of the fifteenth-
century moated manor-house, this side of its courtyard being
open; today, the entrance range (left) is the most imposing,
having a neat little gatehouse remodelled in the late sixteenth
century by Henry Ferrers, a noted antiquary for whom
Baddesley was substantially rebuilt.

Below right IGHTHAM MOTE (Kent) A moated manor-house of
the mid fourteenth century, extensively rebuilt in the 1520s by
the Tudor court official, Richard Clement, to whom the
building owes much of its picturesque timber-framing; at
Ightham, the great hall is fourteenth-century, the gatehouse was
raised into a tower in the mid fifteenth century, and the north
range (as rebuilt by Richard Clement) contains one of the most
complete private chapels in England, restored but otherwise
little changed since Clement's time.

Above left ASHLEWORTH TITHE BARN
(Gloucestershire) The barn of the canons
of St Augustine's (Bristol) on their
important rectorial manor at Ashleworth,
of which the church and fifteenth-
century rectory also survive; the barn was
built by Abbot Newland in *c.*1500.

Left CLERGY HOUSE, ALFRISTON (East
Sussex) Next to the big parish church,
Alfriston's former vicarage dates to the
fourteenth century and is a rare intact
survival of its class.

Above FOUNTAINS ABBEY (North Yorkshire) A fine tower, added to the north transept at Fountains in the early sixteenth century, rises above the already grand Chapel of the Nine Altars, itself an extension of the east end of the abbey church three centuries earlier to accommodate relics and their altars.

Overleaf LACOCK ABBEY (Wiltshire) William Sharington's tower (*c.*1550), built on the site of the former abbey church, carried octagonal banqueting rooms and a viewpoint chamber; in Lacock's east range (right), much of the original medieval building east of the cloister survives, including the nuns' chapter-house and their warming room.

Above ADLINGTON HALL (Cheshire) A country gentleman's hall of *c.* 1500, made more theatrical by its late seventeenth-century redecoration (including the insertion of the great organ), but always an apartment of some drama.

Left GREAT CHALFIELD MANOR (Wiltshire) The hall porch and west oriel of Thomas Tropnell's fine new manor-house, built between 1460 and 1480.

Below SIZERGH CASTLE (Cumbria) A great fourteenth-century tower-house, subsequently much modified internally, to which in the fifteenth century a hall range (far side) was added as the menace of Scottish raiding parties subsided.

place over the years at Sizergh Castle, a major National Trust property in Cumbria. Yet even here the usual basement, the first-floor hall, and the two storeys above of private chambers, so familiar in tower-houses wherever they may be, are easily identifiable in the present fabric. Nor have we far to look for purer specimens. Belsay Castle, in Northumberland, recently stripped back to its medieval stonework, is similar both in date and in scale to the Trust's Sizergh. Both the Middletons of Belsay and the Stricklands of Sizergh were major landowners and military leaders in the North. Consequently, their castles were of above average size. Nevertheless, each shares the plan of much smaller tower-houses, with a kitchen at the bottom, in the basement or ground floor, with a big first-floor hall across the full length of the building, and with a great chamber on the next level above. Sizergh's fourth floor is missing at Belsay, to be made up instead by an adjoining service wing, in which – in a not untypical example of sophisticated internal planning – both the staircase and private bedchambers were accommodated. Crowning the whole, Belsay's machicolated parapets and cor-belled-out bartisans are the tower's most memorable characteristics. They recall that pomp of chivalry already witnessed below in the once lavish heraldic wall-paintings of the hall.

Pomp of this kind is abundantly displayed in the exceptional sophistication of a Scottish tower-house like Cardoness, the McCulloch stronghold in coastal Galloway. Cardoness, indeed, is a miniature palace in which six tiers of living-space are stacked within one frame to provide accom-modation every whit as complete as that of many manor-houses of the South. But Cardoness, built within a few decades of 1500, is unusually well equipped. And certainly more typical of tower-building generally is the National Trust for Scotland's Castle Campbell, in Dollar Glen.

Castle Campbell owes much of its present appearance to very extensive sixteenth-century additions. Yet its dominant feature is still a great tower, dating here to the late fifteenth century. Castle Campbell's tower is not a welcoming building. It is as austere externally as the tower at Cardoness. Internally, in the contrasting simplicity

CASTLE CAMPBELL (Central) A big fifteenth-century tower-house which, although extended in the late sixteenth century with residential ranges, originally held within it all the elements of the gentle life, from the ground-floor vaulted store to two levels of chambers above the hall.

93

of its fittings, Castle Campbell departs little today from its earliest image – 'the tower of the place of Gloom'. Nevertheless, the essential elements of the gentle life-style are all present. The ground floor, too dark and dank for normal living, is given over to a vaulted basement, or cellar store. Above, a first-floor hall is heated by a big fireplace in the eastern wall and lit by a window on the south. Good private chambers on the second and third floors are each separately equipped with a garderobe and bed-space, contrived in the thickness of the walls.

For the tower-house, then, a vertical plan had been reached which, in all its essentials, was scarcely different from that achieved elsewhere on the flat. Some of the simplest of the class were built in Ireland. Consider Audley's Castle, in County Down, or the almost identical Kilclief and Jordan's Castle, just a few miles along the same coast. All three are of the fifteenth century, and although superficially having little in common with such contemporary English manor-houses as Rufford, Lytes Cary, or Great Chalfield, repeat the same accommodation in all but scale. Audley's Castle, unlike the other two, preserves the foundations of an accompanying walled courtyard, or bawn. Within that enclosure, additional lodgings, stores and barrack-rooms once had their place. But the family at Audley's, as at Jordan's and Kilclief, resided in a tower equipped in the same style as Castle Campbell's. Two full-height turrets, on the entrance facade of each of these three Irish tower-houses, protect the door and provide space internally for a newel stair and for garderobes against the upper floors. Over a ground-floor store, the first-floor 'hall' has a large fireplace, wall-cupboards, a slop-drain for waste water, and a garderobe of its own, with windows (all with fitted window-seats) on each face. Kilclief and Jordan's Castle both have two levels of chambers above the hall; Audley's has only one. Although not all separately heated, every chamber has its garde-robe; most have wall-cupboards and all are well lit, with good windows offering fine views.

Beyond doubt, whatever the quality of earlier accommodation on these sites, the tower-house promised something better, in line with ascending expectations. These were expectations, further-more, that were widely shared, and that were in no way confined to the ruling classes. We can talk with confidence, for example, of a 'dietary optimum' in the fifteenth century, when both peasants and townspeople enjoyed better bread, ate more meat and drank more ale than they had ever done before the Black Death. Yet over the identical period, aristocratic diet is thought to have changed very much less. For all classes, too, clothing became richer and more varied in the Late Middle Ages, giving rise to those curiosities, the sumptuary laws, which attempted to regulate apparel by social rank.

PRIEST'S HOUSE, MUCHELNEY (Somerset) A vicarage built by the monks of Muchelney in the early fourteenth century and little altered since, though the windows (restored) are fifteenth-century insertions.

In building, the same pressures operated still more obviously.

Among the properties, for example, of the National Trust is a clutch of late medieval priests' houses, as precisely graded by rank in their time as are the married quarters of one of our present-day armed services. Easton-on-the-Hill, the smallest of these houses, is of the late fifteenth century. It has one room above and one below, and was probably the residence of chantry chaplains. Yet even Easton, despite its small scale, was a building of some quality, with well-finished windows, a good newel stair, and with a fireplace to warm the upper chamber. Vicarages could be very much grander. From the thirteenth century, when reforming bishops for the first time took an interest in such matters, a house 'fitting for the status of the vicar' became increasingly a requirement even of rural parishes. Thus when the monks of Muchelney, in 1308, negotiated an outright take-over (appropriation) of the parish church, they had to build their vicar a new dwelling which, as it survives today, is a

95

house of which none of us would feel ashamed. Like its contemporary and close parallel, the Clergy House at Alfriston, Muchelney's former vicarage has the central hall and flanking chamber blocks of a much larger building, closely resembling a late medieval manor-house in plan. At both houses, too, the decorative detail is of above average quality, whether in the ornamental carving of Alfriston's internal beams or in the fine fenestration of the south front at Muchelney, renewed in the late fifteenth century. Corbridge, in Northumberland, preserves a contemporary 'Vicar's Pele', immediately next to the parish church, which is the exact tower-house equivalent of these vicarages. The Pele has a vaulted store at its base, with a hall above, and with a chamber on the next level, below the parapet. In the hall, the vicar's wash-basin, his wall-cupboards and a fireplace remain; in the chamber, what appears to have been

his reading-desk. Corbelled-out bartisans at the angles of the tower once gave the Corbridge Pele a military style which reinforced the status of the priest.

Ranking still higher, the rectory at Martock – called the 'Treasurer's House' after Martock's appropriator, the Treasurer of Wells – can have differed little in scale from the now vanished manor-house in the same parish. Martock has the full-sized hall of such a house, with an earlier two-storeyed solar block (thirteenth-century) at right angles to this hall, and with a kitchen (fifteenth-century) later added to it. Martock's generous buildings, the occasional country residence of a high official of the Church, are of above average quality. But they are certainly far from unique.

One of the better preserved rectorial complexes of the Late Middle Ages is Ashleworth, in Gloucestershire, formerly the property of the canons of St Augustine's (Bristol), who were also lords of the manor. Just to the west of the parish church at Ashleworth, itself extensively rebuilt in the fifteenth century, is an impressive stone tithe-barn of about 1500, now in the care of the National Trust. To the north, the fine rectory is a little

CLERGY HOUSE, ALFRISTON (East Sussex) A fourteenth-century vicarage, with central hall flanked by two-storey chamber blocks, the service rooms at the lower end of the hall having no direct access to the priests' chambers (right).

earlier. It is a large building of the mid fifteenth century, scarcely touched by time, of which the constituent parts are a big central hall, a two-storeyed solar range at the upper (northern) end, and another chamber (over pantry and buttery) to the south. There were good-sized windows at Ashleworth and handsome timber roofs to both hall and solar, the accommodation fully matching the requirements of the bishop who, a century before, had had this to say of a Somerset vicarage, similarly the responsibility of Augustinian canons: 'We think the vicar should have a house . . . nearer the church . . . fitting for the status of the vicar, viz., with the hall and two solars and two cellars, one solar with the cellar at the front end of the hall, and another solar with the cellar at the back end of the hall. Also a kitchen, a grange, a stable for three horses, and a dovecote. . . .'

If the late medieval parish clergy expected accommodation of this standard, so inevitably did the classes out of which they sprang – the better-off farming families and small-town burgesses. There is little, certainly, to separate their housing. Alfriston Clergy House, although an early example of its kind, was a building of the familiar Wealden type, differing only in the deliberate isolation of its service range, to keep clergy and maidservants apart. Yet Alfriston's central hall, open to the rafters, with two storeys of chambers at each end, anticipates the same basic plan as the rectory at Ashleworth. And it was this plan again, identical in arrangement but on every kind of scale, that continued to feature everywhere in secular building, reconciling new pressures for private family space with the traditional shared fellowship of the hall.

The National Trust's holdings include several of these buildings. And they point the way (as do rectories, vicarages, and chantry priests' lodgings) down the common path of late medieval domestic architecture, unchanging in its inventory of accommodation. Lower Brockhampton, in its rural isolation, might today seem little more than a large farmhouse, especially picturesque in its timber-framing. Yet it retains the ground-floor hall, with adjoining chamber blocks (only one of which has survived), of a much larger contemporary stone

manor-house like the Oxfordshire Broughton. Like Broughton, too, it has a water-filled moat and detached gatehouse approach. Neither Westwood (Wiltshire) nor Stoneacre (Kent), again properties of the Trust, have the overstated 'defences' of Lower Brockhampton. Built in the 1480s, or at about the same time as the little gatehouse at Brockhampton, they post-date its hall range by as many as three generations. Yet each, while as modest in scale as Lower Brockhampton, repeats the same ground-floor hall and annexed chamber arrangements, as if the formula, by this date, were immutable.

In point of fact, within another three generations or less, the halls at Westwood and Stoneacre had been subdivided horizontally, floored over to provide additional accommodation at first-floor level. However, what such halls continued to demonstrate, right up to the end of the medieval period, was the obstinate strength of the old traditions, even at buildings ranking merely among farmhouses. Westwood, in particular, though now dignified as a 'manor', had at no stage been more than a small estate, one of the lesser properties of the monks of Winchester, which they were content to lease out to a lay tenant. Yet when Thomas Culverhouse, the cathedral priory's farmer at Westwood, extended his quarters in the 1480s, what he felt to be appropriate was a new central range of which the principal element was a big open hall, originally taken up into the rafters. At Stoneacre similarly, John Ellys' hall (now cleared of its later floor and restored to full height) is a major apartment, complete with the screen and the crown-post roof which from the first added dignity to volume. Subsequently much extended, Stoneacre preserves only the hall from its original building period. But its plan, on the Brockhampton model, is easily reconstructed as a conventional central hall, open to the roof, with two-storey cross-ranges at each end. Fully two centuries had passed since very similar arrangements had been adopted at Old Soar, another Kentish house of middling rank. In the interval, scarcely anything had changed.

The carpentered staircase and the cheap brick chimney-stack broke this mould in mid Tudor

LOWER BROCKHAMPTON HOUSE (Hereford and Worcester) A pretty fifteenth-century gatehouse bridges the moat of this late fourteenth-century timber-framed manor-house, of which the hall (centre) and one of its attached chamber blocks (right) have been preserved.

99

England. For the first time, upper chambers were to become as accessible and as easy to heat as those below. However, the virtues of the old plan had always included convenience, and the earlier houses were not lacking in material comfort. The Wealden (open-hall) houses of the southeastern counties, with their northern aisled-hall equivalents in the Pennines, have survived in such numbers precisely because they proved so adaptable over the years to the perceived needs of generations of farming families. Inevitably, this continuous use subjected many Wealden houses to destructive modernization, as has indeed been the case at Stoneacre. Yet Synyards, in the same Kentish parish of Otham, is another Wealden house which, perfectly intact and only slightly later in date, preserves the usual jettied chamber blocks at each end of the building and the big hall (formerly open) across the middle. Cherished today, it is a house well suited to modern living.

Similar survivals are not uncommon through the region. They include the fifteenth-century Pilgrims' Rest by the market-place at Battle, the handsome former parsonage at Headcorn west of

THE OLD SHOP, BIGNOR (West Sussex) A fifteenth-century cottage in which the central hall has been reduced to a single bay, though the usual chamber blocks at each end have been preserved.

the churchyard, and the contemporary early sixteenth-century Old Bell Farm at Harrietsham. Each of these houses, sharing Synyards' characteristics, is of generous size. But the plan lent itself also to scaling-down, resulting in such cottages as the mid fifteenth-century Old Shop at Bignor, where the single-bay hall is already so reduced as to constitute little more than a gesture. Both the stubborn retention of the hall in a house the size of Bignor, and its effective reduction and later flooring over, are important. Smallhythe Place, smaller than Synyards but of identical date, shows the next move towards greater convenience. This comfortable post-1514 Kentish farmhouse, the home for nearly thirty years of the actress Ellen Terry, in whose memory the Trust maintains it as a small museum, was equipped with a full-height chimney-stack from the beginning. It is, and always has been, of two floors throughout. The medieval hall and parlour, although still present at Smallhythe, were limited (like the modern reception rooms into which they have been transformed) to the ground floor. Above them, then as now, were the bedchambers.

Smallhythe Place is already of the new era. But comfortable middle-class housing had long anticipated it in rural England, and the phenomenon requires explanation. Certainly, at least some of these Wealden houses were put up by wealthy iron-masters, exploiting the recent technology of blast-furnace and finery forge to meet the demand, among other things, for iron cannons. But the majority were farmhouses, neither more nor less. And they demonstrate the emergence of a vigorous new class, grown wealthy on the retreat of the great landowners. Unprofitable manors on the big estates, often rented out for the first time from the mid fourteenth century, gave the lesser men their opportunity at last. The Wealden house, characteristically, was the home of a thrusting entrepreneur.

It is not always clear who leased the former demesnes, nor what profit was expected by their farmers. Obviously, more than one class was involved in these transactions, and motives inevitably were mixed. Thomas Culverhouse, for example, lessee of Westwood Manor and its rebuilder, probably had his roots in the minor official class which had long looked after this distant Winchester estate. Men of his kind, expert and locally based, were especially well equipped to reverse the trend to loss-making on such lands. But Culverhouse's successors, Thomas Bailey and Thomas Horton, were both Wiltshire clothiers. For them, the prestige of such a holding, elevating them unmistakably to the ranks of the country gentry, may always have been more important than their receipts.

Everywhere in the country, what followed the dispersal of the great demesne estates was a re-concentration in different hands. At first, farmers of the entire demesne had been hard to find, and partitioning in virgate (30-acre, *c.* 12-hectare) units was not uncommon. During the late fourteenth and early fifteenth centuries, when much of this occurred, every major village family, if it survived the plague, might have expected to take its share in the distribution. But such equality, inevitably, was short-lived. The abler and more ambitious, in an active land market, rose quickly to the surface and beyond. Consolidations brought individual virgates together into small family farms, one of which – Yardhurst, in Great Chart – was still identifiable as such in the 1960s. Yardhurst was a 'yeoman' holding of no more than 80 acres (*c.* 30 hectares), split into what might now appear an uneconomic number of little fields. Yet it supported, from the mid fifteenth century, a prospering family of Kentish farmers, with a fine Wealden house of such style and substance as to keep it continuously in occupation until today. Yardhurst's most remarkable individual feature is the original wooden tracery of its window-heads: a rare survival of expensive decorative display. No penny-pinching is evident in this building.

Yardhurst – both house and farm – precisely fitted its family unit. Its owners, home-grown and unshifting, were yeomen of Kent, keeping their name on the land. But consolidation, of course, could be taken much further. The gentlemen farmers of late medieval and early modern England – the Lytes of Lytes Cary, the Moretons of Little Moreton Hall, the Leghs of Adlington and many more – prospered on the back of the great estates. Among others, the Goddards of Aldbourne were to make a speciality of multiple demesne leasing on a very big scale, accumulating great wealth in the concentration of lands and dragging themselves up into the Wiltshire gentry. Aspiring to such status, the clothier Thomas Horton, lessee from 1518 of that other ex-monastic Wiltshire manor at Westwood, had already built lavishly in the towns he frequented: at Trowbridge and at Bradford-on-Avon. Like yeomen or gentlemen, whether stable or rising, the more substantial burgesses of late medieval England had similarly acquired the habit of living well.

One of the towns in the locality in which Thomas Horton would almost certainly have done business was Axbridge, towards the northern tip of Somerset. Axbridge, like Bradford and Trowbridge, was a regional centre of the late medieval cloth trade. And it preserves today a merchant house of the period such as Horton himself may very well have built on his own profits from the wool of Mendip sheep. On the corner of Axbridge's market-place, the misleadingly named 'King John's Hunting Lodge' is a big timber-framed house of about 1500, recently restored by the National Trust. Looking today much as it would have done when Horton knew it, the house had small lock-up booths on the street frontage at ground level, originally let separately to market traders. Behind these was the kitchen, with yard and service rooms, while a well-carpentered newel stair (again entirely of oak) gave easy access to both upper floors.

Characteristically for its date and situation, the Axbridge house is jettied at two levels, having the double overhang which, for all its current vertiginous appearance, contributed rigidity as well as extra floor-space to the entire structure. Partly as a consequence of these overhangs, the upper chambers are of good size, being well-lit and handsomely timbered. Kept meticulously clean in their day, they would have been hung with painted cloths, softened with many cushions, and 'strawed over with sweete herbes', no less cherished by the house-proud matrons of late medieval Axbridge than by their restorers and guardians of today.

Inevitably, the great majority of such townhouses has long since been destroyed, the victim of neglect since the sixteenth century or of those repeated improvements and redevelopments of town centres which began in earnest, at county capitals like Ludlow, from quite early in the Georgian period. Even Ludlow, however, preserves its fine fifteenth-century 'Corner Shop', a big three-storeyed building with prominent overhangs, on the junction of King Street and Broad Street. And there are other surviving timber-framed town-houses of astonishing virtuosity, among them the lately fully restored Booth Hall (or 'Round House') in the market-place at Evesham, continuously jettied on every quarter.

Inside or out, there is not much to separate the late medieval town-house from its farmhouse or manorial equivalents. Burgesses, returning to their roots, re-created in the countryside precisely the type of house they had enjoyed through years of affluence in the towns. Earlier, they had taken country standards to town with them. When Thomas Wall, a rich salter of London, retired to

the little village of Grundisburgh, in Suffolk, he did two things to enrich and reassure his final years. The first was to add a very grand chapel to Grundisburgh parish church, decorated on the parapet with his merchant's mark and with the arms of the city company of salters. It still carries a huge inscription which reads (in translation) 'Pray for the souls of Thomas Wall and of Alice, his wife, AD 1527'. The second was to build a fine house immediately east of the church, again appropriately decorated with his symbols. Wholly rural in its setting, Wall's house (now known as 'Bast's') was as precipitously jettied, on its two upper levels, as his home must have been in the city.

Clearly, the accommodation that suited the well-off country gentleman must equally have been the choice of his companion in affluence, the successful merchant or industrialist in the towns. The National Trust's Grantham House, next to St Wulfram's Church, is now to all appearances a big eighteenth-century town-house, characteristically symmetrical in plan. Yet its core is the late fifteenth-century mansion – hall in the centre, with chamber blocks at each end – of a rich Grantham wool-merchant, Thomas Hall, whose works had included, like those of Wall of Grundisburgh, the addition of a chantry chapel to the adjoining parish church, both as personal memorial and family resting-place.

Floored over and disguised by later modernizations, neither the hall at Grantham House nor the other medieval characteristics of the building are easy to unpick. Nevertheless, more complete survivals on this scale include the impressive stone house, a full century earlier in date, of William Grevel (d.1401), wool-merchant of Chipping Campden, still one of the bigger buildings in the town. And there is a more direct parallel at Strangers' Hall, in Norwich, built by William Barley in the mid fifteenth century, and subsequently much improved by Nicholas Sotherton. Sheriff of Norwich in 1530 and mayor in 1539, Sotherton was a prosperous grocer. Yet he furnished his hall in precisely the way a nobleman might have done in his time. Thus the hall at Strangers', as rebuilt by Sotherton, has a fine entrance porch, a handsome contemporary crown-post roof, and a big stone bay, gracing its high-table

TUDOR MERCHANT'S HOUSE, TENBY (Dyfed) A fifteenth-century town-house in which the hall and chambers, on three levels, have been compressed to fit an existing small urban plot.

end. Like the hall at Athelhampton, built a few years earlier for a retired London skinner, Sotherton's hall at Norwich, for a grocer and his family, lacked neither state nor gentility.

Of course, Strangers' Hall is no model for urban building. Few town sites could offer as much space, nor were burgesses usually as rich as Nicholas Sotherton. But the fact remains that the accommodation at Strangers' – its hall, kitchen, and parlour (or parlours) – was as much standard form in town as in country, as firmly determined in its inventory of living units as the modern three-bedroomed house. Taking its shape from the more usual urban plot, stretching back from the street on a narrow front, such a house might turn on its axis. At Southampton, the *Red Lion* is one of many tenements of this class, preserving a full-height central hall (lit by a roof-light only) between chamber blocks on street and garden fronts. Alternatively, where land was at a premium and sites were very small, the main elements of the same plan could be achieved (as in a tower-house) by stacking them one on the other. Tenby's 'Tudor Merchant's House', a National Trust property, is squeezed within the walls of a fortified town, packed in by neighbouring tenements on both sides. On three floors, each with its chimney, the Tenby house had a hall at ground level, equipped with a convivially large fireplace. Above it, two floors of bedchambers, with garderobe provision, were joined by a stair turret now demolished.

The Tudor Merchant's House at Tenby is small but of good quality. On a similar scale, Lavenham's 'Little House', sited more spaciously on the market square, lays out its central hall and flanking chambers end-to-end. This again would have been the basic plan of the Trust's older and more complex 'Aberconwy House' at Conway. And many were the variations attempted on this model, not least by speculative builders. Among such, the monks of Tewkesbury's development of their precinct next to Church Street still survives as a remarkable testimony to their enterprise. Here more than twenty terraced cottages of uniform plan were built for letting in the mid fifteenth century. Each had a shop on the road front, with a kitchen at the rear, separated by a two-storeyed hall and partly overlain by a solar.

With the exception of the shop, these again were the plan units of a neat range of cottages on Spon Street, Coventry, built contemporaneously as a terrace of six. On the ground floor at Spon Street, the two-bay hall was open to the roof in one of its bays, the other carrying a first-floor chamber jettied forward. At the hall's upper end, a tall window lit the master's table. In the lower bay, under the chamber, a partitioned-off screens passage, with facing doors to street and yard, precisely reproduced in absurd miniature the arrangements of a mighty hall of chivalry.

Tenacious though they were, the relevance of such arrangements to the gentle life of the towns had become questionable by the early sixteenth century. The National Trust's 'Paycocke's House', in Coggeshall, is thought to have been finished in 1505. And here already the planning of the family apartments, while traditional in essence, came closer to the practice of today. Built for rich clothiers, Paycocke's had a central hall which, in the manner of the hall at Smallhythe Place, was overlain from the beginning by a parlour. Its chambers, well-lit by handsome oriels on the street facade, were comfortable rather than grand. Paycocke's, undoubtedly, was an expensive house, with carving (both outside and in) of the highest quality. Nevertheless, the purposes to which these moneys were assigned point clearly to a major shift in fashion. Nothing at Paycocke's, for all its prestigious expense, was sacrificed to the entertainment of that exigent company for which the common hall had been provided in the past. For better or worse – and there is a case to be made for either viewpoint – the Paycockes thought only of themselves.

PAYCOCKE'S HOUSE, COGGESHALL (Essex) The family house of rich Coggeshall clothiers, lavishly timbered and jettied at first-floor level, with a fine set of oriels on the street front; datable to *c.* 1500.

[4]

Spoil of the Abbeys

Except in England, where the entire process took less than four years, the suppression of the religious houses was no elegant final solution. Between 1536 and 1540, Henry VIII successfully rid his kingdom of monks and nuns. But neither Henry's Reformation nor his Dissolution were exportable. Both, in Ireland, were of strictly limited application. Even among the loyal Old English, Protestantism had few permanent converts; in the Gaelic Irish lands, whether conquered or still free, the friars kept rebuilding their nests. Nor was Scotland, at first, any better territory for the reformers. James V's neat alternative to his uncle's wholesale suppressions was to tax the monks, with full papal agreement and at no loss to himself, into failure and eventual self-destruction. The Reformation, delayed by such strategies, came to Scotland only in 1559–60. It had been anticipated by mob attacks on the urban friaries and by some preliminary suppressions of religious houses. But the remaining monasteries (after 1560 as before) were never formally dissolved. They simply wasted away.

In other respects, however, the three territories offered close parallels. In each, there had been a scatter of late medieval monastic bankruptcies, the product of hard times or mismanagement. Yet the overwhelming majority of communities had held on by their fingernails through the post-plague crisis, to display by 1500 at least some positive indications of recovery. Most of this recovery was economic. It would show itself especially in new building works and in the hospitality, for example, of the Welsh abbots. But it had another aspect also in self-renewal. Both in England and in Scotland, individual enlightened superiors led their communities into better discipline. In Ireland, the Observantine movement had its obvious successes, while even the demoralized Irish Cistercians began rebuilding, although too late to halt the tide that ran against them.

It was not, of course, just religion that brought the monks down. James V's cynical exploitation of the Scottish houses followed his father's earlier scandalous abuse of clerical appointments in support of his own Stewart relatives. Under both kings, the lay commendator system – entrusting the monastic houses to land-hungry noblemen – grew unchecked. English troops, using the pretext of religion, were to plunder and destroy the great Border abbeys in the 1540s. And it was the English gentry's profit from the ex-monastic lands that remained, under Elizabeth, the government's chief protection against recusancy. Only in Ireland was an uninterrupted monastic presence widely supported by the aristocracy, while even there it was the lean landless friars rather than the fat possessioners who were encouraged to remain part of the community. Whether in swift execution or in lingering death, there was little to redeem this sorry tale.

ABBOT'S KITCHEN, GLASTONBURY (Somerset) The great late fourteenth-century kitchen, with its big central louver to release the fumes, of the abbot's lodgings at this wealthy Benedictine community.

Those comforts we cherish on our own account, we tolerate less readily in the Church. Yet churchmen, too, are just as likely to be drawn to the gentle life, none more damagingly than monks. Long before the 'spoil' of the abbeys at the formal suppressions of 1536–40, Henry V's indictment of the English Benedictines in 1421 had included three especially significant charges. In contempt of the Rule, the 'black monk' abbots had withdrawn to their personal households. Senior monks, for no better reason than that they preferred it that way, had set themselves apart from the community in private lodgings. At the better-off houses, pocket money and special privileges were routine.

St Benedict, legislating for a sixth-century community, had abhorred private property. It was, he said, a vice which must be 'utterly rooted out of the monastery'. Yet by the Late Middle Ages, such principles (fundamental in their day) had come to be neglected or ignored. Fountains Abbey, now in the guardianship of the National Trust, had begun in the twelfth century as a pioneering Cistercian ('white monk') community, to grow enormously rich on its popularity as a spearhead of the contemporary reform. In its final decades, Fountains still retained something of that role under Abbot Marmaduke Huby (1494–1526), praised at the time as a 'golden and unbreakable column in his zeal for the order' and since claimed to be 'by far the most distinguished Cistercian abbot of his age'. But Huby was a builder. For all his zeal as a legislator and reformer, driving a straight furrow through the hesitancies and compromises of his brother abbots, what Marmaduke Huby has left us at Fountains today is a monument in stone to Cistercian back-sliding, overturning the precepts of St Bernard.

Most obvious of Huby's contraventions of early Cistercian practice was the great tower he built against the north transept of his abbey church, so handsome as to inspire immediate (and unsuccessful) imitation at Bolton Priory, an Augustinian near-neighbour. Huby's tower was as grand as the contemporary western tower at Furness, in Lancashire: the pride of a rich and factious white monk community with which Huby, as commissioner and visitor of his order in England, had

FOUNTAINS ABBEY (North Yorkshire) Abbot Marmaduke Huby's great tower (centre) was an addition of the early sixteenth century, acceptable by his day but earlier anathema to Cistercian purists as out of keeping with the austerity of their Order.

dealings dispiritingly often. But whereas Huby was active in the correction of the conventional misdemeanours of Furness, he was neither able nor willing, so far as we can tell, to call a halt to the programme of expensive rebuilding which, at Furness as at Fountains, characterized the latter years of the community. The towers of Furness and Fountains – like Bolton, had the resources been available to complete it – were prodigy towers in the tradition of the huge Boston 'Stump'. Yet Boston, at least, had a public purpose, 'saluting travellers at a great distance round, and an excellent seamark seen about 40 miles distant'. In contrast, at Furness and Fountains the towers were essentially private, crammed up invisibly against their hillsides, exclusive to the glory of the monks.

Privacy and exclusion can take many guises. And Marmaduke Huby's major works were to include, unsurprisingly, the rebuilding on a grand scale of his personal lodgings, seen everywhere as a characteristic of this period. Huby was not the first to undertake such work even at his own abbey. Nor was it out of keeping in any way with what had come to be the practice of his order. For centuries already, Cistercian abbots had ignored the example of their founding fathers who had slept alongside their monks in the common dormitory. Moreover, Huby's doubling of the size of his private quarters was precisely in tune with the domestic standards of his time, and it took an identical form. Abbot Huby's big new hall at Fountains had the screens passage (at its lower end) and projecting bay window (at its upper) of any equivalent lordly apartment. His great chamber, even in its provision of an adjoining private oratory, differed hardly at all from the private quarters of those contemporary noblemen with whom Huby would naturally have equated himself.

Henry V's criticism of over-extended monastic households had been directed, in the first instance, at the Benedictine abbots. Perhaps he was thinking at the time of the fine new lodgings – complete with hall, bedchamber, study, chapel, garderobe, and 'a decent bath' – recently provided at Canterbury Cathedral Priory for Thomas Chillenden (d.1411), 'the greatest Builder of a Prior that ever was in Christes Churche'. And certainly what we know of the furnishings of such lodgings, as recorded in a Peterborough inventory of 1460, can do nothing but support the king's conclusions. At Peterborough today, the most significant remains of the abbot's quarters are his great gatehouse, dominating the range next to the cathedral's west facade and establishing the scale of an impressive private

mansion since subsumed in the bishop's Victorian palace. Within those quarters, during the lengthy rule of Abbot Richard Ashton (1438–71), a great stock of silver plate and other valuables had accumulated. True, certain of the items had a suitably ecclesiastical flavour. There was a plain silver cup with a cover inscribed 'Blessed is he that cometh in the name of the Lord'; four other cups had the arms of St Peter engraved on them; there was a bowl with 'Ave Maria' on its rim. Yet everything else in Abbot Ashton's establishment was of magnate-style richness and luxury. Ashton and his guests dined off silver. In his hall, the squires, yeomen and grooms of his household were separated at tables of their own. Ashton's chamber had recently been re-equipped with four new feather beds 'bought by brother Richard Harleston', his former steward. There were eight pairs of linen sheets newly bought also, with blankets, bolsters and cushions in abundance, and with six new pillows. The abbot's bed-coverings were of fine red serge. Two silk curtains, 'blood-red in colour', were 'of old stock' ready for renewal.

Prominent in the inventory of Abbot Ashton's effects is the equipment of his larders and his kitchen. At Glastonbury, just such an abbot's kitchen (on an enormous scale) survives to this day, there being no more obvious demonstration of the huge importance that had come to attach to a monastic superior's obligatory hospitality. Expensive though it was, constituting a major charge on resources depleted since the plague, an abbot's generosity was seldom wholly without purpose. Leicester Abbey, although always among the better endowed of the Augustinian communities, was never more prosperous than it became, immediately after the Black Death, under the governance of Abbot William Clown (1345–78). That 'manly man', thought to be among the models for Chaucer's monk and widely acknowledged in his own generation to be a most expert master of greyhounds, was often heard to say to his intimates at the abbey that 'the only reason why he took delight in such paltry sports was to show politeness to the lords of the realm, to get on easy terms with them and win their good will in matters of business'. Conceivably, he meant what he said. In any event, those who joined Abbot Clown regularly in the pursuit of the hare included Edward III and his son, the Black Prince. It was in the glow of their friendship that Leicester Abbey grew rich, in return for incomparable sport.

Others, similarly, would find a welcome at the religious houses, in the convivial company of the

VALLE CRUCIS ABBEY (Clwyd) A Cistercian house of small means but great hospitality in the Late Middle Ages, at which the church was cut down to fit the reduced community and the abbot rebuilt the east range (centre right) as his personal lodgings.

abbot and his guests. Celebrated by their poets, the Welsh Cistercians, in particular, have left a record of free-spending generosity and good cheer. Basingwerk, Neath and Valle Crucis, none of which were especially rich, each became known for the warmth of its hospitality, attracting poets and poor scholars as flies to fly-paper, so numerous that (at Basingwerk) 'they have to be accommodated at meals at two sittings, when they have a choice of the wines of Aragon, Spain and Brittany'. Basingwerk's new guest-house, built specifically for the crowd, has not survived. Yet both Neath and Valle Crucis still exhibit today what is surely best described as an 'architecture of indulgence', as little in keeping with the prescriptions of the saints as the rebuilt Fountains of Marmaduke Huby.

Abbot Leyshon Thomas, last Abbot of Neath, was a man from the same mould as Abbot Huby. He was an energetic administrator, a skilled politician, a scholar, patron and builder. In his lodgings, rebuilt on a grand scale at the south end of the east range, into which the monks' dormitory had

formerly extended, he practised the arts of a good host. As the poet sang,

Sacred is this dwelling by the cheerful sea;
In this compact retreat will be found the
    warmth of hospitality
And welcome banquets, and deer from the parks
    of yonder hill above
And salmon from the ocean, and wheat and
    every kind of wine.

Neath, while Leyshon Thomas ruled, was 'the fairest abbey in all Wales'. But such comforts had not been gained without some sacrifices. The abbey's estates, leased to the local gentry on lengthy terms and for the best rents then obtainable, had escaped its control for ever. In 1539, there were just eight monks in residence at buildings that had once, in better days, accommodated three times that number. Abbot Thomas and his associates could keep themselves in luxury on an income intended for many more. They craved fellowship to fill their empty halls.

Neath's diminished dormitory and expanded abbot's lodgings corresponded with the company (much reduced) of its monks and with the steady erosion of their ideals. Thoroughly domesticated, the abbey site after 1539 was well suited for redevelopment as the country mansion that, under the Herberts, it became. Valle Crucis went the same way. During the fifteenth century, Neath's sister house at Valle Crucis had undergone a transformation of its own. Praised by the poets for the splendour of its buildings and (of course) for the hospitality of its abbots, Valle Crucis was less a functioning Cistercian community in these latter years than the private dwelling of an ecclesiastical grandee.

There is important surviving evidence of this new purpose. Well before 1500, the great church at Valle Crucis was already, very largely, an empty shell. As in so many of the Irish Cistercian houses of the same period, worship had become concentrated in a walled-off chapel at the east end of the church, made up of the presbytery and of only about half the former choir. Bereft of lay brethren and reduced in their own establishment, the monks of Valle Crucis reorganized their resources to live well. Abbot David, towards the end of the fifteenth century, was known (like Leyshon Thomas of Neath) as a builder. It was probably he who transformed the entire upper storey of the east range at Valle Crucis (traditionally the common dormitory of the monks) into fine private quarters for himself. Here, in his handsome new hall with personal chamber adjoining, Abbot David and his successor, Abbot John, entertained those guests who, through the last Indian summer of the Welsh monastic houses, immortalized their hospitality in grateful song. They could not have wished for a more convivial memorial.

Hailes Abbey, in Gloucestershire, was another such fellowship, relaxed and hospitable, once roundly rebuked for its 'many great oaths and horrible'. Yet those same champion oath-crackers were the fortunate guardians of a most precious relic, the Holy Blood of Hailes, given to them for their support as early as 1270 and still working its miracles two centuries later. At Hailes, it was the deliberately revived cult of the Holy Blood, beginning in the 1430s and confirmed by papal indulgences, which helped provide the resources for a major rebuilding, again taking a significant

HAILES ABBEY (Gloucestershire) The radiating chapels (right) at the east end of the abbey church provided space and altars round the shrine of the Holy Blood of Hailes, a precious relic given to the abbey in 1270; it was a revival of the cult in the fifteenth century which enabled the monks to rebuild their cloister (centre), to provide new abbot's lodgings in the west claustral range, and to reconstruct – as at Cleeve Abbey – their refectory.

Above CLEEVE ABBEY (Somerset) The fifteenth-century refectory of a Cistercian community, as rebuilt more comfortably in the Late Middle Ages to replace an earlier over-large apartment.

Right LACOCK ABBEY (Wiltshire) Always a wealthy community, attracting recruits from among the best families in the region, the nuns of Lacock were able to build themselves a fine cloister in the fifteenth century while less lucky houses were struggling to make ends meet.

direction. The west range, emptied now of those 'work-horse' lay brethren who had once been recruited by the Order, was converted into splendid new lodgings for the abbot; the refectory was rebuilt; the cloister was entirely remodelled.

A similar reorganization at Cleeve, in Somerset, more readily identifiable in the surviving buildings, included (as at Hailes) the reconstruction of the west range as a fine house for the abbot, the redesign of the refectory on a more comfortable and appropriate scale, and the subdivision of the common dormitory into private cells. None of these modernizations could have struck contemporary monk-watchers as unusual. Everywhere the life in common, once practised by men and women of religion as an article of faith, was at an end. Partitioned dormitories were familiar from the late fourteenth century, if not before. By the same date, private rooms in infirmaries had become normal. Over-large refectories, cold and unwelcoming, ceased to be used except for special occasions, the community preferring to dine in private 'messes'. Guest lodgings multiplied. Reconstructed cloisters, glazed for the first time, protected individual studies – those little panelled cubicles, known as 'carrells', where the monks might read, doze or meditate by themselves.

Just such a cloister rebuilding was undertaken in the fifteenth century at the wealthy nunnery at Lacock, a fashionable community of Augustinian canonesses, now (like Hailes Abbey) among the properties of the National Trust. It was a costly work, lavishly vaulted, and it still conveys the tone of an exclusive sorority, dear to the hearts of the Wiltshire gentry but hard on the pockets of an anxious parent. When Joan, daughter of Nicholas Samborne, took the veil at Lacock in 1395, her father found himself having to find the money for all sorts of additional expenses. He had, of course, to buy her clothes – her veil and linen cloth, tunic and three mantles (one of them fur-lined for winter use). But that was not all. For Joan's cubicle, a new bed had to be provided, with mattress, coverlet, blankets and canopy. She was expected to come equipped with a silver spoon and with a drinking-cup (mazer) of her own.

At the end of an era, in 1536, a full inventory survives of the contents of the nuns' chambers at the ancient priory of Minster in Sheppey, founded as far back as the late seventh century by that model of piety, St Sexburga. The inventory was taken on the occasion of Minster's suppression. And it makes a point of identifying the personal property of the nuns as distinct from what had passed to the

State. Dame Agnes Davye had 'brought with her' a set of painted hangings, three pairs of sheets and a counterpane, a chest, a carved cupboard, two andirons, a pair of tongs and a firepan. Amongst the 'stuff given her by her friends', Agnes Browne had a feather bed, a bolster, two pillows, a pair of blankets, two 'coarse' coverlets, and four pairs of sheets 'good and badde'; she had a big chest and two little ones, a carved cupboard 'in the window', a goblet with a silver cover, and a mazer 'with a brim of silver and gilt'; she had her own pair of candlesticks, several pieces of pewter, and all the equipment she needed (firepan, tongs and andirons) to keep herself warm through the winter. Anne Loveden had borrowed a coverlet from St John's Chapel, but her 'ship-chest' and feather bed were her own. Dame Elizabeth Stradlynge, along with other possessions, kept 'a little silk cushion' for her comfort. In Anne Clifford's chamber, the painted wood crucifix and 'image of our Lady' seem to have been regarded as private property.

Not long after, the monks of Roche Abbey would stand next to their chambers, trying to get a price for their smallest possessions, even to the doors of their cells. In the words of Michael Sherbrook, whose uncle was present: 'when they were put forth of the House, one of the Monks, his Friend, told him that every one of the Convent had given to him his Cell, wherein he lied: wherein was not any thing of Price, but his Bed and Apparel, which was but simple and of small Price. Which Monk willed my Uncle to buy something of him; who said, I see nothing that is worth Money to my use. No, said he; give me ii d for my Cell Door, which was never made with v s. No, said my Uncle, I know not what to do with it (for he was a Young Man unmarried, and then neither stood need of Houses nor Doors). But such Persons as afterward bought their Corn or Hay or such like, found all the doors either open or the Locks and Shackles plucked away, or the Door itself taken away, went in and took what they found, filched it away.'

No doubt, as Sherbrook says, it 'would have made an Heart of Flint to have melted and weeped to have seen the breaking up of the House, and their sorrowful departing'. Yet the calamity was neither undeserved nor without harbingers. There were, of course, exceptions. The community at Mount Grace, dispersed in 1539, still included three novices in its number, and was clearly looking ahead to better times. Other Carthusian houses, together with the reformist Observant Franciscans (long favoured in Ireland but only lately admitted to England by the Tudors), had made themselves

ROCHE ABBEY (South Yorkshire) Sold off for demolition soon after its suppression in 1538, little except the crossing and gatehouse (off the photograph to the left) of this Cistercian house remains above foundation level, although the plan is exceptionally complete.

unpopular with the authorities of the day precisely because of their uncompromising adherence to their beliefs. Even at some of the great Benedictine abbeys – Winchcombe, Evesham, and Glastonbury among them – at least a whiff of self-renewal was in the air. But that renewal was too late and the hunt had begun. Property, great and small, was at stake. Sherbrook's father, too, had been at Roche at its suppression, and had bought timber on the demolition of the abbey church. Had he not, Sherbrook later asked, 'thought well of the Religious Persons and of the Religion then used? And he told me Yea: For, said He, I did see no Cause to the contrary: Well, said I, then how came

it to pass you was so ready to destroy and spoil the thing that you thought well of? What should I do, said He; might I not as well as others have some Profit of the Spoil of the Abbey? For I did see all would away; and therefore I did as others did.'

Doing as others did was all the easier because it had been done so frequently before. The paring down of the monastic establishment, while leaving much fat by the 1530s, had been proceeding for almost two centuries. In advance of their formal suppression in 1414, the so-called 'alien priories', in particular, had suffered steady erosion. Many of them, in any event, had never supported a full conventual regime. And they would come to be treated in their latter years as freely disposable property. The National Trust's Steventon 'Priory', in Oxfordshire, was one of these. In 1324, when Steventon was still nominally a possession of the Norman Benedictines of Bec, an inventory had been taken of the 'movables' (furnishings) of its dwelling-house. Clearly, although remaining the charge of a 'prior', Steventon had come to function by that date as a simple estate centre, adequately furnished and with some silver of its own (two cups, twelve spoons, and a mazer), but of that hall-chamber-kitchen plan familiar at every equivalent lay manor-house. Not much later, Bec summoned its 'prior' home, and Steventon was found a private buyer. From the 1360s, if not before, the estate had become thoroughly secularized.

By 1400, having come to Westminster Abbey, Steventon was again, in some sense, Church property. And it is certainly true that very few 'alien' lands totally escaped Church control before the Dissolution. Ottery St Mary, bought from the 'unreasonable and exorbitant' canons of Rouen Cathedral as early as 1335, had been converted by its purchaser, Bishop Grandisson of Exeter, into a well-endowed college of remembrance. After 1414, important properties like St Michael's Mount (Cornwall) and Lancaster Priory would be assigned to the newly fashionable Bridgettine nuns of Syon, while a few years before, Swavesey Priory (Cambridgeshire), once of St Serge at Angers, had gone to the almost equally favoured Carthusians of Coventry. Newent (Gloucestershire), a former priory cell of Cormeilles, was to be transferred in 1411 to the endowment of the Yorkist collegiate chantry at Fotheringhay; Pamber (Hampshire), a cell of Cerisy-la-Forêt, went first to Eton, then to Queen's College (Oxford); Isleham (Cambridgeshire), of the Breton St Jacut-de-la-Mer, had passed by 1450 to Pembroke College (Cambridge), with Wootton Wawen (Warwickshire), of the Norman abbey at Conches, transferring to Henry VI's King's College, at the same university. God, it might be argued, could do little but profit from a reinvestment of His portfolio in this fashion. However, the life of religion, at least as St Benedict had understood it, had failed at each of these places. Whatever their purpose, whether laudable or perverse, the possessioners' enemies had scented the kill.

Finally brought to ruin by the Hundred Years War, the alien priories had been vulnerable also for other reasons, principally connected with their size. When Cardinal Wolsey, in 1524–5, launched that first systematic round of suppressions which, far more conclusively than the earlier confiscations, provided the model for wholesale Dissolution a decade later, he described his victims as 'certain exile and small monasteries' where 'neither God was served, nor religion kept'. In many cases, although not in all, he was patently right in his assessment. But if pruning can result in better

fruit, it can also be the death of the tree. In principle, nobody could have seen Bishop Alcock's suppression of St Radegund's (Cambridge) as anything but a reform. The community had collapsed by 1496, and its buildings, well sited on the edge of the university town, were ideally suited for conversion to a college. Similarly, when Creake Abbey failed in 1506, the logic of the reassignment of its revenues to the support of Christ's College was plain for all to see. Both Cambridge colleges, Jesus and Christ's, were intended primarily for the better instruction of the clergy. Yet it was Cambridge, too, that gave Erasmus a home and provided an audience for his analysis. In the merciless spotlight of the great humanist's contempt, the credibility of the monks was destroyed.

Like it or not, the English monasteries by 1536 had few friends in high places to speak up for them. Moreover, the ground for the first suppressions was well chosen. Self-regeneration, last attempted in Wolsey's late neglected reforms, had consistently failed at the smaller houses 'by the space of two hundred years and more'. Consequently to the king, now 'supreme head in earth under God of the Church of England', fell the duty of checking this waste and of converting God's property to better uses, 'forasmuch as manifest sin, vicious, carnal and abominable living, is daily used and committed amongst the little and small abbeys, priories, and other religious houses of monks, canons, and nuns, where the congregation of such religious persons is under the number of twelve persons, whereby the governors of such religious houses and their convents, spoil, destroy, consume, and utterly waste as well their churches, monasteries, priories, principal houses, farms, granges, lands, tenements, and hereditaments, as the ornaments of their churches and their goods and chattels to the high displeasure of Almighty God, slander of good religion, and to the great infamy of the King's Highness and the realm if redress should not be had thereof.'

The ranting tone of the Act of Suppression was offensive and not a little unjust. At Ulverscroft Priory, remote and poor, there was 'not one religious person there but that they can and doth use either embroidering, writing books with very fair hand, making their own garments, carving, painting, or engraving'. And Ulverscroft, like the similarly poor but worthy Polesworth – a house of 'virtuous and religious' Benedictine women – in fact survived another three years. But although there were many such exceptions to the Act of 1536, the relative ease of this initial round of suppressions pointed the way inevitably to more.

Closely following the purge of the 'lesser' houses, defined as those with incomes of £200 or less, the piecemeal surrender of the 'greater' houses began in earnest in 1538. By 1540, even the stragglers had gone down. With nothing to gain by resistance to the king's commissioners, and with the pensions they had been promised yet to lose, few communities put up much of a fight.

What then followed for the majority of the religious houses was very much what happened at Roche. The commissioners had been instructed to 'pull down to the ground all the walls of the churches, steeples, cloisters, fraters, dorters, chapter-houses, with all other houses, saving them that be necessary for a farmer'. And at Roche Abbey, indeed, as Sherbrook tells us, 'the Church was the first thing that was put to the spoil; and then the Abbot's Lodging, Dorter [dormitory], and Frater [refectory], with the Cloister and all the Buildings thereabout, within the Abbey Walls: for nothing was spared but the Ox-houses and swinecotes and such other Houses of Office, that stood without the Walls. . . . It would have pitied any Heart to see what tearing up of the Lead there was, and plucking up of Boards, and throwing down of the Spars; and when the Lead was torn off and cast down into the Church, and the Tombs in the Church all broken . . . and all things of Price, either spoiled, carped [plucked] away or defaced to the uttermost.'

Little, it is true, survives of Roche today. Yet the wholesale barbarism of England's Dissolution was not to be without its compensations. With so many surplus buildings up for disposal at the same time, the market for materials was quickly glutted. 'There be more of great houses in Lincolnshire', wrote the commissioner for that county, 'than be in England beside suppressed . . . with thick walls and most part of them vaulted, and few buyers of other stone, glass, or slate which might help the charges of plucking down of them.' Rather than face the cost of complete demolition, he proposed 'to take first down the bells and lead . . . and this done, to pull down the roofs, battlements, and stayers and let the walls stand, and charge some of them as a quarry of stone to make sales of, as they that have need will fetch.' Many 'bare ruin'd choirs', although skeletons only of what had stood there before, stabilized in precisely that condition. Others, for one reason or another, never reached it. Mottisfont and Lacock, Anglesey, Buckland and Canons Ashby, were all religious houses, adapted at a later time by lay owners. And each of these mansions, now National Trust property, conceals a

significant element of the pre-suppression building out of which, in the sixteenth century, it was reshaped.

Mottisfont was one of the very earliest of these conversions. A small but well-sited Augustinian priory, it had been suppressed among the lesser houses in 1536, to be granted then to the king's Lord Chamberlain, William Lord Sandys. Sandys was an old man by the time he acquired Mottisfont. He had already built himself a great house in northern Hampshire, at The Vyne. In matters of faith, he is thought to have been cautiously conservative. Such a man might have been expected to treat the former priory buildings with sensitivity. In point of fact, he did nothing of the kind. Taking the entire nave of the disused priory church as the core of his new mansion, Sandys joined others in the locality – Thomas Wriothesley at Titchfield, William Paulet at Netley – who were similarly experimenting with conversions of this kind, in each of which the church (albeit gutted and rebuilt) was retained.

Buckland Abbey, remodelled as late as the 1570s, was another such church conversion, in which the nave became a hall (with parlour over) and even the tower was retained on the crossing. But the works at Buckland were of a later generation, after the worst tensions of the Dissolution had been resolved. In the meantime, a new sensitivity had been evoked. When, soon after 1536, 'a Lancashire man' had taken the largest remaining building at the priory cell of Calwich (Staffordshire) to make 'a parlour of the chancel, a hall of the church [nave], and a kitchen of the steeple [west tower]', he would have given little thought to the wrath of God or to the scandal that such conversions might provoke. Calwich Priory, with an income of just £3, fell so clearly within the scope of the Act of 1536 as to deserve immediate closure on every count. In the same way Mottisfont, although distinctly richer than Calwich, was still arguably insufficiently endowed. In the circumstances, neither lay owner need have had cause for self-reproach, and each

Overleaf BUCKLAND ABBEY (Devon) A conversion of the 1570s, Sir Richard Grenville's new country house preserved the big crossing tower (centre) of the former Cistercian church; in this view from the south, the arch and roof-line of the demolished south transept show clearly against the tower, the body of the church – nave, crossing, and chancel – being floored over to make the Elizabethan house, of which the great hall was right of the porch.

believed himself entitled to do what he chose with his new buildings.

Less than two years later, Thomas Wriothesley's usurpation of Titchfield Abbey was markedly more difficult to accept. Titchfield, a comfortably endowed Premonstratensian house with an income of £249, had survived the first round of suppressions. It had only recently been extensively rebuilt. Yet the canons' forced surrender of 18 December 1537 was to be followed immediately by a sweeping conversion which could not have failed to cause offence in the locality. Before 1542, as the antiquary Leland reported it, 'Mr Wriothesley hath builded a right stately house embateled and having a goodely gate and a conducte [conduit] casteled in the midle of the court of it, yn the very same place where the late Monasterie of Premonstratenses stoode, caullyd Tichfelde.' Thomas Wriothesley's 'goodely gate' is still there today, cutting a path through the body of the abbey church. Behind it, the canons' cloister was assigned to Wriothesley's court; their former refectory to his hall. Contemporaneously at Netley, a few miles to the west, Sir William Paulet met the problem of reshaping a Cistercian house by reversing the plan used by Wriothesley. Netley's refectory made way for Paulet's gatehouse; its church became his hall and his kitchen. Conversions like these, characteristically insensitive to local memories and so plainly in the interest of private individuals, understandably provoked public outrage.

In the event, while many monastic churches were permitted to survive the Dissolution for one purpose or another, the conversion of former churches to domestic use was already exceptional by the later 1530s. In part, this was simply a sensible precaution, destroying the nest 'for fear the Birds should build therein again'. But it resulted, too, from a genuine reluctance – fed by horror stories about those who acted otherwise – to make improper use of holy ground. Most of these stories were apocryphal. When assembled later, in seventeenth-century collections like Sir Henry Spelman's *The History and Fate of Sacrilege*

Below TITCHFIELD ABBEY (Hampshire) Thomas Wriothesley's fine gatehouse cut through the nave of a former Premonstratensian church, suppressed in 1537 and immediately converted into a country mansion.

(1632), the purpose of their revival would be polemical. Nevertheless, the pulling down of monastic buildings inevitably led to fatal accidents. And the 'many strange misfortunes and grievous accidents' which befell new owners undoubtedly played their part in the progressive discouragement of what might be seen as irreverent conversions. Sir John Cope, at Canons Ashby from 1538, continued to use the nave (but not the choir) of the former Augustinian church as his private chapel, otherwise demolishing the bulk of the canons' conventual buildings and keeping only the prior's lodgings for himself. Such decisions were common at the time. And they followed reasonably enough from that secularization of superiors' lodgings which had already taken place at so many religious houses in the decades immediately preceding the Dissolution. Fine suites of lodgings,

only lately rebuilt, were subsequently preserved in this way at Muchelney (Somerset), Battle (East Sussex), Castle Acre (Norfolk), St Osyth (Essex), Thame (Oxfordshire), Much Wenlock (Shropshire), and Milton (Dorset), among others. Where monastic buildings of another kind might present insuperable problems of conversion, an abbot's lodging was a manor-house ready made.

Of course, there were always those, provoked by difficulties, who gladly accepted the greater challenge. At the core of the National Trust's Anglesey Abbey, where it is entirely hidden by a rebuilding of about 1600, is the former chapter-house of a community of Augustinian canons, along with their adjoining *calefactorium* (warming-house). The preservation of a chapter-house is unusual. Once the common meeting-place of the brethren, it had lost its purpose in a secular building and was fatally associated, in any event, with a way of life better forgotten. At Anglesey, the survival is probably an accident. Not so at Lacock, where the deliberate preservation of both chapter-house and cloister was an important constituent of the major rebuilding undertaken there by Sir William Sharington in the 1540s. Most new owners of monastic sites would have opted by this date for demolition. But Sharington was an antiquary, an enthusiastic builder, and a man of sophisticated tastes. No longer prepared – as Sandys, Paulet and Wriothesley had once been – to find another purpose for the disused abbey church, Sharington nevertheless kept the nuns' cloister, using its surrounding ranges to support his private quarters, including a fashionable long gallery. South of the cloister, the church was demolished. To its north, Sharington built a second 'service' court, completing the conventional double-courtyard plan of almost all country mansions of his period.

The monastic cloister had once itself played a role in the widespread dissemination of the court-yard plan in manor-houses, hospitals and colleges. Accordingly, at the Dissolution, the disused cloister must have seemed to many the obvious beginning for any projected remodelling. In point of fact, a successful and permanent conversion like Sharington's at Lacock was rare. The task was more difficult than it looked. Sir Richard Lee, the new owner of another former Benedictine nunnery at Sopwell, in Hertfordshire, was a military engineer of high repute. He knew everything there was to know about forts. Nevertheless, Lee's original scheme for the conversion of Sopwell Priory, which he renamed 'Lee's Place' after himself, was a complete and humiliating failure. He had intended at first – like Sir William Paulet at Netley – to convert Sopwell's church into his hall, with the nuns' cloister as his court to the south. But

LACOCK ABBEY (Wiltshire) William Sharington's conversion of the suppressed Augustinian nunnery at Lacock preserved the former cloister (left centre), using its south range to support a long gallery (nearest the camera), at the southeast corner of which he built an octagonal viewpoint tower; the path and lawn in the foreground conceal the foundations of the nuns' church.

the constraints of the existing buildings were too much for him. It proved easier, on mature thought, to start from scratch. Lee's second scheme for Sopwell was cut short by his death in 1575. In the interval, he had demolished the nunnery and his own initial works, beginning again on a much more ambitious double-courtyard mansion in which only the orientation of the former priory was preserved.

Understandably, what was kept by the lay inheritors of monastic England was principally what they could hope to put to use. These were the buildings, 'necessary for a farmer', which the commissioners had been told to leave intact. Among them, of course, were those abbots' lodgings most suitable for conversion to farmhouses. Detached gatehouses, again, at some distance from the ruins, often lent themselves similarly to remodelling. There were the stables and outhouses of the big farm courts. And there were the huge so-called 'tithe barns', even then stranded relics of the monks' high farming days, which have continued to do good service for their successors on the land, as at the Trust's Middle Littleton and Great Coxwell.

Monastic churches too, where they survived, usually did so for the very good reason that they continued to meet the needs of a congregation. Isolated churches, especially those of enclosed orders like the Cistercians, had of course been made redundant by the diaspora. The merest handful of Cistercian churches was preserved. But it had been the frequent practice of other orders, Benedictines and Augustinians among them, to find room in their churches for parochial worship, customarily in the nave or adjoining aisle. Shared use of churches – monks in the choir, parishioners in the nave – inevitably caused conflict between the parties. One solution, as at Abbotsbury and Evesham, Guisborough, Muchelney and Kenilworth, had been to separate the two in distinct buildings. At each of these locations, following the Dissolution, it was the parish not the monastic church which was preserved. Where no such separation had been permitted to take place, the chances of a monastic church's survival were much improved.

Wymondham Abbey (Norfolk) was one of these shared churches: a great carcase of a building as it stands today, the victim of many mutilations. The scars tell a not uncommon tale. Here, next to a little market town and amongst foundation-churned fields, is the 'spoil of the abbeys' in microcosm. Wymondham's huge west tower, built in the 1440s at the charge of the town, humbles the already handsome (but much smaller) crossing-tower which the prior had raised a few decades before. Both towers post-date, yet themselves help explain, a succession of riots in the early fifteenth century, when the monks and their parishioners had come to blows. Also of that time, a thick dividing wall cuts the church west of the crossing. It once separated the monks' choir from the parochial nave, emphasizing a distinction which had always been present but had not previously been made so invidiously.

That distinction, in the event, would determine what survived the Dissolution. At their own particular request, Wymondham's townspeople were allowed to keep the monks' crossing-tower for the bells it still carried, together with everything west of its base. To the east and south, where the abbey buildings had been, nothing but rough foundations has remained. What was left of the church, though, is still striking. The townspeople's nave, blocked off from the choir since the early fifteenth century, was never subsequently equipped with a new chancel. However, its fifteenth-century remodelling had included the addition of a big north aisle, with the usual re-roofing of an East Anglian church of its quality, the handsome porch and ambitious west tower. Grander by far than the majority of such buildings, Wymondham tells us more also about the pressures of its period – about building programmes characteristically fired by jealousy, and about men of religion who, in pursuit of private interest, had lost the hearts and allegiance of their folk. Where the breaking of old bonds was so obvious in the localities, what hope had the monks left at court?

WYMONDHAM CHURCH (Norfolk) A former abbey church which has lost its choir (left), but not the parochial nave (centre); here the monks' crossing tower is overshadowed by the huge west tower (right) raised by the townsmen in the 1440s in undisguised rivalry with the Benedictines.

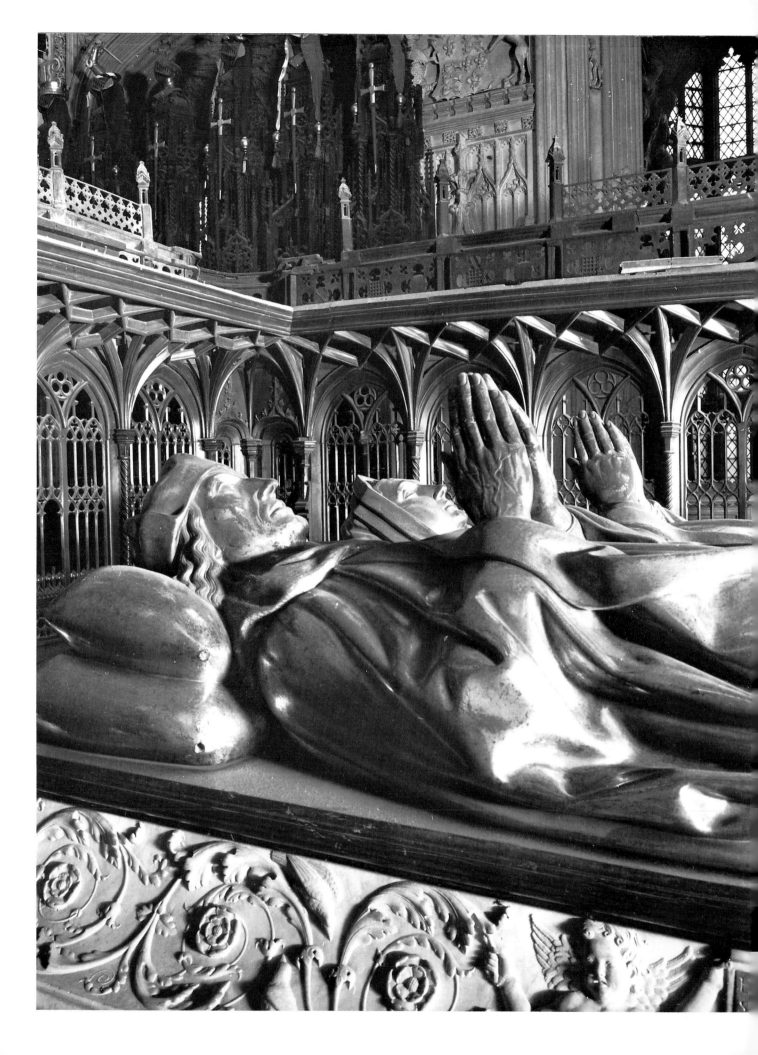

[5]

Royal Phoenix

Henry VIII succeeded to the English throne in 1509. Ten years later, along with Charles of Spain and Francis of France, Henry was a candidate for the imperial title to which Charles secured election on 28 June 1519 as the Emperor Charles V. In such company, and with such elevated aspirations, Henry developed a taste for international intrigue. His standards became those of the great Continental courts. His model was his rival, Francis I (1515–47), with whom he debated in the splendour of the Field of Cloth of Gold (1520) before treating at Gravelines, again on equal terms, with the newly appointed Holy Roman Emperor.

The times were stimulating. Already the Americas had been discovered and their wealth tasted. Portuguese explorers, pushing round the Cape, had set up their bases in the Spice Islands. In their contrasting fashions, Erasmus and Luther had set fire to discontent within the Church. Every king, not least the king of Scots, wanted a part in this action, though on a plane which few could afford. One of Henry VIII's earliest military successes, the overwhelming English victory over the Scots at Flodden in 1513, was the direct consequence of an ill-considered entanglement in international politics which ended fatally for James IV and his nobility. Disregarding the lesson of Flodden, James V kept the intrigues alive, entering marriage alliances with France in the 1530s which were a clear provocation of his uncle. At Solway Moss, in November 1542, he too met humiliating defeat.

The next month, James V died – of despair, it is sometimes said – in the Francophile setting of Falkland Palace, which he had beautified for Mary of Guise. Falkland's Renaissance-style ornament, so different from the vernacular tradition but seen again at James V's extensions to Stirling Castle, proclaimed the new values in the North. In England, Henry VIII had likewise become their champion. Before him, it had been Henry's father, the usurping Henry Tudor, who had been chiefly responsible for bringing the Renaissance to England. And major projects – the great Savoy Hospital and Henry VII's Chapel at Westminster – dated to the earlier reign. However, it was Henry VIII's overweening ambition and his spendthrift ways which flung wide the floodgates of patronage. Henry was not, by most standards, a connoisseur. In the arts, his judgement was liable to be defective. But he seldom stopped to think about the cost.

Henry was a great collector of palaces, the archbishop's Knole being among those he personally solicited. On a fresh site altogether, Nonsuch Palace was to be his individual achievement: a grotesque English answer to the challenge of the more sophisticated Fontainebleau. Yet just at the moment Henry began on Nonsuch, his Continental checks and balances fell apart. In July 1538, Henry's long-term rivals, Charles V and Francis I, agreed a common policy against Protestants and Turks, which left England dangerously exposed. For years, Henry had played one sovereign off against the other. But now the threat of concerted invasion was very real. Characteristically, Henry's reaction was to return to cherished preoccupations of earlier years in the design of a great chain of coastal forts. The Scots, too, had loved their guns, and had felt the more youthful for having them. The ageing Henry reverted to artillery like a drug. Down the sink of coastal defence went a large part of the Crown's profit from the Dissolution. Henry VIII, twice hammer of the Scots and 'most excellent King of England, France, and Ireland', had found the opiate he needed to see him out.

WESTMINSTER ABBEY (London) Pietro Torrigiani's fine realistic effigies of Henry VII and his queen on a tomb-chest decorated with Renaissance ornament; notice the still Gothic inspiration of the enclosing screen.

In truth, little at the court of Henry VIII bore much resemblance to that conservative world in which the monks, for the most part, remained enmeshed. Henry was not the originator of the English Renaissance. His father had been there before him. But the young king's passion for the new had an infectious single-mindedness that put him at the head of his generation. Henry's contemporaries and rivals in patronage were Francis I and Charles V, King of France and Habsburg Emperor respectively. Later, Henry's emulator in Scotland would be his energetic nephew, James V. Each was a great builder in the Renaissance manner, 'as well of fortresses as of pleasant palaces'. On his own territory and in both regards, Henry VIII had indeed a good claim to be 'the onelie Phenix of his time for fine and curious masonrie'.

Tragically little of this work remains intact. Of what there is, not everything even so was 'fine and curious', where no purpose might be served by such extravagance. Henry's Green Court at Knole, added to the palace after its appropriation in the 1530s from Archbishop Cranmer, was functional and disappointingly routine. But that accommodation at Knole was required, as we have seen, not for the king personally but for his servants. At

THE VYNE (Hampshire) The panel above the altar in the east window of William Sandys' chapel shows Henry VIII kneeling before an image of the Virgin, with his patron saint, Henry II of Bavaria, close behind him; the many Renaissance details confirm that this is the work of Netherlandish artists thought to have also been employed by Lord Sandys at Basingstoke.

Hampton Court Palace, where Henry spent more time, the contrast is clear between the comparative austerity of the household lodgings of Wolsey's Base Court and the 'curious' invention of what is left of the royal apartments. In Henry's great hall, the surviving hammerbeam roof is of exceptional richness and complexity, as is the fine ceiling with which the king re-equipped the chapel of his cardinal's former palace. Neither was bettered in its period.

It was probably at the palace of Nonsuch, built thirty years into his reign, that Henry and his architects were at their most inventive. However Henry, since his youth, had been a pioneer in art patronage, and his leadership was influential from the start. Thus it was Pietro Torrigiani, trained by Ghirlandaio alongside Michelangelo, who was employed by Henry VIII to complete the Tudor family tombs at Westminster Abbey. Torrigiani's Italianate example can be seen again in the huge Salisbury Chantry at Christchurch Priory. In much the same way, the Northern Renaissance glass of St Margaret's (Westminster) anticipated the Flemish window in Lord Sandys' chapel at The Vyne, and Henry's fine Renaissance ornament on the choir-stalls at King's (Cambridge) set a standard for imitation throughout the country.

Everywhere, the transition was swift. Torrigiani's Renaissance effigies were protected by a screen, commissioned just before, which in every detail of its ornament was Gothic. Their setting was a chantry chapel, soon to be overtaken by the Reformation and only lately completed in an architectural mode which owed nothing to Italian ideas. At the contemporary royal chapels of St George's (Windsor) and King's College (Cambridge), the conflict is obvious between a Perpendicular building in the medieval tradition and furnishings which belonged rather to the Renaissance. Such models could not pass unobserved.

Consider, for example, the striking change in mood between the monuments of the two Henry Frowyks (d.1527 and 1540) at South Mimms Church, the first medieval, the second unmistakably Renaissance. The Frowyks were City merchants, more sophisticated than most. But there is plentiful evidence of other similar transitions, and some of them belong even earlier. Take the Renaissance portrait bust at Tong of a Henrician divine, Arthur Vernon (d.1517), in the new chantry chapel of Sir Harry Vernon (d.1515) who had himself chosen a more old-fashioned and traditional memorial. Tong is in Shropshire. Still more remote from current high fashion was the parish church of Bodmin, in Cornwall. Yet even here Torrigiani's mannerisms – medallions within wreaths, cherubs (or *putti*), and twisted balusters – were already on display by 1533 on the monument of the late Prior Vyvian.

Inevitably, the spread of the new styles owed much to individuals who had originally encountered them at court, at the universities, or in the capital. Henry Frowyk the Younger was no doubt brought up in the cosmopolitan society of rich merchants. Arthur Vernon was a Cambridge graduate who may have known Erasmus and would certainly have been an admirer of Margaret Beaufort. Prior Vyvian of Bodmin was one of those lesser princes of the Church – Abbot Vintoner of St Osyth, Abbot Charde of Forde, and Abbot King of Thame were others – whose tastes had developed along humanist lines, fostering the study of Greek and Roman antiquities, and who may very well have made the pilgrimage to Rome. On the painted dado of a screen at Bunbury Church (Cheshire), classical motifs of astounding purity look as if they have been rescued from Pompeii. They date to 1527 and were part of the furnishings of a new chantry chapel intended as Sir Ralph Egerton's memorial. Sir Ralph, unremarkably, had been well-known at court, the personal standard bearer of Henry VIII. Like Arthur Vernon at Tong or Prior Vyvian at Bodmin, he brought the Renaissance home.

One of the most significant of these early cultural migrations occurred in Hampshire, at the newly-built mansion of another courtier, William Lord Sandys of The Vyne. Sandys had been a close associate of the king since the start of his reign, beginning as Knight of the Bedchamber. He had fought overseas, in Spain, France and Flanders, and he had been present at that spectacular confrontation, the Field of Cloth of Gold, of which indeed he had been one of the organizers. Sandys' experience undoubtedly shaped his tastes, and The Vyne is the house of a pioneer. In particular, Sandys' long gallery, completed before 1528, was well in advance of its time. At Fontainebleau, the French king's *Galerie François I*, often considered the model for such apartments, had yet to be completed. Already fashionable in Italy, covered exercise-spaces of this kind were rare, if not unknown, in the North. Yet Sandys built a wing specifically to accommodate his gallery, which ran the entire length of its first floor. Expensively panelled from floor to ceiling, the apartment offered strollers a rich display of commemorative heraldry, interspersed with Renaissance motifs.

Sandys' long partnership with the king had raised him to prominence in the decades before the royal divorce. Accordingly, his panelling at The Vyne carried the pomegranate device of Queen Catherine of Aragon – represented again in his chapel window – with the cardinal's hat and escutcheon of Thomas Wolsey. After the disowning of the one and the disgrace of the other, neither would have been remembered in this way.

Among the posts held by Sandys in the 1520s was the Treasurership of Calais, in which he was succeeded by Sir Richard Weston, another long-serving courtier. Both were much-travelled, especially in Flanders and north France. And each would take advantage of what he had experienced on his journeys to confer some special character on his home. At Richard Weston's Sutton Place, the existing long gallery is a later feature, not

Far left KING'S COLLEGE CHAPEL (Cambridge) In the Late Gothic setting of this famous college chapel, begun by Henry VI (d.1471), the choir-stalls introduced by Henry VIII are very much of the Renaissance in their ornament, with cherubs and foliated pilasters in the Antique manner framing the repetitious Tudor heraldry.

Above THE VYNE (Hampshire) A good mid seventeenth-century chimney-piece and other later alterations have done much to conceal the originality of this apartment; nevertheless, William Sandys' long gallery at The Vyne, completed before 1528, was one of the first of its kind, and the fine carved wainscot (though painted at a later date) is original.

attributable to the first building programme. Even without it, however, Sutton Place was as innovative as William Sandys' The Vyne, its quality showing rather in the exploitation of terracotta, for which Italy, by way of France or Flanders, was the source.

Moulded terracotta ornament, as used at Sutton Place in the later 1520s, was a relatively short-lived fashion. In the Home Counties, the model was probably Giovanni da Maiano's terracotta roundels of Roman emperors, commissioned by Cardinal Wolsey for Hampton Court. Through East Anglia, the only other region where terracotta ornament occurs in any quantity, a more likely influence was the Netherlands. In any event, terracotta was rarely seen in England before 1520, nor after the 1540s. At Sutton Place, Sir Richard Weston's enthusiasm for the new material, shared with other courtiers, was entirely up to date and *à la mode*.

Certainly, terracotta's decorative potential was considerable. Already at Layer Marney, earlier in the same decade, Henry Lord Marney had employed terracotta in the ornamental cresting of his tower, on which shells and dolphins in the Renaissance taste replaced the more conventional battlements. Another use, more appropriate to the material, was in Layer Marney's window mullions. And Weston, while doing the same at Sutton Place,

SUTTON PLACE (Surrey) Sir Richard Weston's fine new country house (*below*) of the late 1520s has lost the gatehouse range which formerly closed off the inner court; but the careful symmetry of the entire composition shows well here in the central hall range and its flanking residential wings, very much in the incoming tradition of the Tudor Renaissance. The facade of Weston's mansion was enlivened with fashionable terracotta ornament (*right*), featuring banks of cherubs and other Renaissance devices in the latest taste of Henry VIII's court, of which Sir Richard was a prominent member.

was to take terracotta's exploitation one stage further in an ostentatious exhibition of moulded panelling and friezes, plinths, turrets, and battlements. The big quatrefoils of Weston's frieze over the hall door at Sutton Place are medieval. His window heads, like those of Layer Marney, remain Gothic. But whereas the comparably elaborate carved and moulded brickwork of Sir Henry Fermor's contemporary East Barsham Manor (Norfolk) showed nothing of the Renaissance in its ornament, Sutton Place is replete with Italian naked cherubs and with Roman-style trophies of arms.

Briefly, the two styles (Gothic and Renaissance) lived together – in the houses of courtiers like Marney or Weston, as also at such mansions as Hengrave Hall, in Suffolk, built for a London merchant, Sir Thomas Kytson, and completed in 1538. The more innovative Weston had made little show of his hall door, sacrificing it rather to the overall Renaissance harmony of his facade. In contrast, Kytson kept the old traditions going with a central showpiece window of deliberate splendour, conferring dignity on the entrance below. Kytson's trefoiled bay was in the final medieval style of such influential recent works as Buckingham's Thornbury Castle (on its garden front), or the east end of Henry VII's chantry at Westminster. Its arched lights were again pre-Renaissance. Nevertheless, the bay rested on moulded supports of classical inspiration, while at its base were the familiar naked cherubs, close cousins of the Sutton Place terracottas.

Terracotta ornament, at its most extravagant, is probably best studied at first hand in the abundant detail of contemporary sepulchral monuments: on the Marney tombs in the parish church at Layer Marney, on the Bedingfeld monuments at the surviving family chantry in Oxborough, or on the tomb of Abbot Ferrers at Wymondham. All date to the 1520s, and what they illustrate together is a common delight in new materials and styles that transcends the mere whim of the moment. At Layer Marney, terracotta and moulded brick had

HENGRAVE HALL (Suffolk) The spectacular centre-piece of Sir Thomas Kytson's mansion (1525–38) was its gatehouse (*right*), crowned with ornamental turrets and equipped with a big trefoiled bay, still Gothic in inspiration but carrying sculptures that are clearly of the Renaissance. *Overleaf* Detail of the classically-inspired mouldings and cherub supporters at the base of Kytson's bay window.

been used simultaneously in Sir Henry Marney's spectacular prodigy tower, overlooking his rebuilt church and family tombs. A generation earlier, Oxburgh Hall, although entirely of brick, was already of the most lavish and ingenious construction. The Marneys and the Bedingfelds, in the company of such other progressive builders as Sir William Cordell of Melford Hall, Sir Thomas Lucy of Charlecote Park, and Sir George Throckmorton of Coughton Court, were fully as open to the new influences of the day as was Henry VIII, their king. Of the remarkable houses they have bequeathed to us since, only Layer Marney is not cared for by the Trust.

Henry, for his part, would never rest content with what he had built already, characteristically reaching out for more. His palace at Nonsuch, begun in 1538, was intended to live up to its name. While still traditional in plan, with the plainly-built outer quadrangle (for household lodgings) of such other royal palaces as Knole, 'Nonsuch' earned its title in the royal quarters, a shop window for every known decorative technique. Henry had poached an Italian artificer, Nicholas Bellin of

Modena, from the rival works at Fontainebleau of Francis I. And he set Bellin to work on two new materials in particular: on plaster-stucco and on carved and gilded slate. Ornamental effects might be obtained in both of these which, in stone or moulded brick, were impossible. They dictated the commissioning of a timber-framed supporting structure, certainly one of the largest and most elaborate ever built.

Nonsuch had decayed by the mid seventeenth century, to be demolished in 1682. Always bizarre rather than beautiful, it had exemplified the 'curious' quality of Henry's building, and proved impossibly expensive to maintain. Nevertheless, no structure as boldly exhibitionist as Nonsuch Palace could fail to leave its mark in the record. Particularly significant, and still recoverable in outline, is the complex iconography of its facades.

STIRLING CASTLE (Central) The east front of James V's quadrangular palace (*c.* 1540) within the royal fortress at Stirling, showing the rich external sculptures of the *piano nobile* stage, on which were the royal apartments.

The royal apartments at Nonsuch, as at other palaces of its date, included a King's Side (west of the private inner court) and a Queen's Side (in the range to the east). Each had its separate scheme of stucco 'statues, pictures and other Antik formes of excellent art and workmanshipp and of noe small cost', a figure of Scipio guarding the king's entrance, and of Penthesilea protecting the queen's. Nonsuch mirrored the learning of Henry himself and promoted, in anticipation, the humanist education of his son, Prince Edward, born in 1537. Against the king's apartments, the Labours of Hercules were recorded in stucco; against his queen's, Patientia and Humilitas, with the Seven Liberal Arts and Seven Virtues. On the next level above were mythological figures, crowned by busts of Caesars at the top. Carved and gilded slates, in striking colour contrast with the stucco, sheathed the supporting timbers of the structure. They, too, were richly worked in the fashionable 'antique' (or neo-Roman) taste, with fruit swags and with trophies of arms.

Direct echoes of Nonsuch are hard to find. One, certainly, is the lively Fontainebleau-style chimney-piece at Broughton Castle (Oxfordshire), installed during Richard Fiennes' major remodelling of the castle in 1554. Another great chimney-piece, at Loseley Park in Surrey, is as ornate and allusive as anything that Nonsuch could have shown, the inspiration being surely the same. At the National Trust's Dunster Castle, Hans Eworth's allegorical painting (dated 1550) of Sir John Luttrell, one of the very few notable works of English Mannerism, is close both in spirit and in execution to the School of Fontainebleau and to the art of the competing royal palaces of the time. But Henry VIII's death in 1547, although not the end of building at Nonsuch, had effectively put the cap on it as a model. The next major advance in English architecture, shedding the alien bravura of Henry's Nonsuch, owed more to the comparative restraint of the Protector's Somerset House and to home-grown professionals like Smythson and the Thorpes, fully alive to what was happening overseas.

In point of fact, the works at Nonsuch were more closely paralleled north of the Border than in the buildings of Henry's own realm. James V's new, or remodelled, palaces at Falkland and Stirling were the exact contemporaries of his uncle's Nonsuch. And they shared a common source in a Northern Renaissance of which France was unquestionably the leader. The Scottish king's marriages, in rapid succession, to Madeleine of France (d.1537) and to Mary of Guise, brought him into direct contact with Francis I's court at Fontainebleau, already well known to many prominent Scots of his generation. Further, in building for his queens, it was natural for James V to call French craftsmen to his aid, freely adopting the Renaissance styles of his foreign mentors. Consequently, it was at Falkland Palace and then again at Stirling Castle that the Renaissance entered Scotland in full dress. That dress, as at Nonsuch but with greater purity of execution, was essentially in the current mode of France.

Falkland Palace today is a hybrid. Scottish Gothic (late) on its outer facade, it is French Renaissance (early) towards the garden. Internally, it has been ruthlessly rebuilt. Yet the palace's high importance to Scottish architecture is obvious. James V's surviving garden front at Falkland, built between 1537 and 1539, antedated the more complete work of the early 1540s at Stirling Castle, with which it had many features in common. Both palaces were originally quadrangular. At both again, the royal apartments – as at Nonsuch and earlier at Linlithgow – occupied separate suites on the first floor. Emphasizing the importance of this *piano nobile* on which the main living quarters, in the Continental fashion, were concentrated, pilasters decorated the facades. At Stirling, the pilasters are placed in niches and are highly ornamented in a style which, in Scotland, had no precedents. At Falkland, they are separated by large medallions, equally unfamiliar in the North. Neither could have occurred here as early as this without the intervention of the French.

Indeed, the medallions at Falkland, carved with the heads of the heroes of Antiquity, are the work of a French mason, Nicholas Roy. Such ornaments were already well known in northern Europe. Seen in Wolsey's terracotta roundels at Hampton Court, they had probably come there directly from Italy. In Scotland, their source was unquestionably French. Still more splendidly again, carved medallions of an identical style were re-used by James V in the great coffered ceiling of the formal presence chamber of his new royal apartments at Stirling. However, for these, significantly, the closest parallel was neither in England nor yet in France, but far away in Wawel Castle (Poland), where they had occurred in the ceiling of the Ambassadors' Chamber, built a few years earlier for Sigismund I. Wolsey's roundels at Hampton Court date to about 1520; Sigismund's medallions at Kraków to the early 1530s; James V's ceiling at Stirling Castle can be no later than 1542. By the 1540s, where Europe was concerned, such Renaissance tastes had spread convincingly to the uttermost parts of the earth.

Of the Stirling medallions, displaced since that time, the finest are those carved by another Frenchman, Andrew Mansioun, who must have come to Scotland, like Nicholas Roy of Falkland, under the patronage of Mary of Guise. Mansioun's portrait heads are of fashionably dressed individuals, thought to be members of James V's circle, whether of his family or his court. This glittering company had its cousins elsewhere, in Kraków, Nonsuch and Fontainebleau. And what we know of its routines – its cavalcades and entertainments, its hunting parties and its picnics – establishes a degree of social sophistication far exceeding that of most élites, including (one surmises) our own.

Such a life-style required its own buildings. Generally, its surviving hunting lodges, banqueting pavilions and viewpoint towers, few of which were ever intended to be permanent, date to a later generation: to Sir David Lindsay, for example, creator in 1604 of the remarkable Renaissance garden at Edzell (Angus), or to Sir Thomas Tresham, scholar and eccentric Northamptonshire builder of the summer pavilions at Rushton and Lyveden New Bield, both of the 1590s. But the line, of course, had begun much earlier in such prodigies as Lord Marney's great entrance tower at Layer Marney, or Sir George Throckmorton's wall-of-glass gatehouse at Coughton Court, both of the second decade of the sixteenth century. At Nonsuch in the 1540s, the 'fine and curious masonrie' of the palace's facades was fully matched by the accommodation within.

Already, the gatehouses of Layer Marney and of Throckmorton's Coughton Court had functioned primarily as prospect towers. From both, huge windows offered views over the surrounding countryside, while the lofty platforms of their roofs were far better suited to taking the air than to any earlier purpose like defence. Evidently, the shift in priorities had begun, in court circles, from towards the start of Henry's reign. Moreover, long before the 'royal phoenix' had himself stopped building, many others had taken up his tune. That 'loftie and fresch' tower which ascended, for example, from Melbury Sampford, in Dorset, was equipped at the top with an early version of the glazed prospect lantern – at Melbury, a comfortable viewing chamber of hexagonal plan, with windows in all but one face – seen on so many of the great houses of the later sixteenth century after a further taste for such novelties had developed. Giles Strangways built

Melbury Sampford in the 1530s. Over the next decade, Nonsuch set the pattern for much more.

Among those who knew Nonsuch at the close of Henry's reign, as well as other more restrained buildings like the Protector's Somerset House (1547–52), was William Sharington, purchaser of the nunnery at Lacock. In the early 1540s, Sharington's modifications of Lacock had begun conservatively. However, the addition in about 1550 of a new corner tower brought his mansion more convincingly up to date. Lacock's tower, like the much grander angle towers on the garden front at Nonsuch, was octagonal. And its purpose was no more military than those. Furnished with banqueting chambers at two levels, the upper of which doubled as a belvedere, the tower was a refuge for civilized conversation and for repasts of Arcadian simplicity. Sharington and his guests, among them Sir John Thynne who would apply similar ideas at Longleat, took their meals at purpose-built tables, carved in the Italian style by an English sculptor, John Chapman, who had been trained in the workshops of the king. Every detail of such entertainments, and of the furniture that went with them, was of Mediterranean rather than Gothic inspiration.

Sharington's deliberate cultivation of an 'antique' life-style owed much to the late king, whose own banqueting house at Nonsuch Palace had been approached through its 'Grove of Diana'. Today, only the foundations of Henry's pavilion can be traced. However, a survey of 1650 recorded its two-storeyed timber-framed construction, its many windows 'quite round the whole house', and the 'balcone placed for prospect' at each corner. Another feature of significance in the building's plan was uncovered during recent excavations. Of course, Henry's pleasure pavilion at Nonsuch was as much a rich man's plaything as the other elements of his palace: extravagant, frivolous, and self-indulgent. Yet it was planted squarely on a bastioned platform laid out with the military precision of a fort. Those, indeed, were the two faces of his reign.

By the later 1540s, when the Nonsuch banqueting house was built, there was nothing new in Henry's military preoccupations. He had been interested since youth in armour and in innovative

LACOCK ABBEY (Wiltshire) The octagonal table, echoing the plan of the tower itself, in one of William Sharington's banqueting chambers, thought to be the work of John Chapman and to date to c. 1550.

weaponry. And he had made it his business to keep abreast of his commanders in the new technologies of war, whether by land or sea – in fortifications, in gunfounding, and in naval architecture. These concerns, shared by many of his subjects, had led him, early in his reign, to experiment with simple artillery towers like those of Camber, on the Sussex coast, and of Wark, facing Scotland across the Tweed.

But Englishmen, in general, remained novices in fortification, complacent behind the barrier of their Channel. Dartmouth Castle, England's first major coastal artillery fort, dated to the 1480s, fully two decades after the building of Ravenscraig, its Scottish equivalent on the Firth of Forth. And Dartmouth, even so, was the private initiative of merchant adventurers in the haven, applying lessons they had learnt on the Breton coastline, which at home were otherwise ignored. Characteristically, when artillery engineering came to be acknowledged as a science in Britain, it was Scots who again took the lead. Still, early in the 1500s, James IV's new forework at Stirling Castle was a medieval fortification, dependent on great bulk for its strength. Yet within half a century, at Stirling again, that same forework had the significantly-named 'French Spur' as cover – a modern artillery platform. In between, came the pioneering Craignethan.

Sir James Hamilton of Finnart, building at Craignethan from about 1530, had spent much of his youth overseas. There, in France and in Italy, an effective siege gun had only lately been developed. Craignethan was purpose-built to resist it. Hamilton's fort, though well protected by steep descents on its three other quarters, was overlooked by a tall bluff on the west. Against this, Hamilton opposed his principal lines of defence. A deep vertical-sided ditch, cutting straight across the headland, fronted a massive curtain wall pierced by gunports. Hidden by the stone curtain from siege artillery on the bluff, Hamilton's residential tower-house was set towards the back of a bawn, or inner court, itself adequately protected by a lower curtain. The tower was an innovative building, in harmony with the

CAMBER CASTLE (East Sussex) Built to protect the seaward approaches to Rye, Henry VIII's expensive coastal fort at Camber was never put to the test; it began in 1512 as a simple artillery tower (centre), subsequently raised and supported by semi-circular bastions in successive building campaigns of 1539–40 and 1542–3, separated by a major rethinking of the defences.

145

defences, in which a tall vaulted hall, rising through two stages, was turned at right angles to a spacious vestibule. The plan, effective but unusual, had not been seen in Scotland before that day.

Hamilton's work at Craignethan, certainly complete by 1540, anticipated the better known artillery forts of the English king by almost a decade. Certainly, it was every bit as ingenious. One feature, especially, stands out. Across the base of Craignethan's moat, Hamilton laid a stone *caponier* (or vaulted passage), pierced by loopholes to command the ditch floor with raking fire. The contraption was Italian: a very new invention. And its rapid transmission to the North in the merest handful of years is good evidence of the contemporary pace of change. Such speed could result in costly errors. Craignethan itself was already out of date before Stirling received its French Spur. Even while the first works were in progress at Henry's forts, expensive modifications were introduced.

The incentive for a new programme of coastal defence in England, for which the blueprint was the so-called 'Device by the King' of February 1539, came with the crumbling of Henry's Continental alliances that previous summer and the coming together of his enemies for invasion. After decades of destructive rivalry, deliberately fomented by Henry, Francis I and Charles V had at last made common cause against him. With the Pope's assistance, they had hoped to prise Henry and his subjects apart, restoring the English Church to its old allegiance while settling their accounts with its king. The plan soon came to nothing. But the danger, while it lasted, had appeared very real. And a major programme of fortification, once launched by the government, was difficult to halt or divert. The king, moreover, had set his heart on it. The Henrician defences of mid Tudor England were Henry's in much more than name. That 'perfect builder' had found another cause to engage him. In only seven years – the last of his reign – Henry spent substantially more on his coastal fortifications than on everything else he ever built. The royal phoenix, ac-

CRAIGNETHAN CASTLE (Strathclyde) At Sir James Hamilton's pioneering artillery fort of the 1530s, the great fronting wall shows now only as foundations (centre), but the *caponier* (vaulted firing passage) can still be seen crossing the base of the defensive ditch (centre left), while Hamilton's blockhouse stands to almost its full height towards the back of its neat rectangular enclosure (towards camera).

knowledged expert in 'plattes [plans], blocke howses, bulwarkes, walles, castelles . . . and fortresses', had risen reinvigorated from his ashes.

Hamilton's Craignethan had been designed as an artillery blockhouse, shielding guns behind the stonework of its curtain. The function of Henry's forts was much the same. Before the crisis, the king and his advisers had learnt all they knew of artillery defences in Northern Europe. Long familiar with the gun-tower as a key unit in such works, they had yet to come to terms with the angle-bastions of the South, low in profile and hidden in the earth. Very probably, even had they done so, they would not have seen the value of bastions of that kind for the purposes immediately in view. What was required was concentration of fire-power. The enemy was shipping; the duel was with the sea. Every one of Henry's forts, of which there were many, bristled like a porcupine with guns.

Deal Castle, north of Dover, was the largest. Its defences, on five tiers, carried no fewer than 145 firearm embrasures. Almost next door, Walmer Castle had four tiers of batteries, with at least sixty embrasures for guns. Formidable though these fortresses undoubtedly were, they had more than one value for their builder. On the walls of St Mawes Castle, completed late in Henry's programme, are proud inscriptions, specially composed in Latin hexameters by the royal Chaplain and Antiquary, John Leland. One of them reads (in translation): 'Henry, thy honour and praises will remain for ever'; another, 'Honour Henry VIII, most excellent King of England, France, and Ireland'; a third, 'May Edward resemble his father in fame and deeds'. And then, recalling all those traditional memorial practices that Henry, in his greed and impatience, had overthrown: 'May the soul live for ever of Henry VIII who had this made in the thirty-fourth year of his reign [1543].'

St Mawes, with three semicircular bastions springing from a central artillery tower, or keep, was of elegant clover-leaf plan. On the opposite shore of the same estuary, Pendennis Castle was a simpler but nevertheless graceful composition of concentric circles. At Deal and Walmer, Hurst and Camber, there were other variations on the concentric theme, with similar emphasis on pure geometry. Very much the exception in this company, Portland's half-moon batteries faced the

DEAL CASTLE (Kent) Built in a single campaign in 1539–40, Deal perfectly exemplifies the geometric planning of Henry VIII's coastal forts, repeated even in the outline of the moat.

sea without ever completing the full circle. Such economies, generally, were unnecessary. Resources were at hand in the disposable lands and buildings of the suppressed religious houses. The king could build what he wished. Henry himself was at Dover in September 1538, returning there the following spring. His three great castles 'which keep the Downs' – Deal, Walmer and Sandown (now eroded by the sea) – rose regardless of expense and at remarkable speed from 'ground-plats' prepared for 'the most excellent' Henry and under his personal supervision.

That dispatch could only have been achieved – as indeed it was – by teamwork of an exceptional order. Henry used men on his Kentish forts who had worked for him before, at Nonsuch and on the new extensions at Hampton Court. Between them, they devised castles of characteristic ingenuity, at least as 'fine and curious' as the palaces. The spiralling newel stairs at the core of Deal, though since replaced, originated as an artful double helix.

ST MAWES CASTLE (Cornwall) One of the smallest but most perfect of Henry VIII's artillery fortresses, completed in 1543 with a proud coat-of-arms over the entrance and a series of laudatory inscriptions.

Below them, a neat supporting pillar, surrounded by fine vaults, incorporated a well precisely at the centre of the building. Ventilators cleared the smoke from the covered fighting galleries, and there were ammunition recesses by the guns. The planners of these castles loved artillery. At Deal and Walmer, the gunports were as numerous on the landward quarters as against the more vulnerable sea shore. Everything was symmetrical. In an expensive gesture which must always have been hard to appreciate except in plan (or nowadays, of course, from the air), the stone revetments of the moats repeated precisely each pinch and every curve of the bastions.

There was much of pure art in buildings such as these. But there was evidence also of engineering on a frontier, not least in alterations of plan. At Pendennis, the handsome multangular curtain is clearly an afterthought, masking the ground-floor gun embrasures of the keep. Similarly at Camber, the original groundplat of Stephen von Haschenperg was amended, first in detail and then overall, within the less than four years of the building programme. Haschenperg's work at Camber, starting from the core of the still comparatively new artillery tower of 1512, began in May 1539. By

the following spring, activity had peaked, to tail off to a temporary halt in September. Even during that time, Haschenperg changed his mind about the gatehouse and curtain wall, the first (originally rectangular) being given a new D-shaped front, the second having to be raised a full storey. Haschenperg's design had been too daring. He had kept Camber's profile low in the new Italian manner, protecting his outer curtain with a shingle glacis, and employing such devices as flankers with

PENDENNIS CASTLE (Cornwall) Here a relatively simple Henrician artillery tower, built in the early 1540s, has been enclosed within sophisticated Italian-style ramparts of 1598, almost entirely filling the headland.

orillons (spurs) to provide covering fire along its length. These were techniques, still barely known in the North, with which the king was essentially out of sympathy. Within a very few years, Henry himself would be converted to them. In the meantime, Haschenperg's scheme for Camber Castle was put on ice.

A second building programme, twice as expensive as the first and only two seasons following its conclusion, began in April 1542. Camber's central tower, raised already in the first campaign, was taken up another full storey. Haschenperg's glacis was removed and his flankers demolished, to be replaced instead by a strong polygonal curtain, with big semi-circular bastions on each quarter. By late August 1543, after another £10,000 had been spent on Camber, the castle at last was complete. It had begun life in 1512 as a simple artillery tower: a blockhouse of the most primitive kind. Then, in 1539–40, it had been the setting for an advanced and unique experiment in the new Italian techniques, albeit somewhat fumblingly applied. Camber's final form – a bold upstanding artillery

fortress in the Henrician full-dress of the three castles of the Downs – was a compromise, peculiar to England, between old and new: progressive, in its symmetry and in the advanced equipment of its fighting galleries; backward, in the target it presented to bombardment had any enemy taken the trouble to invest it.

In point of fact, Camber never faced such a challenge and was in service for less than a century. Surrounded and beached by silting-up waterways, it became about as effective as a stranded man-of-war. In Henry's programme, it had been a costly and vexing mistake. Nevertheless at Camber, for the first time, the new Italian theories of artillery defence had been given a preliminary hearing.

CARISBROOKE CASTLE (Isle of Wight) Sophisticated artillery fortifications, with arrow-head bastions, enclose the medieval defences (centre) which originated as a Norman motte-and-bailey earthwork castle, itself later refortified in stone; the Italianate ramparts are by Federigo Giambelli, dating to 1597–1600.

CRAIGIEVAR CASTLE (Grampian) Danzig Willie's 'fortress in the air' – a conventional tower-house which, at wall-head level, takes on all the aspects of a country house; completed in 1626.

Above TRIANGULAR LODGE, RUSHTON (Northamptonshire) Sir Thomas Tresham's Trinitarian conceit, built with maximum symbolism in 1594–7 as a witness to his allegiance to the 'old religion' and rejection of the Tudor Reformation.

Left HAMPTON COURT (London) The timber vault of the Chapel Royal (1535–6) was one of Henry VIII's additions, characteristically splendid, to Cardinal Wolsey's former palace; the stars on the ceiling panels date to Pugin's restoration of the 1840s.

Above MOTTISFONT ABBEY (Hampshire) One of the first conversions of a former monastic house, the gable (left) marking the west end of the transformed church, with the wings (centre and right) of the eighteenth-century mansion re-using the lines of the west and east claustral ranges; the initial conversion, by the courtier William Sandys, was begun soon after 1536.

Right HARDWICK HALL (Derbyshire) The south (side) elevation of Bess of Hardwick's great house, built for her by Robert Smythson in 1591–7; note the importance given to the second floor, where the state apartments were sited, and to the viewpoint chambers in the towers. The long gallery (*below*) is the most impressive of the state apartments, far exceeding the ground-floor hall in size and running the entire length of the building.

Left AUDLEY END (Essex) The west front of Thomas Howard's Jacobean prodigy house, as rebuilt on the site of a former monastery between 1605 and 1614; notice the attention to symmetry in the provision of two porches, as in the central placing of the tall bay window, lighting the great hall but a stage removed from the high-table end. The great hall (*above*), which was the centre-piece of this ambitious mansion, still has its original carved oak screen, embellished with caryatids and other characteristic Northern Renaissance ornaments.

Left BLICKLING HALL (Norfolk) The east range at Blickling, dating to the 1620s, carries the long gallery on the first-floor *piano nobile*, and is the principal garden front of Sir Henry Hobart's fine country house, built for him by Robert Liming who had worked previously for Robert Cecil at Hatfield.

Right ASHDOWN HOUSE (Oxfordshire) A country lodge built in the Dutch urban manner for Lord Craven shortly after the Restoration; designed by William Winde who had been brought up in Holland as the child of exiled royalists.

THE VYNE (Hampshire) John Webb's austere classical portico of 1654 makes a striking centre-piece for Lord Sandys' 1520s brick mansion, of which the big chapel can be seen to the left; sash windows replace William Sandys' original mullions.

They had failed to gain acceptance; but not for long. In 1547, at Yarmouth on the Isle of Wight, a single arrow-head bastion, in the pure Italian style, made its first appearance in the royal works. In between, Henry had experienced his conversion.

The little fort at Yarmouth was a reflex response to the threat of yet another invasion. More serious as a stimulus to advanced engineering were the proposals being promoted for urban enceintes, one of them an abortive project for the naval base at Portsmouth, always an interest of the king. Portsmouth's defences were to have been in the Italian style, already challengingly in use by Henry's old rivals, Charles V and Francis I. Not to be outdone, Henry too had Italian engineers in his employ before his death, to exploit their techniques, during his last French campaign, in the new ramparts of Boulogne and Ambleteuse.

At the start of the next reign, it was Italians again who were chiefly influential in the Duke of Somerset's defensive works for the holding down of Scotland after the Protector's invasion and defeat of the Scots army at Pinkie (1547). Other major projects, including the refortification of Berwick-upon-Tweed, were launched on that occasion, a comparatively minor element in all this activity being the building of the little fort at Holy Island (Lindisfarne), which is now among the properties of the National Trust. Lindisfarne's squared-off batteries are not noticeably Italian, nor has much of the interior of the fort of 1549–50 survived its rebuilding by Edwin Lutyens. Nevertheless, for Holy Island too a contemporary scheme had been prepared for the defence of the former priory buildings (on the flats next to the village), with two demi-bastions of the Italian system. In the event, it was the towering natural strength of Beblowe Crag that determined the more traditional location.

Lindisfarne Castle today has the appearance of a medieval fortress. Only just up the coast and of similar date, the garrison town of Berwick is wholly modern. In 1550, when Sir Richard Lee prepared his first, unrealized plan for Berwick's citadel, his scheme was Italian to the core. In the huge ensuing enterprise, on which nearly £130,000 (ten times the cost of Camber) was spent during the major building campaign of 1558–70, disputes between Lee and his Italian consultants were bitter and prolonged. However, what resulted in the end was a complete set of landward defences, with arrow-head bastions (incorporating flankers and *orillons*) in the Italian manner: by far the largest project of

its kind in Britain, with only Londonderry to rival it in the next century.

Nowhere are the lessons of the new military engineering more forcibly brought home than in the late Elizabethan refortification of Henry's blockhouse at Pendennis, once again in the ripe Italian manner. Paul Ivey, Elizabeth's engineer at Pendennis, had been the author of a handbook, *The Practise of Fortification* (1589), a lucid exposition of all that was best in the Italian system. He had received his training in the Netherlands during the 1570s, had been employed on Elizabeth's works since at least 1584, and by 1598, when he came to Pendennis, was already highly skilled and experienced in the queen's service. What resulted thereafter was utterly unlike the existing (and still comparatively new) fortifications on the same site. Where Henry's artillery tower had been bold and upstanding, making conspicuous play with its prominence on the headland, Ivey's geometrical Italian-style earthworks were deliberately low-lying and part-hidden. Henry's castle had had no flankers; at Elizabeth's, they were the salient characteristic of Ivey's design, every wall-face covered against dead ground.

Broadly, a full-blooded Italian system, as applied by Ivey at Pendennis or simultaneously to Carisbrooke by Giambelli, was better suited to urban than to coastal defence. Indeed, Sir Richard Lee, much earlier, had shown he was aware of the difference when he designed Italian-style defences for Berwick-upon-Tweed at precisely the period when at Upnor, on the Medway, he was building a more conventional two-storey battery. But even Upnor's defences of 1559–67 included a triangular Water Bastion to the front of the main artillery tower. And Italian principles, however ineffectively applied, had clearly taken root in defence. The disease, if that is what it was, had spread more widely. Already some of the Renaissance experimentalism of the early Tudor decades had faded by the time of Henry VIII's death. Moulded terracottas, for example, although briefly fashionable in Henry's reign, were thereafter highly exceptional. Gilded slates and derivative Fontainebleau-style stuccos never had much impact outside Nonsuch. Yet there would be no return, except in nostalgia, to the evaporating traditions of the Late Middle Ages, whether in the Church, in civil life, or in war. Henry and his companions, acknowledged princes of the Renaissance, had made the first decisive fracture with the past.

[6]

Every Man Almost is a Builder

The old king's reign had ended in disenchantment and confusion. Henry VIII's profoundly conservative religious settlement suited neither reformer nor recusant. His economic policies, practising debasement to finance expensive foreign wars, were widely resented as a fraud. From 1547, Somerset's Protectorship made matters worse. A second Dissolution – of chantries, colleges and hospitals – enraged local communities. The war with Scotland forced another debasement of the coinage. True, deliberate manipulation of the currency ceased after 1551. But other problems multiplied in its place, whether self-induced as in the Catholic reaction of Mary's brief reign (1553–8), or a consequence of natural disasters: the catastrophic harvests of 1555–6 and the savage epidemics of the next two years, of which the queen herself may well have been a victim.

Many of these difficulties refused to go away. The climate had been noticeably deteriorating since the 1540s. Between 1550 and 1700, Europe experienced what has since become known as its 'Little Ice Age', with cool wet summers and with winters so cold as to freeze tidal waters like the Thames. Major harvest failures returned in the late 1580s and 1590s, again accompanied by heavy mortalities. Scotland, although at peace, continued to be troubled by depreciation and inflation, while Ireland endured the successive horrors of the Tudor conquest, of the early plantations, and of Tyrone's bloody rebellion (1595–1603). Yet for her own domain, Elizabeth's accession in 1558 was followed by an interlude of exceptional prosperity. Cecil's calling in of the debased coinage in 1560–1 inaugurated an era of currency stability in England unequalled elsewhere in Europe. With two decades of peace from 1564 and with no serious harvest failures over the same period, all the elements of a revival came together.

In particular, propertied England took advantage of the steady population increase which in Scotland merely added to the nightmare. Between 1540 and 1610, population rose by some 60 per cent, with three or four times that growth occurring in London. The increasing dominance of the capital as a focus of consumption was to syphon trade out of the provinces, being a chief cause of urban decay in the localities. Nevertheless, the first two decades of Elizabeth's reign were accompanied by the development of a standard of living unexampled in earlier generations. Profiting by high prices and low wages, the wealthier classes, in town and country alike, accumulated surplus capital. Without (as yet) many alternative investment options on call, they poured their profits into the security of new buildings.

This greedy hunger for the new had roused many critics before 1600. The war with Spain (from 1585), together with Elizabeth's increasingly expensive campaigns in Ireland, helped generate another economic crisis. In such circumstances, some despised comfort, others resented extravagance. There were even those who, imagining the 'goodly usage of those antique times | In which the sword was servant unto right' (The Faerie Queene), retreated with the poet Spenser into pseudo-chivalry. But fancies of that kind were rightly confined to dilettantes. The realists pushed on with few regrets.

TRIANGULAR LODGE, RUSHTON (Northamptonshire) Detail of the east-facing entrance front of Sir Thomas Tresham's Triangular Lodge, in the grounds of Rushton Hall; on this side, the symbolism alludes to God the Father; on the others, to the Son and the Holy Ghost.

Many indicators of social change exist. We each make our choice of which to emphasize. But the measure of a man's modernity has always been his house: accordingly, a better guide than most. Henry VIII undoubtedly saw it that way, and never stopped building all his life. Through the next generations, others felt the same, the zeal for home improvements scarcely faltering. In 1582, when one observer wrote to deplore it, Elizabethan Southampton, deserted by the Italian trade, had neither wealth nor prospects of recovery. Yet during the brief boom of the early years of the reign, the port's feckless burgesses had spent for the day, as if there were no morrow:

'Then beganne costly apparell: then downe with old howses, and newe sett in their places: for the howses where the fathers dwelt could not content their children. Then must everie man of good calling be furnished with change of plate, with great store fyne lynnen, rich tapistrie, and all other things which might make shewe of braverie. And who then but Hampton for fyne dyett and great cheare.'

New standards, once set, are usually irreversible. So whether Hampton's burgesses were rich or poor was of little real consequence to their expectations. In the late 1570s, before their own local critic took up his pen, William Harrison had written a *Description of England* in which the same general observations were elaborated. 'There are old men yet dwelling in the village where I remain, which have noted three things to be marvellously altered in England within their sound remembrance. . . . One is the multitude of chimneys lately erected. . . The second is the great (although not general) amendment of lodging. . . . The third thing they tell of is the exchange of vessel, as of treen platters into pewter, and wooden spoons into silver or tin.' These things, the greybeards complained, had taken their toll in rising rents, in extortionate rates of interest, and in the 'daily oppression of copyholders'. But for those with property, 'how they set up, how they pull down, how they enlarge, how they restrain, how they add to, how they take from' was keeping 'their heads never idle, their purses never shut, nor their books of account never made perfect'. In short, 'he that has bought any small parcel of ground, be it never so little, will not be quiet till he has pulled down the old house (if any were there standing), and set up a new after his own device', so that 'every man almost is a builder'.

Such high activity depended, of course, on the relative prosperity of the landholder. Without the rising rents and descending wages of a period of population recovery, it might very well not have taken off at all. However, the so-called 'Great Rebuilding' of the late sixteenth and early seventeenth centuries spanned decades of dearth as well as plenty. Like the parish church rebuildings of the Late Middle Ages, it cannot adequately be explained in terms of wealth alone, nor in the exceptional availability of surplus capital. With 'head never idle and purse never shut', Sir Francis Willoughby, through the 1580s, bankrupted himself and his luckless heirs in the building of Wollaton Hall. Why, we might ask, did he do it?

The Willoughbys of Wollaton were entrepreneurs: coal owners and iron founders who would try their hand also, with much reduced success, in ventures in woad and with glass. Certainly, they were far from typical in this regard. Nevertheless, what the Willoughbys wanted, and what they thought they could afford, was no more than an exaggeration of others' wishes. Wollaton Hall, with typical bravura, was equipped with what was surely the biggest Elizabethan prospect chamber ever built. 'Behold this house', the proud inscription runs, 'of Sir Francis Willoughby, built with rare art and bequeathed to Willoughbys. Begun 1580 and finished 1588.' Truly, a legacy of sorrow.

Yet in 1580, when he began work at Wollaton, Sir Francis had reason for optimism. There had been bad times in the mid century, through the expensive overseas wars of Mary's reign, the terrible harvests of 1555 and 1556, and the immediately ensuing epidemics. Elizabeth herself had come to the throne in the wake of political and religious confusion, sorely aggravated by famine and plague. However, the next generation, luckier by far, had enjoyed at least two decades of breathing-space to establish new patterns of consumption. England's entanglement in Continental wars came to an end in 1564, on the conclusion of the Treaty of Troyes; there was to be peace until 1585. Major harvest failures, similarly, were not experienced again until 1586–7, nor was there to be a serious population check, famine-induced and on a national scale, before the catastrophes of the later 1590s. The intervening years, though not without their problems, were a time of growth, not least in those areas in which the

WOLLATON HALL (Nottinghamshire) Sir Francis Willoughby's Elizabethan prodigy house, built for him by Robert Smythson in 1580–8. Smythson kept the medieval great hall but placed a huge prospect chamber upon it, seen here rising through the centre of the building.

Willoughbys especially were active: in mining, in industry, and in rents. Coal-mining, in particular, had been a startling success story, production multiplying many times on the back of a steadily growing demand from both industrial and domestic sectors. Glass-making too, another Willoughby interest, kept its costs stable and its yields ever rising, promoting that generous spread of windows, a direct product of the new technology, with which Wollaton, and houses like it, might be furnished. Even the continuous inflation of these decades, deeply worrying to contemporaries, favoured a great landowner like Sir Francis. Of course his costs went up, both in building materials and in wages. But so also did his rents and other receipts from the land, inspiring him still further to those excessive prodigies of invention which so cruelly burdened his heirs.

Works of the Wollaton kind had two inspirations: the first, a legitimate desire for 'amendment of lodging'; the second, a restless pursuit, certainly harder for us to accept, of 'curious' invention and display. Both are present in Elizabethan building, and each, of course, had abundant precedents in the palaces of Henry VIII, as well as in the houses of his wealthier subjects. The Lytes of Lytes Cary were country squires, the accumulators of broad Somerset acres. There was little of the court in their make-up. Yet even at Lytes Cary, in its deep rural seclusion, the 'amendment' of the Lytes' manor-house in the 1520s and 1530s, traditional though it was in so many ways, had included a most striking innovation. In John Lyte's great chamber, where it could be inspected from the matrimonial bed, there was a fine plaster ceiling, coved and ribbed in the style of half a century later. The ceiling carries the arms of Henry VIII, with those of John Lyte and of Edith Horsey, his wife. It is believed to date to about 1533, and has parallels only in the royal works, being fully as pioneering as those.

At Lytes Cary, the plasterwork is comparatively simple. It has none of that sumptuous Late Elizabethan elaboration of the ceilings of Lyme Park or Sizergh, of Bramall, Gilling Castle or Levens Hall. However, its importance is not simply as an appetizer. The Lytes Cary ceiling was itself an element in a programme of substantial refurbishing which entirely transformed the family

LYTES CARY (Somerset) John Lyte's great chamber, with its innovatory coved and ribbed ceiling, dated by the royal arms over the bed to c. 1533.

quarters. These, in the south wing, now included a great parlour at ground-floor level, immediately below the master's chamber. And each of these apartments was both elegant and comfortable: splendidly lit by a bay and other windows, heated individually by a side-wall fireplace, and either wainscoted or hung with tapestries against the chill.

Such comforts, as the men of Southampton in turn would demonstrate in their 'change of plate', their 'great store fyne lynnen', and the 'rich tapistrie' with which they equipped their new houses, were quickly becoming routine. Of course, many remained in no position to afford them. However, amongst the better-off burgesses and countrymen of the will-making classes, there is plentiful evidence in the inventories of the period of a steady accumulation of household goods. In the past, the great majority of luxuries had been imported. Now, as with glass, they might be made at home, to the mutual benefit of producer and consumer alike. Government policy promoted home industries, seen as stemming a chronic haemorrhage abroad of national stocks of gold and silver. Local markets grew as the population itself rose and as prices continued to increase. In the peace and prosperity of Elizabeth's first decades, household purchases inevitably boomed. Yet it was not just surplus wealth that generated this demand, for men of precisely equivalent status in the recent past had been willing to settle for much less. Significantly, in the inventories of the 1570s and later, household goods began to take a larger share of the average testator's wealth, in proportion to his other possessions. Men had not become accumulators just because they were richer. Their standards had taken off as well.

Increasingly, though, these home comforts were intended for the family alone. Houses of substance like Lytes Cary still required their halls: the old traditions of hospitality were not dead. Indeed, John Lyte spent as lavishly on his hall as on his chambers, even if he preferred to dine more quietly in the adjoining bay. Nevertheless, that emphasis on private apartments which had already begun to show itself in the Late Middle Ages, strengthened appreciably under the Tudors. One of the more significant conversions of the late sixteenth century in the northern counties was that of a former tower-house at Turton. William Orrell, Turton's re-builder, was a landowner of substance: a Catholic recusant like many others in conservative Lancashire, but still wealthy and influential in the 1590s and characteristically anxious to extend and

improve his accommodation. What Orrell chose to do at Turton was to gut and re-floor an existing fifteenth-century pele tower, raising it a further stage, and equipping it (on new levels) with three tall apartments, one above the other, the topmost of which, having windows on all quarters, would serve as a prospect chamber or gallery. At Turton today, the furnishings include the so-called Courtenay Bed: a fabulous state bed of 1593, once of the Courtenay earls of Devon. While not original to Turton and far exceeding, in the elaboration of carving, its likely equivalent in William Orrell's original bedchamber, the Courtenay Bed is some indication at least of contemporary taste and of what a Lancashire landowner, with many others of his kind, increasingly felt the challenge to emulate.

Competition, certainly, was in the air. Before Turton's conversion, there were models already available, from the 1570s and 1580s, in such 'prodigy' great chambers as the 'Inlaid Chamber' at Sizergh Castle, Sir Piers Legh VII's great chamber at Lyme Park, or the 'Fairfax Chamber' at Gilling. None of these chambers survives entirely intact. Sizergh's has lost its remarkable panelling to the Victoria and Albert Museum; at Lyme Park, much was either altered or over-restored in the nineteenth century; and only Gilling retains a substantial part of its original armorial glass. Yet taken together, these chambers preserve an extraordinary record of the most extravagant taste of the period: its continuing fondness for heraldry in the glass and painted frieze of Gilling's Fairfax Chamber, its loyalties in the arms of Elizabeth on the overmantel at Lyme Park, its eclectic use of ornament in the Sizergh panelling, where Renaissance Ionic pilasters frame elaborate decorative inlays, the sources being both German and Italian.

Not uncommonly, in an older building, space for such a chamber might have had to be borrowed from the upper levels of an existing ground-floor hall, as it was, for example, in the refurbishing of Bramall, completed in 1592. Bramall's great chamber (now called the 'withdrawing room') is the floored-over upper storey of a fourteenth-century hall, disguised with a stucco ceiling, with a fine Renaissance chimney-piece, and with panel-

GILLING CASTLE (North Yorkshire) The Fairfax Chamber, decorated in the 1570s, is the most remarkable surviving Elizabethan prodigy great chamber. The inlaid wainscot and painted frieze, carved chimney-piece, plaster ceiling and armorial glass are all perfectly intact, though not seen to advantage today.

ling to the level of the frieze. Like the equivalent apartments at Sizergh, Lyme Park and Gilling, the great chamber at Bramall was a prodigy. But it followed, rather than created, a trend. Anticipating Bramall's modernization in the 1590s, the flooring over of halls had become common in England, especially in houses of modest size, among them the National Trust's Snowshill and Westwood, both reconstructed contemporaneously. Earlier in the same century, entirely new buildings like Smallhythe Place and Paycocke's (see pp. 70, 101, 105) had had the status of their halls much reduced. The reduction triggered changes in its turn.

Harrison's old men had noted, without approval, the 'multitude of chimneys lately erected'. They spoke in the 1570s, and what they observed was not so much a breakthrough in contemporary building methods as an obvious manifestation, like the sprouting TV aerials of our own 1950s, of major social change in the localities. True, it was undoubtedly cheaper and simpler to build tall chimneys, now that brick had become more generally available. The diffusion of coal at moderate prices had helped raise expectations in domestic heating. However, the real motivation for chimney-building had come from quite another direction. Everywhere, the downgrading of the common hall, once (but no longer) the resort of all, had been accompanied by a retreat of the family to private chambers. One of these chambers might, in the new designs, have been sited above the hall, making economical use of the same chimney. But others, if they were to be heated more efficiently than by the firepans of the past, would require separate hearths of their own. The two great chimney-stacks of the National Trust's Moseley Old Hall, dating to about 1600 and designed to serve multiple fireplaces, seem to support the entire building. At Thorington Hall, in Suffolk, another Trust property of equivalent size and period, finely-finished brick chimneys (like those at Moseley) betray the true origins of a subsequently much-altered building. Similarly at the relatively humble Gullege, near East Grinstead, it is the enormous late sixteenth-century brick chimney-stacks at the rear of the farmhouse that prop up an earlier timber frame. Added on the occasion of the flooring over of the hall, they antedate by some decades Gullege's eventual grandiose face-lift, when a Jacobean stonework show-front was pinned to its facade: charming, modish, but absurd.

Of course, the flooring over of the hall at a farmhouse like Gullege created difficulties other than heating. In the past, at houses of comparable

GULLEGE, EAST GRINSTEAD (East Sussex) An early
seventeenth-century stone front (left) has been pinned onto
the existing timber frame of a modest late medieval
farmhouse. The house had already been modernized some
fifty years before on the flooring over of the hall and the
building of tall brick chimney-stacks.

standing, access to the upper stages had quite
commonly been by ladder. Nor were ladders
unsuited to sleeping-lofts. But when, in the
sixteenth century, the family's favoured living-
space moved upstairs, some fresh solution had to
be found for its approaches. The answer at Gullege
was to add a new stair turret between the chimney-
stacks, like the comparable (but grander) turret at
Churche's Mansion in Nantwich, a major town-
house of 1577. But neither at Gullege nor at
Churche's were these oak newel stairs, although
durable and well-crafted, treated as features of
style and importance in the building. Still hole-

and-corner affairs, they were hidden away, cupboard-like, behind doors.

While the contrast with seventeenth-century building practices could hardly be more striking, the change was not as sudden as it might seem. Except as formal approaches to a first-floor hall, as at John of Gaunt's Kenilworth or James I's Linlithgow, staircases had never been prominent in medieval building. Yet already, early in the sixteenth century, one of James IV's improvements at Linlithgow was the amendment (by general increase) of its stairs. And the model of the great Italian-style staircases of contemporary France was not slow in making the next leap across the Channel to the British Isles.

Unquestionably the most remarkable Renaissance building of the late sixteenth century in Scotland was Francis Stewart's residential range at Crichton Castle, south of Edinburgh. Bothwell the 'wild earl', described as 'a terror to the most

desperate duellists of Europe', among them 'the gasconades of France, the rhodomontades of Spain, fanfaronades of Italy, and braggadocio brags of all other countries', had come to know the Continent well on his escapades. At Crichton, his architect almost certainly was Italian. In complete contrast to the rest of the castle, Stewart's north range flaunted the bold diamond-faceted facade, authentically Mannerist in style, of the precisely contemporary *Palazzo dei Diamanti* at Ferrara. It had the pillared ground-floor loggia of the Mediterranean tradition. Most impressively, it had a broad staircase, rising in straight flights to the top of the building, which was entirely southern and classical in its execution. Of the 1580s but still in

CRICHTON CASTLE (Lothian) The isolated late medieval context of Francis Stewart's flamboyant Mannerist north range (right), built in the 1580s and among the trendsetters of the Scottish Renaissance.

advance of its time, the Crichton grand stair had nevertheless come to Scotland to stay.

Before Crichton, similar grand staircases had begun to feature already at major building projects south of the Border. At Burghley House, William Cecil's innovative 'Roman Staircase' may date as early as the 1560s. And it led the way up, as in any building of like pretensions, to the principal public staterooms of the *piano nobile*. As a young man, Cecil had served under Edward Seymour, Duke of Somerset, himself a leading figure in the brief and over-sophisticated classical revival which had inspired the Protector's own (now demolished) Somerset House, and the comparably pure detailing of William Sharington's tower at Lacock, or of Sir John Thynne's great pile at Longleat. Indeed, Cecil's treatment of the staircase at Burghley was as authentically Antique as that of the stairs which, at Wolfeton (Dorset) a few decades later, would ascend majestically just two straight flights to the pedimented doorcase of the saloon.

In the meantime, Cecil himself had pioneered a grand stair so unrestrained in the profusion of its decorative carved ornament as to appeal more directly to contemporary builders. Theobalds, the mansion Cecil refashioned in the 1570s to break his journeys north to Burghley House, has been lost almost as completely as Henry VIII's palace at Nonsuch. However, the great staircase at Theobalds was rescued on demolition, to be reinstated in the 1920s at Herstmonceux Castle. With caryatids on the balusters and heraldic beasts on the posts, the Theobalds stair is a clear and direct forerunner of such later grand ascents as the fine surviving stair at Hatfield House. It would, moreover, have been especially splendid in its day, carved with 'grotesk-work' and as lavishly painted as the Hatfield stairs for which, in 1611, the accounts record 'gilding & working of the naked boys and lions standing upon those stairs holding of instruments and his Lordshypps arms'.

Hatfield itself was built for Robert Cecil (the Treasurer's son) who, on the urging of James I, had taken this and other manors in exchange for Theobalds. Cecil's principal agent on the site was the carpenter, Robert Liming, previously employed in works at Theobalds, and there are many echoes of the earlier house in its construction. In turrets and balustrades, in loggia and clock-tower, as well as in the stair and its embellishments, the two houses were closely related. Then, after finishing at Hatfield, Liming took the same stair to Blickling Hall, in Norfolk, where he was at work for Sir Henry Hobart in the 1620s. And at Knole, meanwhile, Thomas Sackville's great staircase must have been at least similarly inspired, as were assertive new staircases all over the country, from the substantial framed stair of the Yorkshire (Humberside) Burton Agnes to the carved newel posts and balustrading of Shropshire's Benthall.

Like everything William Cecil built, Theobalds helped establish the new fashions. It was splendid both outside and in. One of its features, the open pillared loggia, was repeated no fewer than four times. Theobalds' turrets were as numerous and as fanciful as those of Burghley House, slate-hung in the earlier Nonsuch style, yet a clear advance on the older tradition which, at houses like William Clifton's contemporary Barrington Court, had finished off each gable with a trio of pinnacles, cluttering the roofline with chimneys. Symmetrical and many-windowed, Theobalds had all the dignity that Nonsuch lacked, while yielding nothing to it internally in display. On Theobalds' garden show-front, the ground-floor loggia was 'well painted with Kinges and Queenes of England and the pedigree of the old Lord Burley [Cecil himself] and divers other antient families, with paintings of many castles and battailes, with divers subscriptions on the walls'. Immediately over it, the great chamber was a room of myth and fable. It had a fountain ('a very high rock, of all colours, made of real stones'), of which the bowl was a 'basin supported by two savages'. Its ceiling was 'very artistically constructed', painted with 'the 12 signs of the Zodiac, so that at night you can see distinctly the stars proper to each: on the same stage the sun performs its course, which is without doubt contrived by some concealed ingenious mechanism'. To complete the effect, the side walls carried 'six trees, having the natural bark so artfully joined, with birds' nests and leaves as well as fruit [that] when the steward . . . opened the window birds flew into the hall, perched themselves upon the trees and began to sing'. Little wonder that even Cecil came to rue his own extravagance.

Elizabethan decorative programmes of this kind, having much of the character of a courtly masque, were not necessarily intended to be long lasting. It was probably no later than the next generation that

HATFIELD HOUSE (Hertfordshire) The highly ornamental balustrade, with cupids and heraldic beasts on the posts, of Robert Cecil's grand staircase, datable to 1611 and clearly modelled on his father's stair at Theobalds.

Theobalds' great chamber was panelled and re-roofed more conventionally. And relatively few such painted schemes have descended through the years, making those that survive the more precious. One of the earliest and best preserved is in the palace wing at Kinneil House, begun in 1553 by James Hamilton, second Earl of Arran and Duke of Châtelherault, during the last year of his governorship of Scotland. The scheme in the 'Parable Room' at Kinneil House is not, even so, complete. But it retains, in good condition, a number of picture panels of superior quality, including that fine treatment of the Parable of the Good Samaritan which has given the chamber its name. Hamilton, for all his vacillations and deficiencies as a statesman, was a man of wide interests and rare refinement. He was rich, a good host, and a discerning patron. What he chose for his new palace was a scheme of tempera decoration on plaster which reproduced in paint both the subjects and the style of the French tapestries of his period, already familiar to his circle. Such deliberate

conceits and optical games were the everyday exchanges of contemporary high society, whether in Scotland, in England or in France. Hamilton was wealthy enough, certainly, to buy his own tapestries. He opted for murals by intent.

The same must have been true of the English statesman, Sir Thomas Smith, when he commissioned the murals for the 'goodly and faire house' he rebuilt in the late 1560s at Hill Hall. Smith's paintings, now thought to date to about 1570, are later than the Earl of Arran's pseudo tapestries at Kinneil. But they repeat the convention of big picture panels between broad tapestry-style borders, realistically overflowing with fruit and flowers. Smith had been a scholar before he was a statesman, and he maintained a lively interest in the Classics. Accordingly, while many of his panels

KINNEIL HOUSE (Central) A mid sixteenth-century decorative scheme of high-quality tapestry-style wall-paintings survives in the Parable Room of James Hamilton's palace range at Kinneil, datable to 1553–4.

were still biblical in theme, others reverted to the Antique World and to that perennially popular myth of Cupid and Psyche, lovingly rendered in Roman disarray.

Thomas Smith was no ordinary citizen. Earlier in the 1560s, his lengthy embassy in France had developed tastes for a culture very unlike his own. The ingenuity of his painters, stretching even to *trompe l'oeil*, need have had few parallels at Theobalds or indeed anywhere else in England at that time. But in other respects, not least in the provision of a long gallery at Hill Hall, Smith fell in with the current conventions. Theobalds too had been equipped with a great gallery, lavishly panelled and ceiled, and with a memorable frieze of 'divers citties rarely painted and sett forth'. It was the diagnostic state apartment of Tudor England, as of Scotland and Ireland also in the same period.

Certainly, the duties of the hall in medieval Britain had now usually been taken over by the great chamber and long gallery, whether for public entertainment or private ease. Nonetheless, new houses of the period might keep their halls, among them the magnificent and otherwise innovatory mansion of William Cecil at Burghley House. There the great hall of the early 1560s, one of the first elements in Cecil's building programme, was still reminiscent of an ancient hall of chivalry, even to the Gothic detailing of its anachronistic double-hammerbeam roof. Over the next four decades, until Elizabeth's death in 1603, the hall would reappear in properties of widely differing character, as at the National Trust's Charlecote Park, Melford Hall and Barrington Court, Wilderhope and Trerice, Lyme Park, Montacute, Gawthorpe and Hardwick. Nor would the opening of another political era, with the accession of the Scottish James VI and I, have any appreciable effect

TRERICE (Cornwall) Behind the fine show-front of *c.* 1570, the hall of Trerice was still traditionally sited, with the great window (left) upsetting the symmetry of the facade; both the ceiling and the chimney-piece, with its Renaissance caryatids, are original.

initially on the old customs. The two most significant private building enterprises of the start of the new reign, Thomas Howard's Audley End (from 1605) and Robert Cecil's Hatfield House (from 1608), each featured grand halls in the old tradition. And again, continuing through the 1610s and 1620s, great halls would be preserved as a prominent element as much of such big traditional Home Counties residences as the National Trust's Ham House, in London, as of its Felbrigg and Blickling, in remoter Norfolk.

Nevertheless, the signs were everywhere, where innovative architects and patrons were at work, of a fundamental rethinking of the hall's functions. Burghley's 'medieval' great hall had been furnished from the start with a wholly classical fireplace in the Protector Somerset tradition, crowned with an oddly-placed Roman pediment and lifted in every detail from the Italians. At the Countess of

Shrewsbury's Hardwick, before 1600, Robert Smythson had turned the great hall at right angles to the show-front, effectively demoting it to entrance hall or lobby. At Gawthorpe (1600–1605), it was probably the same pioneering architect who hid the hall away at the rear of the building, more like a billiard room than a state chamber. The hall at Montacute (late 1590s), although traditionally sited and equipped (as before) with a screen, was no bigger than the great chamber on the first floor of the north wing, and was entirely out-classed by the gallery.

Below CHARLECOTE PARK (Warwickshire) The inner face of Sir Thomas Lucy's late 1550s gatehouse, such stately entrances still being considered an essential introduction to Tudor country houses of any size.

BARRINGTON COURT (Somerset) A very complete example of the Tudor E-plan manor-house, especially handsome on this southern show-front, everywhere furnished with a lavish display of spiralling pinnacles and chimneys, all datable to a single programme of work in the 1550s.

With the family removed to a first-floor *piano nobile*, or (as at Hardwick) to the still greater seclusion of the top storey, both luxury and display travelled with it. At Theobalds, the grandest chimney-piece of Cecil's lavish mansion, and probably his finest ceiling also (described in 1592 as 'a frett seelinge with divers pendants, roses and flowerdeluces, painted and gilded'), had been located not in the great hall but in the gallery. Similarly, it was in the competitively ambitious long galleries of Hardwick and Knole, Powis and Hatfield, Haddon and Blickling, that the great Elizabethan patron and his Stewart successor sought to obtain just those same effects once looked for exclusively in the great hall. The audience, in the meantime, had changed significantly. It might still be possible for George Wheler, author of *Christian Oeconomicks* (1698), to uphold hospitality's traditional definition as the 'Liberal Entertainment of all sorts of Men, at ones House, whether Neighbours or Strangers, with kindness,

especially with Meat, Drink and Lodgings'. Indeed, 'Hospitality is an excellent Christian Practice.' However, open-handedness to all comers, if it had ever truly existed outside the religious houses, had long retreated in practice to the remotest regions, wherever visitors remained an event. Only the folk whose status and social class took them successively through every filter of door, lobby and stair could marvel at Bess of Hardwick's great gallery. Bess and her kind entertained in style. But they did so with mounting discrimination.

Galleries, once established as socially desirable, spread quickly amongst all who could afford them.

One fine example, with intact 'loyal' stuccos of the 1570s, including busts of Elizabeth supported by Justice and Equity, has survived unexpectedly in Tipperary, at the Earl of Ormond's castle at Carrick-on-Suir: a nice reminder of the divided allegiances of that troubled period when the Tudor conquest of Ireland was under way. In the next generation, at Earlshall Castle in Fife, the whole top floor of this compact little tower-house was to be given over to a single broad gallery. Chastleton (Oxfordshire), built in 1602–10, would not have been complete without its top-floor gallery; nor

Left BLICKLING HALL (Norfolk) The long gallery which, in the 1620s, was still inevitably a part of any self-respecting gentleman's accommodation; both the ceiling and the frieze are original.

Below LITTLE MORETON HALL (Cheshire) The south wing, built by John Moreton in 1570–80, with a long gallery running the entire length of the top floor. Moreton's addition brought the accommodation up-to-date at this otherwise comparatively modest manor-house.

would Burton Agnes (Humberside), Doddington (Lincolnshire), or Montacute (Somerset), at each of which a common hall and private great chamber coexisted still as alternative areas of display. Giving Little Moreton that Noah's Ark look which is now its most memorable characteristic, a gallery ran the length of the new south wing completed for John Moreton in the 1570s. It was on the second floor of the building, a full storey higher than anything else, and it did duty also as a viewing chamber like the other top-floor galleries of its class. Plasterwork figures of Fortune and Destiny, ornamenting the inward-facing gables, conveyed a message of Protestant self-help closely in sympathy with the Moretons' consuming drive as engrossers of the lands they surveyed.

Galleries continued to be built for some time yet. One, at Chirk Castle, is as late as the 1670s. But the Chirk long gallery is already less an exercise and conversational area than a pulled-out saloon, decorated authentically in the classical style with acanthus-leaf cornices and broken pediments over the doors, 'its oaken panels evincing the superior taste of such furniture in such a building'. By then,

much of the free-for-all inventiveness of Northern Renaissance craftsmen had been curbed in the interests of decorum. The discipline, in some respects, was timely. Before Inigo Jones, almost single-handed, returned unadulterated Italian classicism to England after its earlier temporary flowering in the mid sixteenth century under the patronage of the Protector Somerset and his circle, even the best English architects like Robert Smythson and the Thorpes, father and son, had re-used designs from French architectural treatises, spatchcocked in between with Netherlandish motifs in frequently bizarre combinations. Thus in Sir Thomas Smith's library, before he began his final remodelling of Hill Hall in 1568–9, there had been copies of Jacques Androuet du Cerceau's *Livre d'architecture* (1559) and of Philibert de L'Orme's *Nouvelles inventions pour bien bastir* (1561), as well as three editions of Vitruvius. And Hill Hall indeed, in its prominent projecting dormers and its boldly exaggerated entablatures, is very much in the style of the contemporary French châteaux with which Smith had become familiar on his embassies.

In England, Hill Hall's closest parallel is Kirby, in Northamptonshire, probably among the works of the older Thorpe. Kirby, like Hill Hall, took its engaged pilasters from France, its pediments and parapets from Italy. Contemporaneously, Robert Smythson at Wollaton, along with all else, made free and full use of Flemish strapwork and other ornament, which he copied directly from de Vries. Wollaton, even to Mark Girouard, Smythson's architectural biographer, has to be ranked as 'something of a monster'.

Few Elizabethans would have experienced any such misgivings. In plan, as in ornament, they were to toy obsessively with the 'ingenious device' – with geometry and with the alphabet, with self-conscious antiquarianism, and with symbolism both religious and occult. In the Late Middle Ages, there had been frequent picture-plays on names, especially in the use of the personal symbol, or rebus, as the emblem of a patron or donor. Under the Tudors, the delight in such games went much further. Nothing pleased educated men better than the 'wittie devise expressed with cunning woorke-

manship', defined as 'somethinge obscure to be perceived at the first, whereby, when with further consideration it is understood, it maie the greater delighte the behoulder' (1586).

Later, it would be said of that notorious Elizabethan builder, Sir Thomas Tresham of Rushton (Northamptonshire), that he was 'more forward in beginning than finishing his fabricks'. And certainly his garden lodge, the National Trust's Lyveden New Bield, was abandoned incomplete on his death in 1605. Yet, as Fuller observed of him, it was 'hard to say whether greater his delight or skill in buildings', and Lyveden is remarkable on many counts. Built in the form of a Greek cross, Tresham's Lodge took the Passion of Christ and Our Lady of Sorrows (the *Mater Dolorosa*) as its themes. At the end of each wing, the seven faces (five round the bay and two supporting) are each of five feet: seven for the Godhead, five for Salvation. Inscriptions in the upper entablature, praising Christ and the Virgin, were chosen with care for their eighty-one letters: itself an allusion, in their pattern of nines, to the trefoils of the Tresham family heraldry. On the lower entablature, the emblems of the Passion again repeat the mystic number seven.

Scholarly ingenuity was one characteristic of Tresham's work at Lyveden; another was his unconcealed affirmation of the Old Faith. Like William Orrell, the rebuilder of Turton, Tresham was a prominent local recusant. With other major Nottinghamshire landowners, he is thought to have received Jesuit missionaries at his family home, though his own brand of Catholicism, overwhelmingly traditional, stopped short of their assault on the State. 'Country-house Catholics' like Orrell and himself – or indeed Edward Norris, their contemporary at Speke Hall – kept the lamp of Rome alight in England after the Marian *débâcle*, just as it would continue to glimmer, albeit more faintly, under the protection of the conservative magnates of northern Scotland.

Yet the price paid for this loyalty could be high. The Norrises of Speke Hall saw their fortune greatly reduced by heavy fines for recusancy, which of course is one of the reasons why their splendid Tudor mansion, continually extended and improved during the years of their prosperity, has come down to us so little altered through later centuries. And Tresham himself made such slow progress at Lyveden not least because of the fines which, before his death, had already cost him much more than he had ever had available for building projects. Among those works he did complete was

KIRBY HALL (Northamptonshire) Tall engaged pilasters give a French Renaissance outer skin to what is still a great hall (right of the porch) in the old manner, as built for Sir Christopher Hatton (d.1591), probably by Thomas Thorpe; other decorative elements like the pedimented doorcase over the entrance are clearly taken from contemporary architectural pattern books.

the little Triangular Lodge in the grounds at Rushton which was intended both as 'the Warryners Lodge' (for the keeper of rabbits) and as a conceit-ridden sermon in stone. From the inscription over the door, TRES TESTIMONIUM DANT, to the self-conscious ingenuity of its crowning triangular central chimney, Tresham's entire little building was an architectural working-out of the message of St John: 'there are three that bear record in heaven, the Father, the Word and the Holy Ghost: and these three are one.'

Neither at Rushton nor at his contemporary Lyveden New Bield would Tresham make any

attempt to disguise the loyalty to the old religion which had cost him so much both in fines and imprisonment, and which, in the year of his death, would further fatally implicate his son in the abortive Gunpowder Plot. 'Who shall separate us', he asks (quoting Paul) on Rushton's northern facade, 'from the love of Christ?' As the apostle had concluded, so Tresham resolved: 'Nor height, nor depth, nor any other creature, shall be able to separate us from the love of God, which is in Christ Jesus our Lord.'

At Rushton, the Trinity theme was deliberate and explicit. Sir Thomas Gorges' Longford Castle (Wiltshire), similarly triangular in plan, may have been intended to make the identical point, and this certainly was the way contemporaries saw it. Equally, though, abstract geometry appealed to Gorges and his fellow patrons, as had once been the case in the Henrician forts and with as little regard to expense. Longford, with prominent drum

LYVEDEN NEW BIELD (Northamptonshire) Sir Thomas Tresham (d. 1605) never finished his garden lodge at Lyveden, which remains now much as he left it; rich in Catholic symbolism, it was built in the form of a Greek cross to dimensions determined by the mystical significance of certain numbers (e.g. seven for the Godhead).

towers at the angles like the much earlier Edwardian Caerlaverock, dates to the 1580s. At Chilham (Kent), in the next generation, Sir Dudley Digges' polygonal brick mansion, turreted and crenellated like a fortress of chivalry, was built under the frown of an octagonal tower-keep attributable to Henry II. Both houses were laid out to geometric 'devices', though neither (any more than was Tresham's lodge at Lyveden) was well adapted thereby to practical living. Both, moreover, reflected another preoccupation, characteristic of their period, in the return to a dream world of

LONGFORD CASTLE (Wiltshire) Built for Sir Thomas Gorges in the 1580s and, although much extended and rebuilt by Salvin in the 1870s, still preserves the triangle of Gorges' original plan with its highly exceptional two-storeyed loggia on the northwest facade (another Salvin reconstruction, but authentic); note the re-use by Gorges at Longford of drum angle towers in the medieval style shortly afterwards to be seen at other pseudo-castles like Lulworth and Bolsover, often labelled Spenserian.

183

castles, knights and maidens: those 'fierce wars and faithful loves' of Spenser's *Faerie Queene*, with which all contemporary men of intellect were acquainted.

It was in this Spenserian tradition that Robert Smythson, architect of the recent multi-style prodigies at Wollaton and Hardwick, and associated also with the earlier Somerset-inspired classicism of Longleat, turned his hand late in life to Bolsover Castle (1612), his fantasy 'keep' for Charles Cavendish. Likewise, there were to be four-square 'sham castles' at East Lulworth (1608) and Ruperra (1626), for Viscount Bindon and Sir Thomas Morgan respectively, inspired rather by knight errantry than by defence. These fictions were mere games for the English gentry. Bolsover was in Derbyshire, Lulworth in Dorset, Ruperra in the long anglicized Welsh county of Glamorgan. Elsewhere in Britain, the law could do less for the individual. In colonial Ireland especially, in striking contrast to what had happened in the better governed and more sophisticated societies of its neighbours, the time had arrived for a new type of 'strong-house', combining (as had always been the case in castle architecture) a statement of lordship with practical self-help against the enemy. No longer an anachronism and certainly no joke, the castle rediscovered its role.

CHILHAM CASTLE (Kent) Chilham's geometric polygonal plan, laid out for Sir Dudley Digges in the early 1600s, shows well from the air, as does its situation next to the late twelfth-century polygonal keep (left), which may have helped inspire it.

185

[7]

The War of the Three Kingdoms

James VI of Scotland, acceding to his new throne in 1603 as James I of England and Ireland, had hoped for greater unity than he got. In point of fact, neither legislature could be persuaded to accept a complete merger. However, there was good cause for general optimism on other grounds. The rebellion in Ireland was at an end, offering fresh opportunities to aspiring colonizers. Markets widened throughout James' joint realm, with the repeal of restrictive trade laws. The king himself, in complete contrast to the long-standing parsimony of Elizabeth, launched regardless into a programme of free-spending.

Very soon, that spending had lost control. Too much evaporated on lavish court entertainments, on the pensions of royal favourites, and on offensively vulgar display. Nevertheless James, who had worked hard for his inheritance, kept in touch with his people in a way that his son, the more cultivated Charles I, would never do. Certainly, although ignoring his promise to return regularly to Scotland, James understood his Scots and left them, on his death in 1625, more prosperous than any could remember. Among the benefits he gave them was the Ulster Plantation: perhaps not, in the long term, the happiest of legacies, but a rich spur to enterprise in the short. 'Hungrie Scottis' settled Ulster as the 'undertakers' of the Stewart plantation. Better-situated compatriots travelled south with James himself to the overflowing cornucopia of Whitehall. Both proved difficult to unseat.

It was Charles I (1625–49) who made most of the mistakes, revealing early in his reign that he knew little about the Scots and cared less. Charles' Act of Revocation (1625), which threatened to resume Church lands, alienated his natural allies among the Scottish aristocracy; he was fatally at odds with his churchmen in the General Assembly in 1636–7; by 1638, confronted by the many signatories of the Covenant, he had a popular revolutionary movement on his hands. In England, his affairs had gone no better. Charles' experiment with personal government, beginning with the dissolution of Parliament on 2 March 1629, had failed by 1640. With Scotland already aflame, Gaelic Ulster rose in 1641. The king had nowhere else to turn.

For almost two decades from 1642, civil war and continuing political uncertainties put paid to effective growth in the economy. Then, as if in a hothouse, all blossomed again at the Restoration. Many long-term exiles had come home with Charles II in 1660. During their spell abroad, in the Netherlands or in France, they had developed new tastes, losing the suspicion their fathers had felt of alien innovation in the arts. Furthermore, fresh sources of funding were now available. One token of contemporary business confidence was the speed with which London rose again from the ashes of its Great Fire of 1666. Another was the rapid development of financial institutions, among them the Bank of England, as a means (hitherto unknown) for obtaining credit. Agricultural improvements and entrepreneurial activity, whether in industry or commerce, all benefited from easier access to new capital. Gone was the crisis management of the past. In the easy commercial optimism of the 'Mercantile Age', the spectre of dearth at last was laid, and the Middle Ages had come to their end.

LULWORTH CASTLE (Dorset) One of a group of fantasy castles built by antiquarians – or by those with Spenserian chivalric longings – in the early seventeenth century, and never intended for defence; the builder of Lulworth (1608) was Thomas Howard, Viscount Bindon.

Ireland, by the end of the sixteenth century, was no place for a man to sleep secure. The long and bitter struggle of the Tudor conquest of Ireland, beginning in the 1540s under Henry VIII and completed only in 1603 during the last weeks of Elizabeth's reign, had left almost everybody cherishing a grievance. It was not just the native Irish who had been alienated. Catholic 'Old English' landowners, the inheritors of what was left of the original Anglo-Norman territories, were the foes of Protestant 'New English' government officials and planted settlers. That 'land of peace' that had once been the Pale was almost as prone to rebellion as any other. True, Tyrone's submission in 1603 brought peace of a kind for forty years. Nor was the Irish economy, almost entirely agricultural, slow to pick up from the abysmal trough into which Tyrone's sustained rebellion (from 1595) had pitched it. But Ireland was a land of 'swordsmen' still: the fractious retainers of great magnates. Feuds were common and brigandage was everywhere endemic. Those assumptions about property and the law which had come to govern England, and much of Lowland Scotland and Wales, ceased to apply west of Cardigan Bay.

The consequences in Irish building are very obvious. The great house at Kanturk, in County Cork, has many of the same features as the Dorset Lulworth, being less than a decade its senior. It is a four-storeyed mansion, rising to five levels at the angle towers, with its principal accommodation on the three upper floors, beginning with a first-floor hall. Both Kanturk and Lulworth share the same Renaissance-style doorcases, with identical continuous decorative string courses on their facades, and an equivalent provision of large windows. Yet, in one particular especially, the difference between them is significant. Thomas Lord Bindon's 'little pile' at Lulworth was designed to meet the tastes of a wealthy English courtier, the close associate of such other great builders, uninhibited by cost, as Robert Cecil of Hatfield or Thomas Lord Howard of Audley End. Bindon's 'Castle' was a hunting lodge: a banqueting pavilion: a conceit. The defences of Kanturk, in complete contrast, were in earnest. Like other major Irish houses of the same class and period – Mallow (1590), Portumna (1618), and Burncourt (1641) among them – Kanturk (1601) was designed for self-protection, furnished with an array of purposeful musket-loops, and with limited access only at ground-floor level.

Of course, the defensibility of such 'strong-houses' was never great. But their owners' purpose was always essentially just to make them fast, and landowners rich enough to build on this scale, accommodating their swordsmen with themselves, could usually put their faith in their friends. Kanturk, in point of fact, was never finished. Burncourt, originally known as 'Everard's Castle' from the surname of its builder Sir Richard, came to grief very quickly in 1650 at the time of the Parliamentarian attack: 'it was seven years in building, seven years living in it, and fifteen days it was burning', ran the jingle. Mallow underwent successive assaults and rebuildings, and only Portumna (burnt out eventually in 1826) could be said to have enjoyed a full span. However, the precautions felt necessary in these greater establishments were still more obviously a requirement in the smaller. Many Irish noblemen, as one English visitor had cause to remark, continued to shelter in fortified houses even as late as the 1680s. They were only a generation removed from the brutal killings of the Ulster Rising of 1641, itself the trigger of the English Civil War.

Ulster, originally a stronghold of the dispossessed Gaelic Irish, was particularly sensitive territory. From 1607, the flight of the earls, Tyrone and Tyrconnell, had left the entire province exposed to Protestant colonization on a hitherto unprecedented scale. There had been examples of resettlement in Ireland before, the most successful being the Elizabethan plantation of Munster (1581–98), overturned during Tyrone's rebellion. Similar colonizations were contemporaneously being practised outside the British Isles, in particular (by this date) in North America. Accordingly, the pattern of such settlement was well established. With the reluctant but financially essential co-operation of the City of London, it took the form in western Ulster of a comprehensive development and fortification of the two main towns, Derry (subsequently Londonderry) and Coleraine. To this period belong the remarkable surviving defences of Londonderry (1613–18), retaining almost complete the stone-faced ramparts, with artillery angle-bastions in the Italian style, that reflect the best military thinking of their day. In the countryside, market towns were expanded and smaller settlements planted, each with its 'English' houses (as distinct from Irish cabins) round the defensible nucleus of a fortified manor.

Two such manors, fine examples of their class, are the 'castles' at Monea and Tully, in Fermanagh, situated within a few miles of each other to the south of Lough Erne, close to the garrison town of Enniskillen. Both had walled bawns, with towers at the angles and with many gunports. Both also were equipped with a handsome stone manor-house – a turreted rectangular building closing part of the circuit, in which the hall was situated at first-floor level, with bedchambers either alongside it or above. Monea was built in 1618–19; Tully at roughly the same date. In each case, the manor-house was captured by the rebels in 1641 when Enniskillen itself was besieged.

Many of those who settled western Ulster in the 1610s were Protestant Scots, including Malcolm Hamilton and John Hume, 'undertakers' at Monea and Tully respectively. And indeed it was the Scots, already long resident in the northern and eastern sectors of the province, who were to put up the most successful resistance to the Irish rebels. They had been schooled in a society not so different from the one in which they found themselves, and had developed an architecture which came to terms with it. A close parallel to Monea, yet impossible to match in any contemporary English context, is the

little 'tower fortalice and manner place' of Claypotts, near Dundee, built on a former monastic estate between 1569 and 1588. The two dwellings share the same circular angle towers, squared-off at the top with heavy corbelled turrets and crow-step gables. Fearsomely equipped with an array of carefully sited musket-holes, they are unmistakably furnished for the wars.

Castles like Claypotts and like the contemporaneously refortified Burleigh, near Kinross, made good models for the military settlement of Gaelic Ulster. In Scotland, they offered the protection still required by men of property for as long as the blood feud continued to be tolerated as a

CLAYPOTTS CASTLE (Tayside) Corbelled-out crow-step gables are the outstanding characteristic of this elegant little Z-plan tower-house, built in the 1570s or 1580s and representative of a large class of similar fortified dwellings still being erected in both Scotland and Ireland.

form of substitute law. In such conditions, William Forbes' comfortable courtyard-based extensions to Tolquhon Castle, completed between 1584 and 1589, understandably presented a defensible face to the world, while at Castle Campbell, in the same generation, a new gatehouse carried gunports as routine. But the context was changing, and so was the response. Tolquhon itself was the welcoming home of a cultured and bookish laird: a man of peace, devoted to his library, who chose his remedies less in bloodshed than in the law. At Castle Campbell, too, the late sixteenth-century gatehouse was one element alone of a more general and consciously civilizing rebuilding which included the construction of a Renaissance 'palace' range, elegantly equipped at ground-floor level with the now obligatory pillared loggia. Not so long afterwards, in the 1610s, Alexander Seton's new pleasure grounds at Pinkie House (Musselburgh) would be finished off with a significant inscription. Translated from the Latin, it read:

'For himself, for his descendants, for all civilized men, Alexander Seton, lover of mankind and civilization, founded, built and adorned his house and gardens and these out-of-town (*suburbana*) buildings. Here is nothing warlike, even for defence; no ditch, no rampart. But for the kind welcome and hospitable entertainment of guests, a fountain of pure water, lawns, ponds and aviaries.'

Alexander Seton, first Earl of Dunfermline (d. 1622), was a near-neighbour of William Forbes of Tolquhon, having extensive interests also in Aberdeenshire. And it was at Fyvie that he undertook another major project in the three linked tower-houses of the ambitious castle-palace on which he began work in about 1600. For Seton and landowners like him, the inflation and continuous price rises of the late sixteenth century had been, as in England, a source of profit. Even the harvest failures, famines and plagues of the disastrous 1590s had done little but dent their prosperity. Then, as James VI's long reign entered its last and most favoured decades, following the Union of the Crowns in 1603, others increasingly took their share of the bonanza. Among those, in particular, who profited from the Union were the courtiers and officials, many of them lawyers, who followed

FYVIE CASTLE (Grampian) The south facade, showing the three linked tower-houses of Alexander Seton's early seventeenth-century country mansion; the big sash windows are later insertions.

the king down to London. But another group also did notably well in these circumstances, that of the merchants and industrialists.

Late sixteenth-century Scotland had experienced a significant commercial recovery even before the Union of 1603. And indeed the royal burghs, privileged monopolizers of Scotland's overseas trade, had always been relatively prosperous. Nevertheless, the sudden expansion of markets after 1603 was the immediate occasion for a boom. Prosperity soon showed itself in urban building. A big but representative town-house of this period, stoutly built in stone and dating to the late 1610s, is Gladstone's Land, in the Lawnmarket (Edinburgh), now in the care of the National Trust for Scotland. Like many houses of its class, it makes intensive use of its restricted plot, with shopping booths (sheltered by an arcade) at ground-floor level, and with five storeys of accommodation above, each of them a self-contained lodging. Let out by Thomas Gledstanes, rebuilder of the 'land', to Sir James Creichton, knight, the great (or 'Painted') chamber on the first floor at Gladstone's Land was a warm, commodious and colourful apartment, certainly better suited to Edinburgh's sharp climate than its later equivalents in the Georgian New Town. Such a building indeed, ideally adapted to site and purpose, was a triumph of the vernacular tradition.

That tradition, exported to Ulster by the Protestant 'undertakers', was otherwise peculiar to Scotland. Not all Scottish urban tenements were as constricted or as tower-like as Gladstone's Land. Set on more generous plots, John Hamilton's near-contemporary house at Preston (1626–8) and Sir George Bruce's 'palace' at Culross (1597–1611), both now owned by the Trust, were each comparatively spacious and low-lying. However, even Culross contrives a deliberate loftiness, emphasized by the strong verticals of its southern facades. And the pedimented dormers of these separate buildings, their crow-stepped gables and steep-pitched roofs, are all clear borrowings from the tower-houses of their time: familiar badges of the architecture of the Scots.

Bruce of Culross, a notable merchant and entrepreneur, would choose to remain in the town he

GLADSTONE'S LAND (Edinburgh) The Painted Chamber, decorated with a bold architectural frieze and colourful painted ceiling, at first-floor level in Thomas Gledstanes' tall tenement of 1617–20; let out with the other rooms on this floor as a separate apartment.

had made prosperous, to be buried in the kirk on the hill. In contrast, his near-contemporary William Forbes – also known as 'Willie the Merchant' or 'Danzig Willie' – took what was undoubtedly the more conventional path in a retreat, with his fortune, to the countryside. As Bruce had been, Forbes was a gentleman-trader. And having risked life and capital in ventures overseas, his understandable preference, towards the end of his time, was to revert to the life of a laird. Culross Palace had been earth-bound – a sprawling set of buildings making little obvious show of climbing skyward. In contrast, Craigievar was a fortress in the air.

Remotely sited, close to the lawless Highlands, Forbes' tower-house still wore military uniform. But Craigievar's posture was only incidentally defensive. Like its near-neighbours, those other contemporary residential towers at Crathes and Castle Fraser, similarly properties of the National Trust, Craigievar continued and elaborated a style of building which had become part of the living history of the nation. In the high hall at Craigievar, over Danzig Willie's fireplace, a huge Royal Arms celebrated the recent Union of the Crowns so profitable to Willie and his friends. It was a demonstration of confidence in the times, exhibited in another way in the skill and daring of the Bels of Aberdeen, famous local masons who were to make each of these towers into a lofty pedestal for the oversailing bulk of a Renaissance mansion.

These extraordinary tower-houses of Mar, with their galleries and balustraded viewpoints, their fine plasterwork and painted ceilings, are comfortable, sophisticated, and picturesque. Understandably, they were later the models for the national style subsequently dubbed 'Scottish baronial'. But the story they tell is incomplete. Where Willie the Merchant had seen his fortune grow at home with his country's trade, others of his generation joined the exodus to England, taking passage with their king to Whitehall. Not all these 'hungrie Scottis' came home. But among those who did, comfortably enriched, was Thomas Dalyell, Deputy Master of the Rolls and builder of the House of the Binns. Significantly, a rich returned official, living within a day's ride of Edinburgh,

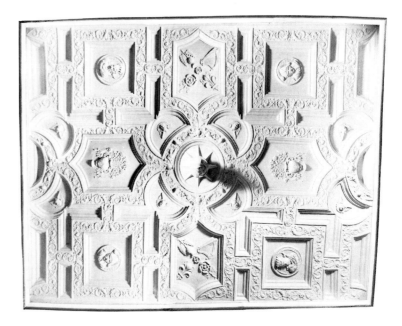

HOUSE OF THE BINNS (Central) The fine plaster ceiling, panelled and moulded in the French style, of the King's Room, prepared in 1630 for an anticipated visit of Charles I.

could afford to neglect genuine defences. Dalyell's crenellations and his 'feudal' staircase turrets are no more than a gesture. They conceal interior furnishings which, as provided in 1630 for an anticipated royal visit, had all the foreign comforts of the English court, itself dependent for its fashions on the French.

Alien tastes, intruding at the Binns, are especially obvious in the astonishingly up-to-date plasterwork of the King's Room, prepared for Charles I, with its richly panelled ceiling in the new French manner and the overflowing cornucopias of its frieze. The allusion to the king's munificence and to the benefits of his government was untimely. Charles did indeed visit Scotland, but not before 1633: a full eight years after ascending the throne of the two kingdoms. When he came, his reception cost more than it was worth. Charles' father, James VI and I, having departed for England in 1603, returned to his Scottish kingdom only once. Absentee government had been less of a problem with James I, who knew and understood the Scots, than with his son, who did not. But, either way, the effect of non-residence was to syphon cultural patronage to the Stewart court at Whitehall, freezing the arts in the North.

In contrast, James' accession to the English throne in 1603 brought the warming breath of spring to his joint kingdom. James viewed England, it has been well said, as 'a new Peru'. The

CULROSS PALACE (Fife) The main building of Sir George Bruce's town-house complex, dating to the 1600s and furnished with the pedimented dormers and crow-stepped gables familiar in contemporary Scottish tower-houses.

characteristic parsimony of the old queen, Elizabeth, was immediately replaced by profligate spending, much of it on the reward of loyal Scottish henchmen like Dalyell of the Binns, but even more on uninhibited display. One manifestation of this extravagance was the ephemeral royal masque – the excuse and occasion for elaborate architectural sets – so favoured by the early Stewart court. Heartily disliked by those of a sober and puritanical temperament, the masque was yet the school in which Inigo Jones, 'our Kingdome's most Artfull and Ingenious Architect', sharpened and perfected his skills. In building as in politics, with related cause and effect, a revolution was in the making.

Although the professional term 'architect' was still very new, Inigo Jones was by no means the first of his kind. Born in 1573, he had been an impressionable young man when, for example, the Elizabethan Robert Smythson was most active. Nevertheless, Jones took a path of his own. From the beginning of his court employment, early in the new reign, Inigo Jones was a committed convert to Italian theory and to the architecture of Serlio and Palladio. Then, just before taking influential office in 1615 as James I's Surveyor of the King's Works, Jones had again visited Italy in 1613–14 to study Palladio's villas and other buildings at first hand. However, those alien classical systems introduced by the new Surveyor and applauded, under his instruction, by the Stewart court, took more time to be received beyond that circle. With good cause, Inigo Jones' newly-finished classical Banqueting House (1622) at Whitehall – the extravagant and innovatory building from which Charles I stepped to his death on 30 January 1649 – was judged by one contemporary 'too faire and nothing suitable to the rest of the house' [the Tudor palace]. And indeed the corollary of the Surveyor's uncompromising classicism was his rejection, much harder to accept, of the existing architectural vernacular. In the troubled preliminaries of the Civil War, Inigo Jones (always a favourite at court) was to find himself tarred with the same brush as his patrons: Charles I, Queen Henrietta Maria, and Archbishop Laud. The Surveyor, for all those manifold talents of which none was more aware than himself, came to be viewed by his Puritan critics as a mere 'contriver of scenes for the Queen's Dancing Barne'. Nor was he – intolerant, arrogant and pedantic: that '*huomo vanissimo e molto vantatore*' – wholly without blame for the catastrophe.

It was in the nature of Inigo Jones' official employment that he should have been a builder of palaces. True, he is remembered also as the architect (for the Earl of Bedford) of the innovatory 'Tuscan' church of St Paul's, Covent Garden – 'the handsomest barn in England' – which would later be such an inspiration to the neo-classicists. But the time he could assign to private clients was limited, while it was always the larger schemes of his undeviatingly extravagant royal master that allowed him the scope his art demanded. Undoubtedly the greatest of these projects, never wholly abandoned by Charles till the day of his death, was for a total rebuilding of Whitehall Palace: so ambitious and so costly as to have been itself, in prospect alone, one of the contributory causes of the Civil War. Only the Banqueting Hall now survives to recall it. Other schemes similarly – most notably the earlier and more formal Queen's House at Greenwich – had to be left incomplete for want of funds.

Nevertheless, the royal Surveyor's personal style had become well known by the 1630s among those in the service of the king. Jones had a penchant for spectacular staircases, as in the so-called 'Tulip Stairs' at Greenwich. He was fond of grand ceilings, which might be coffered as at the Queen's Chapel (St James' Palace), or painted as at the Banqueting House (Whitehall). And he became a powerful advocate of those ornate and total decorative schemes, ultimately French-inspired, which would later reach their apotheosis in the Double Cube Room at Wilton (*c*.1650), completed by Webb to his designs. Each of these influences is already obvious at the National Trust's Ham House, modified in 1637–9 for the Scottish courtier William Murray, less than a generation after its first building.

Ham House, when Murray came into full possession there in 1637, was just the kind of mansion that Inigo Jones' chief detractors would have found reassuringly conventional. It had been built by Sir Thomas Vavasour, James I's Knight Marshal, in (or around) 1610. Modern only in its French-style formal garden, Ham had otherwise kept the H-plan, with central great hall and flanking wings, of the long-established vernacular tradition. Murray could do little to amend those general arrangements. But he was a man of fashion,

WILTON HOUSE (Wiltshire) The Double Cube Room at Wilton, with its lavish French-inspired ornament, is thought to be one of the last works of Inigo Jones, completed by his assistant, John Webb, in *c*. 1650; the great Pembroke family portrait at the far end is by the former court painter Anthony Van Dyck, the oval ceiling panel being by Thomas de Critz.

one of Charles I's close circle of friends, and the redecorations he put in hand of the first-floor state apartments were very much in accord with court taste. Two of these chambers, the north drawing room and the long gallery, are as Murray left them. They are precious evidence – the one still Mannerist in flavour, the other wholly classical – of the advanced decorative styles of the Caroline court: the sort of interiors that Whitehall Palace might have known had the plans of Inigo Jones left the drawing-board.

Such fine apartments – and there were more at Murray's Ham before the further refurbishings of the Restoration period – deserved the appropriately splendid grand-stair approach already pioneered at great houses like Hatfield. At Ham House, accordingly, the great staircase was given

HAM HOUSE (London) William Murray's long gallery, panelled in the refurbishing of 1637–9. It is in the classical taste favoured at Charles I's court, of which Murray himself was a welcome member, high in the confidence of the king.

priority in Murray's refurbishment, and it was a stair of the most modern type. Rising in broad shallow treads round a big open well, its balustrades – abandoning the traditional upright balusters of the Hatfield stair or of a less up-to-the-minute remodelling like contemporary Canons Ashby – were of pierced panels carrying trophies of arms. On its newel posts, carved baskets over-flowed generously with wooden fruit.

In the 1630s, a stair like Murray's was barely known outside the embattled society of Charles' friends. It was a product of the court style, ultimately French at source, and it had much to do with the alien influences lately introduced by Henrietta Maria and her suite. However, neither the queen's home background nor Inigo Jones' genius are sufficient explanation for that more general movement, the so-called 'Artisan Mannerism', which was beginning to invade the English arts. The style had not developed, of course, entirely independently of the king's Surveyor. Nicholas Stone (d.1647), foremost of its practitioners, was to work closely with Inigo Jones

on the Whitehall Banqueting House, with other architectural projects. Nevertheless, Stone's early training had also been in the very different school of Amsterdam. And the ubiquitous Dutch gables of the country houses of this period, including Raynham Hall in which Inigo Jones himself took a hand, must obviously be traceable to such a source. London masons, bricklayers and carpenter-contractors, fully alert to existing Continental models which they might either study in pattern-books or travel to see for themselves, came to practise their skills throughout the country in circles remote from Whitehall. Such exposure to foreign influences would have touched the arts whether or not Inigo Jones were at court.

In nothing is this more obvious than in the contemporary transformation of memorial sculp-ture, also attributable to Nicholas Stone and to others trained abroad as he had been. Chiefly, the trend in sepulchral monuments (as in building) was towards a more exact and scholarly classicism. But this was accompanied simultaneously by a new humanistic realism in effigy-carving, rendering the subject as from life. The meretricious monuments of Elizabethan and early Jacobean England – flashy, bombastic and stiffly-posed – increasingly gave way during Charles I's reign to memorials of equal cost but fine restraint. Imported marbles, in sombre greys and blacks, replaced the gaudily-painted native alabasters of the past. Ornament was either disciplined or eschewed. Fully repre-sentative of the new style is the Chipping Campden memorial to Sir Baptist Hicks (d.1629), the London usurer who had been prominent in the financing of the 'Peruvian' extravagance of James I's court. Raised to the peerage towards the end of his life as Viscount Campden, Sir Baptist might have chosen to make his exit with vulgar exhibition. Up to a few years before, he would certainly have done just that. Yet Hicks' monu-

HAM HOUSE (London) The open well, shallow treads and pierced-panel balustrade of the Ham House staircase all mark it out as a pioneer in its class, highly exceptional in pre Civil War Britain and rarely seen again until the rebuildings following the Restoration.

Terraces
CLOSED
TO THE PUBLIC
TODAY

ment, gigantic though it is, is a model of classical reticence. The chest and columns are plain; the capitals and entablature are free of ornament; the colouring is austerely black and white. Thought to have been by Nicholas Stone, the monument's stark and uncompromising classicism is in the mould of Inigo Jones.

Nicholas Stone was a craftsman-entrepreneur, a London monument-maker on a major scale, whose Long Acre workshop supplied clients all over the country. Inevitably, his commissions reflected their wishes. At Hatfield (Hertfordshire), there was to be the astounding naturalism, far in advance of its time, of the Curle effigy (1617), stretched naked on the floor beneath its shroud. At Chilham (Kent), there was the architectural conceit of the Digges monument (1631–2): an Ionic column supporting an urn, with Justice and Prudence, Temperance and Fortitude, seated life-like in effigy at the base. At Paston (Norfolk), the semi-reclining figure of Dame Katherine Paston (1629), while plainly in an older tradition than the classical urn and columns of Sir Edmund Paston's nearby monument (1632), yet came from the same Long Acre premises. What was new in Dame Katherine's memorial was the reposeful naturalism of her effigy, relaxed and conspicuously at ease. And it was precisely that repose which was recaptured again by another talented sculptor in that famous St Albans monument to the philosopher and statesman, Sir Francis Bacon (d.1626), forever asleep in his chair.

The former Lord Chancellor, departing this life barely a year after Charles I's accession, had chosen a good time to go. In 1629, Charles broke the mould of politics, dismissed his Parliament, and began a decade of personal rule. Yet at court, his extravagance continued unabated. That same year, Peter Paul Rubens, universally acknowledged as the greatest (and most expensive) painter of his day, came to England. He was commissioned, at huge cost, to paint the panels of Inigo Jones' ceiling at the new Whitehall Banqueting House, his major themes being the *Union of England and Scotland*, the *Benefits of the Government of James I*, and a grand central *Apotheosis of James I*, supported by processions of cherubs. In one of the side ovals of this outstanding work, a figure of Abundance,

identified by its spilling cornucopia, triumphs over a bound Avarice below – strange and hurtful irony at a time when the king's exactions had never been more blatant or oppressive!

In point of fact, by the late 1630s, Charles' increasingly desperate financial shifts were losing him more friends than they raised revenue. And standing high among the anxieties current at the time was the king's reckless refusal to economize. Rubens' paintings for the Banqueting House ceiling had cost Charles £3000. And then there was that other busy Antwerp painter, Sir Anthony Van Dyck, a pupil and associate of Rubens, who had been induced by Charles in 1632 to settle in England, to be received with every honour as 'principal painter in ordinary to their majesties'. Charles and his queen were discerning patrons. They were constant visitors to Van Dyck's London studio, just as they deliberately sought the company of Inigo Jones and unaffectedly discussed commissions with them both. But quality at this level came expensive. What distinguished the court style from Artisan Mannerism was both taste and a refusal to cut corners.

Inevitably the Civil War, from the raising of the Royal Standard at Nottingham on 22 August 1642, placed a temporary moratorium on the arts. And one of its better-known architectural casualties was the interrupted rebuilding of Castle Ashby's south front, where a fine classical screen in the style of Inigo Jones still separates wings in the most conservative of Jacobean traditions. Spencer Compton, Castle Ashby's remodeller, was killed in 1643 at Hopton Heath. Inigo Jones himself, trapped that year in the lengthy siege of Basing House, was later captured, humiliated, and fined. But the conflict was not without its winners. Philip Herbert, Earl of Pembroke, was one of those: a personal friend of Charles I who had nevertheless opted for the Commonwealth. Edmund Prideaux, Oliver Cromwell's Attorney General from 1649, was another. Their monuments were to be Wilton House and Forde Abbey: respectively court style and Artisan Mannerist.

The garden front at Wilton, rebuilt for the earl soon after a fire in 1647 had almost completely destroyed the east range, was by Inigo Jones (restored to favour) and by his long-term assistant and amanuensis, John Webb (later designer, for Mr Speaker Chute, of the handsome classical portico at The Vyne). Plain though it was, the Wilton facade hid an interior of surpassing magnificence. There, in his last major work, Inigo Jones was to contrive a suite of state rooms of which

Previous page CASTLE ASHBY (Northamptonshire) Seen through the gates, the central portion of the facade is in the classical style of Inigo Jones, dating to 1625–35 and separating wings which, although only a decade or two earlier, are still very conservative in taste.

the culminating set-piece was the Double Cube Room, the principal repository of the Pembroke family portraits commissioned in the 1630s from Van Dyck. Like the adjoining Single Cube, it had white and gold panelling in the current French style, with applied decoration of carved fruit and foliage, with classical doorcases, and with a fine painted ceiling in the Whitehall style, incorporating panels by Thomas de Critz. Interiors of this kind, known usually only by reputation before the Civil War, were to be made familiar to royalist émigrés during the course of their long exile on the Continent. Not unnaturally, this was the tradition they brought back with them on their return.

Pembroke's work at Wilton was in the grand palatial manner, not inferior in taste or cost to anything commissioned at court. In comparison, Prideaux's remodelling of the former abbot's house at Forde was both provincial and a little naïve. Rarely, however, had the deliberate juxtaposition of grand stair and great chamber (or saloon) been carried out more emphatically than in this building. Such theatrical effects, in part an inheritance from the spectacle of the masque, were to become the recurring motif of better times. Prideaux started from the existing base of Abbot Charde's pre-Reformation lodgings at Forde. But he preserved Charde's hall only to truncate and demote it. Instead, display concentrated on a big new saloon on the *piano nobile* and on the finely-crafted grand stair of its approach. Prideaux's stair, like Murray's earlier model at Ham House, had fruit baskets on the newels and a lusciously-carved openwork balustrade. It had a fine plaster ceiling, dated 1658, more restrained than the ceiling of the adjoining saloon but of similar ambition and quality. The saloon itself, in Prideaux's house, had taken the place of the former abbot's hall as the focus of hospitality at Forde. Nothing was spared in its embellishment. The saloon's panelling, reserved and classical, is very French in flavour. Its plasterwork, in contrast, is complex and deeply-moulded, as rich and as flamboyant, in ceiling and frieze, as anything commissioned during the post-Restoration decades, when universal patronage at last was resumed.

Prideaux died on 19 August 1659. Less than a year later, Charles II was back in London, his enemies were discomfited, and his friends were recovering their estates. Their situation was better than they knew. The Civil War had concealed, but had not significantly postponed, a major readjustment of the economy. In particular, the spectre of catastrophe – the reigning determinant of medieval economic policy – had decisively retreated as prices stabilized and population at last levelled off. True, Cromwell's overseas struggles had helped give the final *coup de grâce* to the once dominant English export trade in woollen cloth. Many small centres, dependent on that trade, went into a permanent decline. But the political solution of the king's return in 1660 set aside, for the majority, two decades of economic stagnation. In the cities and market towns, business confidence was re-born. On the land, the harsh but useful lessons of more efficient farming, learnt by necessity during the war, were not set aside at the peace. Vigorous growth – in trade, in industry, and in agriculture equally – characterized these years. Britain's 'Mercantile Age', beginning at this time, experienced that rare combination of stable prices and economic expansion uniquely favourable to domestic consumption.

Major demographic catastrophe revisited Scotland in the later 1690s. But the famines, even there, were the last of their kind, and a door had been closed on the Middle Ages. Contemporaneously, another was being shut in architecture too, as the old traditions gave place to the new. Consider the difference, effected within half a century, between the south and west fronts of Felbrigg Hall – the one Jacobean of the early 1620s (by Robert Liming of Theobalds, Hatfield and Blickling); the other Dutch Palladian of the mid 1670s (by William Samwell, an associate of Wren). Royalist émigrés and their families, many of whom had spent their exile in the Netherlands, had learnt the simple merits of Dutch classicism. They had admired its order, its comfort and (in the use of brick) its economy. Not unfamiliar, even before the Civil War, with Dutch traditions, they were all the readier to adopt them wholesale on their return. Another associate of Wren, younger and more professional than William Samwell of Felbrigg Hall, was William Winde, born in Holland of royalist parents and active as early as the 1660s in the building of the thoroughly Dutch and urbanized Ashdown House. In the event, it would be the relatively modest Dutch Palladian of a country house like Ashdown, far more than the expensive international Baroque of Christopher Wren and his followers, that would establish a new vernacular in English building: a model that almost everybody could follow.

Other influences, inevitably, were also present. Prominent royalists had returned from France as well as Holland, and they were to build on their experience of domestic life overseas to extend and

Above FELBRIGG HALL (Norfolk) The two faces of Felbrigg
– a Jacobean show-front of the early 1620s, still very
traditional in manner, to which a post-Restoration wing
(left) was added in the 1670s in the Dutch Palladian style.

to improve on their home comforts. As with Dutch
Palladian, direct borrowings from France had
occurred before, most influentially in the pre-war
generation of Inigo Jones and the London
craftsmen-builders: the Artisan Mannerists. However, it was only in the 1660s, with the king restored
to his joint domain, that acceptance of the styles
became complete. Thus it was in the Restoration
period, and not before, that Scottish architecture
made common cause with the South. And this
would be as true of a formal garden in the French
manner like Alexander Seton's Pitmedden (1675),
as of the contemporary, and equally alien,
remodelling of Charles II's Palace of Holyroodhouse by Sir William Bruce, founding father of the
new Scottish classicism.

Bruce had become acquainted with the French
tradition while on clandestine missions, during

Cromwell's Protectorate, to his sovereign's travel-
ling court. Later, in 1665–6, Christopher Wren
(astronomer by profession and still only at the
beginning of his architectural career) took himself
to France with the specific intention of making his
own study of French buildings. Wren is known to
have brought back every pattern-book and engraving he could lay his hands on: nothing less, as he
said, than 'almost all France on paper'. And such
intensive personal exposure to the Continental
styles, shared by architect and patron alike, killed
the reigning English vernacular in its tracks.

One instant casualty was the medieval great hall which, already in its death throes, had outlived its first purpose by many years. Felbrigg, in the 1620s, still had its hall. Yet when William Samwell, in the 1670s, designed his extension, what he provided there instead was a chain of interconnecting state apartments: a miniature palace suite in the château-style of France, with lavish ornamental plasterwork to match. Elaborate moulded ceilings, at least equivalent in quality to those of Felbrigg, reappeared in many contemporary refurbishings. They are to be found, for example, at such fortresses (victims of the late wars) as Colonel Luttrell's Dunster Castle and William Herbert's Powis Castle, both transformed in rebuildings of the 1670s and 1680s. At their most overwhelming in the dining room ceiling at Dunster, as in the lavish gilded panelling and the bold Italianate frescoes of the state bedroom and grand staircase at Powis, these expensive post-Restoration decorative schemes had as little in common with any native style as had once the Palladian of the Queen's House at Greenwich with the Norfolk vernacular of Blickling.

Indeed, local vernacular and imported classicism were increasingly one and the same. Moreover, the fashions had become universal. Thus 'Good Will' Conyngham's Springhill (Co. Londonderry), only two generations following the Protestant settlement of Ulster, would be a comfortable, symmetrically-planned and well-proportioned manor-house, only lightly defended and essentially indistinguishable from any similar-status residence of its period. In Scotland also, many tower-houses, ferociously fortified in the still recent past, were swiftly converted to more domestic uses during the post-war euphoria, in the wake of the Francophile refashioning of Holyroodhouse for a

ASHDOWN HOUSE (Oxfordshire) More influential than Christopher Wren's Baroque in setting the new style for English building was the Dutch Palladian of a country house like Ashdown, built in the 1660s by one returned royalist for another.

monarch committed to the peace. One of these, the National Trust for Scotland's Brodie Castle, had been a casualty (like Dunster and Powis) of the Civil War. But at Brodie, only the present dining room ceiling, crowded and oppressive at such close quarters, survives to recall a decorative programme characteristically foreign and ornate. At the Trust's Kellie Castle, transformed at the same period, the mood is conspicuously lighter. Redecorated for returned royalists who had suffered their share of agony in the wars, Kellie's contemporary Vine Room (the former great parlour) is a cheerful apartment. It has a fine plaster ceiling, outstandingly delicate and elegant, of which the Olympian central panel, by the court painter de Witt, has all the froth and sparkle of champagne.

In the new gallery at Holyroodhouse, Jacob de Witt's commission was to paint, as best he could, the portraits of eighty-nine Scottish kings: imaginary for the most part, but together presenting, in seemingly pre-ordained succession, a triumphant justification of legitimacy. Working in 1684–6, de Witt's final sitter was the luckless James VII and II, last of a troubled line of Stewart kings who had seldom worn their crowns with any ease. James sacrificed his kingdom for his principles. But still,

at that time, what most men wanted was peace and a breathing-space after conflict. Although not an explanation in itself for the growing uniformity of British architecture, Augustan serenity gave it context.

William Bruce, like his peers in England, was the exponent of an architecture urbane but insensitive, from which the conceit, the fantasy, and even the fragile nuances of kin and nation, were all to be ruthlessly expelled. This was not how a man of the Middle Ages would have seen the purpose of a building, nor yet his Northern Renaissance successor. In practice, great though the achievements of the eighteenth century might yet be, in Edinburgh no less obviously than further south, time had come to favour the professional. In the aftermath of the Civil War, it was no longer 'every man' but only the occasional eccentric amateur who, when he had 'pulled down the old house (if any were there standing)', would replace it with 'a new after his own device', challenging his neighbours to think their worst. For architecture as for the law, there may be loss as well as gain in making rules. Arguably, in the consequential failure of native-born traditions, the cure could be worse than the disease.

Gazetteer

The gazetteer locates by county, and gives summary descriptions of, all the buildings cited in the preceding text, together with some indication of access. For particulars of opening (which may change from year to year), see annual guides such as *Historic Houses, Castles and Gardens open to the Public*. The location of each building listed here is shown on the maps on pp. 232–3.

NT   National Trust
NTS   National Trust for Scotland
OR   Open regularly
OO   Open occasionally
OA   Open on application
NO   Not open

1 Abbotsbury (Dorset) Parish church adjoins ruins (scanty) of Benedictine abbey; large but incomplete late medieval monastic barn; delightful coastal setting.

Aberconwy House, Conway See **Conway**.

2 Aberdeen, Old (Grampian) Cathedral of St Machar; Scottish Perpendicular/Romanesque of early 15c, with fine heraldic ceiling of 1520s.

3 Adlington Hall (Cheshire) Manor-house of *c.*1500 with hall in which canopy of honour has been preserved; extensions of late 16c and *c.*1750. (OR)

4 Alfriston: Clergy House (East Sussex) 14c Wealden timber-framed vicarage; central hall open to the roof, with two-storey chamber blocks at each end; no direct communication between the quarters of the priests and their servants. (NT, OR)

5 Alnwick Castle (Northumberland) Big Percy stronghold of second quarter of 14c with multi-towered central keep and fine barbican-protected gatehouse; interiors rebuilt and Victorianized by Salvin. (OR)

6 Anglesey Abbey (Cambridgeshire) Former Augustinian priory dissolved with the lesser houses in 1536; rebuilt in 1600, but, most unusually, the chapter-house and warming-house of the canons were preserved. (NT, OR)

7 Ashdown House (Oxfordshire) A country lodge built for Lord Craven in the Dutch style and datable to the early 1660s; note especially the importance, in this Restoration building, of the staircase and viewpoint cupola. (NT, OR)

8 Ashleworth: Tithe Barn (Gloucestershire) The *c.*1500 tithe barn is part of a group of buildings that belonged to the rectorial manor of the canons of St Augustine's (Bristol). (NT, OR) Next to it are the PARISH CHURCH and contemporary RECTORY (private).

9 Askeaton Castle (Co. Limerick) 15c tower-house on earlier castle mound, with contemporary great hall in bailey below; also very complete Franciscan friary buildings within sight of the castle, mainly 1420–40. (OR)

10 Athassel Priory (Co. Tipperary) Big Augustinian priory preserving substantial remains of late medieval fortifications, with evidence of a reduction in size of the church after the sacking of the priory in 1447. (OR)

11 Athelhampton (Dorset) High quality stone manor-house, built in the 1490s for William Martyn, a London merchant, with especially fine great hall; a new west wing of the 1540s, with interesting Renaissance ornament on its facade, was built to extend the private quarters. (OR)

12 Audley's Castle (Co. Down) 15c tower-house, attractively sited and retaining the foundations of its original rectangular bawn; standard accommodation of ground-floor undercroft, first-floor hall, and second-floor bedchamber. (OR)

13 Audley End (Essex) Originally a converted monastic house (Walden Abbey), but completely rebuilt on a palatial scale (1605–14) for James I's Lord Treasurer, Thomas Howard; much of Howard's great prodigy house had subsequently to be demolished, and there have been major alterations even to what remains; but the hall survived, being especially notable for its grotesquely ornamental Jacobean screen and for a lavish roof, also largely authentic, as is the ceiling of the saloon; Howard's long gallery, certainly among the grandest of its time, was demolished in the mid 18c. (OR)

14 Axbridge: King John's Hunting Lodge (Somerset) Timber-framed merchant house on the market-place at Axbridge, dating to *c.*1500; jettied at two levels, with surviving timber newel stair. (NT, OR)

15 Baconsthorpe Castle (Norfolk) Fortified manor-house of the later 15c, built for the Heydon family, with water-filled moat and impressive gatehouse. (OR)

16 Baddesley Clinton (West Midlands) 14–15c moated manor-house on a comparatively small scale, re-modelled in the late 16c by Henry Ferrers, the noted Warwickshire antiquary; very prettily set. (NT, OR)

Banqueting House, Whitehall See **Whitehall.**

17 Barrington Court (Somerset) Handsome stone E-plan manor-house with fine southern show-front, pinnacled gables and many chimneys; interior much modified and restored; built in the 1550s for William Clifton. (NT, OR)

18 Barsham, East (Norfolk) Brick manor-house of the 1520s, built for Sir Henry Fermor, with much carved and moulded brick ornament; detached fronting gatehouse; private, but easily studied from the road. (NO)

19 Basingwerk Abbey (Clwyd) One of the Welsh Cistercian houses especially noted in the Late Middle Ages for its hospitality; quite extensive remains of broad-naved church, big refectory, and east range (including small chapter-house). (OR)

Bast's, Grundisburgh See **Grundisburgh.**

20 Battle Abbey (East Sussex) Founded by William the Conqueror in 1067 to commemorate his victory at Hastings; remains include an exceptionally handsome gatehouse of *c.* 1338, the late medieval abbot's lodgings (now a school and private), and a guest-house range overlooking the battlefield, rebuilt as lodgings for Princess Elizabeth, ward of the abbey's post-Dissolution owner, Sir Anthony Browne. (OR) Facing the market-place, the PILGRIMS' REST is a good surviving 15c timber-framed hall house.

Beauchamp Chantry, Stoke-sub-Hamdon See **Stoke-sub-Hamdon.**

21 Bective Abbey (Co. Meath) Cistercian abbey founded in 1147 and almost totally rebuilt in the 15c when the site was fortified, a strong tower-house built on the former west range, and both cloister and church reduced in size. (OR)

22 Belsay Castle (Northumberland) Well-preserved late 14c tower-house with handsome corbelled-out bartisans at the angles; ground-floor kitchen with big hall above, in which are traces of contemporary heraldic wall-paintings; adjoining Renaissance manor-house of 1614; also important neo-classical mansion built for Sir Charles Monck in 1807–15; fine gardens. (OR)

23 Benthall Hall (Shropshire) Late 16c stone manor-house with polygonal bays and central porch; fine staircase of 1618 with carved newel posts and pierced strapwork balustrading. (NT, OR)

24 Berwick-upon-Tweed (Northumberland) Major Elizabethan artillery fortifications on the north and east sides of the town, protecting the landward approaches; open access ramparts of 1558–70 with prominent arrow-head bastions in the Italian style.

25 Bickleigh Castle (Devon) One of the Courtenay castles, preserving a big late medieval gatehouse and earlier chapel, but little else earlier than the 16c. (OR)

26 Bignor, Old Shop (West Sussex) The cottage version of a 15c hall house, with diminutive single-bay hall. (NO)

27 Binns, House of the (Central) Comfortable country house built by Thomas Dalyell in 1612–30; fine plasterwork of 1630 in the King's Room and high hall. (NTS, OR)

28 Blarney Castle (Co. Cork) Big 15c tower-house, handsomely fitted with hall, great chamber, chapel, and many individual bedchambers, including the earl's room with little oriel. (OR)

29 Blickling Hall (Norfolk) Ambitious mansion of brick with stone dressings, built in 1619–27 by Robert Liming for Sir Henry Hobart; has many parallels with Liming's earlier work at Hatfield; some fine contemporary ceilings and chimney-pieces; also an especially handsome long gallery. (NT, OR)

30 Boarstall Tower (Buckinghamshire) Moated site with surviving early 14c stone gatehouse, later much transformed and rebuilt but retaining its original dimensions; visible from the road. (NT, OA)

31 Bodiam Castle (East Sussex) Built for Sir Edward Dalyngrigge in the late 1380s; moated and of regular plan, with circular angle-towers and a single central court; complex barbican-protected approaches; exceptional setting. (NT, OR)

32 Bodmin Church (Cornwall) Big Perpendicular church of the 1470s and 1480s; notable features include a remarkable late 12c font and the Renaissance tomb-chest of Prior Vyvian (d.1533), with details recalling Torrigiani's work at Westminster Abbey.

33 Bolsover Castle (Derbyshire) Fantasy keep (Little Castle) designed by Robert Smythson for Charles Cavendish in 1612, recalling the romance of chivalry, with fine intact contemporary interiors; also riding school and terrace range (roofless) of the 1630s. (OR)

34 Bolton Castle (North Yorkshire) Rectangular with angle-towers, built for Richard Lord Scrope in the late 14c; public rooms include a hall and chapel, with Scrope's private quarters in the west range and many flat-like suites for his retainers in the towers; setting of great beauty. (OR)

35 Bolton Priory (North Yorkshire) Parish church preserving the nave of the former Augustinian priory church, with the skeleton only of the choir and transepts, and foundations of the claustral ranges to the south; stump of an unfinished 16c west tower, left incomplete on the priory's suppression; early 14c gatehouse incorporated in 19c mansion (private), with substantial remains of the original precinct wall; beautiful location.

36 Boscobel House (Shropshire) Early 17c hunting-lodge at which Charles II took refuge after the battle of Worcester in 1651. (OR)

37 Boston Church (Lincolnshire) One of the biggest parish churches in England, with a great 15c prodigy tower known as Boston 'Stump'; features include a fine classical pulpit of 1612.

38 Bothwell Castle (Strathclyde) Planned on a grand scale by Walter of Moravia in the late 13c but never completed; rebuilt by the Douglas earls in the late 14c and early 15c, with big public apartments including a great hall and chapel; unspoilt setting. (OR)

39 Bradley Manor (Devon) 15c stone-built manor-house with later embellishments and extensions; original features include the hall and big 1420s private chapel. (NT, OR)

40 Bramall Hall (Cheshire) Big 15–16c timber manor-house, much restored in the 19c but preserving its late medieval hall; hall floored over in the late 16c to provide a great chamber; good 15c roof and 16c tapestry-style wall-paintings in the solar; big private chapel. (OR)

41 Bridlington Priory (Humberside) Big 13c nave of Augustinian priory church preserved for parish use at the Suppression; late 14c monastic gatehouse.

42 Bridport (Dorset) The Chantry, in South Street, has late medieval features, with some of the characteristics of a tower-house. (NO)

43 Brodie Castle (Grampian) Late 16c Z-plan castle transformed by later modernizations and extensions; fine late 17c plaster ceiling in the present dining room. (NTS, OR)

44 Broughton Castle (Oxfordshire) 14c moated manor-house extensively rebuilt and modernized in the second half of the 16c; big 14c private chapel; fine 16c interiors, including a Fontainebleau-style chimney-piece in the Star Chamber. (OR)

45 Buckland Abbey (Devon) Former Cistercian abbey church converted into a residence by Sir Richard Grenville in the 1570s; big 14c monastic barn and a fragment of the original precinct wall, pierced by arrow-loops. (NT, OR)

46 Bunbury Church (Cheshire) Big Perpendicular parish church rebuilt after Sir Hugh Calveley established a college here in 1386; Sir Hugh's tomb remains in a central position in the chancel; south chancel chapel added in 1527 as Sir Ralph Egerton's personal

chantry, the dividing screen still preserving its Renaissance-style painted dado.

47 Bunratty Castle (Co. Clare) Mid 15c tower-house of noble proportions, remodelled internally in the late 16c for Donogh, fourth Earl of Thomond, with good surviving contemporary decorations, especially in the south solar chamber. (OR)

48 Burghley House (Cambridgeshire) Built for William Cecil from the 1560s and completed in 1589; much modified internally in later generations, but includes a great hall of c.1560 and contemporary pioneering Renaissance staircase (the Roman Staircase); one of the great prodigy houses of the Elizabethan period. (OR)

49 Burleigh Castle (Tayside) Early 16c tower-house of conventional plan, with hall (over kitchen) and three levels of chambers above; refortified for Sir James Balfour in 1582, with a neat artillery tower on the roadside angle and with gunports on each side of the gate; an obvious model for the Plantation forts of early 17c Ulster. (OR)

50 Burncourt (Co. Tipperary) Semi-fortified strong-house of the 1640s, roofless since 1650; rectangular in plan, with gabled angle-towers; private but clearly visible from the road. (NO)

51 Burton Agnes Hall (Humberside) Completed in c.1600 for Sir Henry Griffith, with fine contemporary fittings and decorative schemes, including those of the great hall and drawing room; good carpentered stair and top-floor gallery. In the grounds, the OLD MANOR HOUSE is a rare and important example of 12c domestic architecture, with surviving big first-floor hall (over a vaulted undercroft). (OR)

52 Bury St Edmunds (Suffolk) Remains of the Benedictine abbey here include two gatehouses, one 12c and the other mid 14c, with much of the original precinct wall; fine parish churches of St James (now the cathedral) and St Mary, both rebuilt on a large scale in the 15c and early 16c. (OR)

53 Butley Priory (Suffolk) Major Augustinian gatehouse, datable to the 1320s and carrying a fine display of contemporary heraldry, in five rows of escutcheons, on its outer facade; private but visible from the road. (NO)

54 Cadbury Church, North (Somerset) Rebuilt on a grand scale as a collegiate church by Lady Elizabeth Botreaux (d.1431), with the big chancel required for chaplains and choristers; fine 15c nave roof and 1530s benches. Just to the east, and clearly visible from the churchyard, is Sir Francis Hastings' NORTH CADBURY COURT of c.1600 (private). Ideal setting.

55 Caerlaverock Castle (Dumfries and Galloway) Late 13c triangular fortress, built in the 1290s perhaps by English masons; big gatehouse at the apex, with drum towers at the base angles; fine Renaissance range of the 1630s, built for Robert Maxwell, Earl of Nithsdale. (OR)

56 Caernarvon Castle (Gwynedd) Edward I's principal North Wales castle, built with great sophistication and at high cost in the late 13c and early 14c, together with an accompanying walled town; features include polygonal towers and banded masonry (echoing Constantinople), multiple gate defences, and fighting-passages built into the thickness of the walls. (OR)

57 Cahir Castle (Co. Tipperary) Major fortress of the earls of Ormond, with a big 12c keep remodelled in the 15c and supplemented by tower-houses of the same period; approaches protected by a barbican, an outer and a middle ward. (OR)

58 Calwich Priory (Staffordshire) Nothing now remains of this little Augustinian priory cell, although the site (in Ellastone) is known.

59 Camber Castle (East Sussex) Artillery tower of 1512, subsequently raised and defended by a strong bastioned curtain in the major building campaigns of 1539–40 and 1542–3. (OR)

60 Cambridge: King's College Chapel (Cambridgeshire) Built, initially for Henry VI, between 1446 and 1515; features include the famous fan vault, with fine window glass of the early 16c, and Renaissance screen and stalls. (OR)

61 Cambridge: St Radegund's Priory/Jesus College (Cambridgeshire) The choir, crossing and part of the nave of a Benedictine nunnery suppressed in 1496 in favour of Bishop Alcock's Jesus College, which was to re-use the bulk of the priory church as its chapel. (OR)

62 Canons Ashby (Northamptonshire) Country house of the 1550s with subsequent improvements and additions, the last in the early 18c; features include heraldic wall-paintings of the 1590s in the Winter Parlour, a handsome staircase of the 1630s, and a spectacular contemporary plaster ceiling in the drawing room. Built on land of a former Augustinian priory: part of the CHURCH survives to the east. (NT, OR)

63 Cardoness Castle (Dumfries and Galloway) Sophisticated tower-house of c.1500, with accommodation disposed on six levels and many intact (or at least recognizable) interior fittings, among them fireplaces, cupboards and window-seats. (OR)

64 Carisbrooke Castle (Isle of Wight) An important royal fortress with a long life which began with the original Norman motte-and-bailey earthworks of the late 11c; the big late 14c projecting gatehouse has gunports in its upper stages which are among the earliest of their kind, but systematic fortification against artillery attack was delayed at Carisbrooke until Federigo Giambelli, in 1597–1600, laid out the surviving rampart circuit, commanded by arrow-head bastions. (OR)

65 Carrick-on-Suir: Ormond Castle (Co. Tipperary) Elizabethan mansion tacked onto the north side of an existing mid 15c castle, with especially splendid first-floor gallery featuring loyal plasterwork. (OR)

66 Cartmel Priory Gatehouse (Cumbria) Big rectangular mid 14c monastic gatehouse with large

well-lit chamber over vaulted passage. (NT, OA) The priory CHURCH of this Augustinian community, suppressed in 1536–7, has remained in use as a parish church; features include the splendid ornate tomb of John Lord Harrington (d.1347) and a good set of 15c choir-stalls with early 17c Renaissance backs.

67 Castle Acre Priory (Norfolk) Important remains of a Cluniac community founded in the late 11c; expensive 12c west facade of church with adjoining prior's lodgings (formerly the west claustral range) preserved at the Dissolution as a farmhouse. Also in Castle Acre, making this one of the best such groups in Britain, is the great late 11c and early 12c ringwork-and-bailey CASTLE of the Norman Warenne earls of Surrey, founders of the priory, and a big PARISH CHURCH, rebuilt in the 15c and furnished then with good fittings, including a nice contemporary wooden pulpit and font cover. (OR)

68 Castle Ashby (Northamptonshire) A major late Elizabethan and Jacobean house, of which the screen on the south side of the courtyard (inward-facing loggia below, with long gallery above) is in the classical taste, either by or after Inigo Jones (1625–35); contemporary work includes the majestic west staircase and the ceilings of the great chamber and old library. (OR)

69 Castle Campbell (Central) Substantial 15c tower-house to which further fortifications and residential ranges were added in the 16c, the east linking range (late 16c or early 17c) having an Italian-style open loggia on the ground floor. (NTS, OR)

70 Castle Fraser (Grampian) Major late 16c tower-house to which service wings in the French style were added in the 1630s (cf the later Traquair House (Borders) and Springhill (Co. Londonderry)); features include a fine hall and balustraded viewpoint platform. (NTS, OR)

71 Charlecote Park (Warwickshire) Built for Sir Thomas Lucy in the late 1550s, but keeping com-

paratively little of the original Tudor work, having been extensively rebuilt in the 'Elizabethan Revival' style between 1826 and 1867; Tudor features include the location and scale of the great hall (though not its furnishings), and a handsome surviving gatehouse. (NT, OR)

72 Chastleton House (Oxfordshire) Built in first decade of 17c and little changed since; hall still traditionally sited; two big staircases, the one in the east tower being especially handsome; fine contemporary decorations in the great chamber and bedchambers, also in the top-floor long gallery; unique and unspoilt, with much of the original furniture still in use. (OR)

73 Chilham Castle (Kent) Polygonal brick mansion built for Sir Dudley Digges in 1603–16, adjoining a tower keep of 1171–4; good contemporary staircase but most other internal features are modern. (OR) In the PARISH CHURCH, some memorable Digges monuments of the early 17c.

74 Chipping Campden (Gloucestershire) Big parish church rebuilt on a grand scale, like other Cotswold churches, on the profits of the 15c wool trade; in the south chapel, a notable classical monument to Sir Baptist Hicks (d.1629), possibly by Nicholas Stone. On the High Street, the fine stone TOWN-HOUSE of William Grevel (d.1401), north of the market-place, has a central hall and contemporary chamber blocks at each end (private).

75 Chirk Castle (Clwyd) Built originally for Roger Mortimer between 1295 and 1310, with the prominent drum towers of that period; slighted in the Civil War and refurbished in the 1670s, when the present long gallery, with its classical panelling, was completed; most of the other internal fittings are of the 18c and 19c. (NT, OR)

76 Christchurch Priory (Dorset) One of the wealthier Augustinian houses of which the church remained in use following the Dissolution; many fine features, including the great Tree of Jesse reredos of *c.*1360 – a highly exceptional survival – and the chantry of Margaret, Countess of Salisbury, next to the high altar, an important work of the early Renaissance.

Churche's Mansion, Nantwich See **Nantwich.**

77 Claypotts Castle (Tayside) Neat little tower-house built for John Strachan between 1569 and 1588; typical Z-plan with corbelled-out crow-step gables; prominent ground-floor gunports at waist level. (OR)

78 Cleeve Abbey (Somerset) Former Cistercian abbey of which the church has almost wholly gone, although the claustral ranges are unusually complete; notice in particular the 15c refectory in the south range, being a more comfortable rebuilding of the earlier north-south refectory; also the exceptional survival of a full range of 13c dormitory windows over the chapter-house in the east range; a site of great charm and interest. (OR)

79 Clevedon Court (Avon) Much transformed semi-fortified manor-house of *c.*1320, with strong tower to the east and former portcullis defences at each end of the screens passage; surviving great hall and adjoining first-floor hanging chapel, both of the early 14c. (NT, OR)

80 Coggeshall: Paycocke's House (Essex) Fine complete timber-built town-house of *c.*1500, with range of street-facing oriels; built for the Paycocke family of Coggeshall clothiers; good internal timbering, although much restored. (NT, OR)

81 Colchester Abbey Gatehouse (Essex) A big, stately and expensive monastic gatehouse of the 15c, being all that survives of one of the wealthier Benedictine houses; easily seen from the ring road.

82 Compton Castle (Devon) A manor-house of the 14c and 15c to which a military-style facade was attached in *c.*1520, very much in the late medieval chivalric tradition; big 15c private chapel; interiors much rebuilt and restored. (NT, OR)

83 Conway: Aberconwy House (Gwynedd) A late medieval stone-built town-house, much restored and remodelled internally; orig-

inally with hall and chamber on the first floor over a tall ground-floor undercroft. (NT, OR) Other monuments in Conway include Edward I's CASTLE and TOWN WALLS (1283-7); also PLAS MAWR, a remarkable 16c town-house on a grand scale, with fine interiors (especially plasterwork) of 1577–80, and little changed since its construction.

84 Cooling Castle (Kent) Impressive 1380s gatehouse, next to the road, with heavily machicolated drum towers in the French style, giving access to a big outer bailey; moated inner bailey to the west, with a second gatehouse on its east wall and drum towers at the angles; gunports in the two gatehouses and in the tower. (OO)

85 Corbridge: Vicar's Pele (Northumberland) Little early 14c tower-house in the churchyard, with corbelled-out bartisans at roof level; on three storeys – store, hall, and chamber. (OO) Next to the Pele, the PARISH CHURCH has an important 8c Anglo-Saxon tower.

86 Cotehele House (Cornwall) A courtyard-plan manor-house, semi-fortified, dating to the 15c and early 16c, with many original features, including a fine timbered hall roof and substantial domestic chapel; setting of great natural beauty. (NT, OR)

87 Coughton Court (Warwickshire) Big early 16c prodigy gatehouse, now the centre-piece of a Gothick facade of 1780; oriel and turret windows create a wall-of-glass effect, the turrets themselves incorporating viewpoint chambers at fourth-floor parapet level. (NT, OR)

88 Coventry: Spon Street (West Midlands) A terrace of six 15c Wealden-style cottages (private) on the north side of Spon Street just outside the medieval west gate of the city, each with a small ground-floor hall half overlain by a first-floor chamber.

89 Cowdray House (West Sussex) Begun in *c.*1500 by Sir David Owen, but most of the work here is of the 1530s and 1540s, including the great central gatehouse (cf Titchfield) and many multi-light

bays; notice the persistence of many medieval features, among them battlements, the great hall, gatehouse tower, and courtyard plan. (OR)

90 Craigievar Castle (Grampian) The most spectacular of the early 17c Scottish tower-houses, built for William Forbes ('Danzig Willie') and completed in 1626; magnificent first-floor hall with fine stucco work, and other good contemporary interiors; note musket-holes at the base of the corbelled-out turrets, and balustraded view-point platform (cf Castle Fraser); attractive hillside setting. (NTS, OR)

91 Craignethan Castle (Strathclyde) Pioneering artillery castle built by Sir James Hamilton in the 1530s, with rectangular residential blockhouse protected against the rising ground to the west by a strong curtain wall; dry moat across the headland with *caponier* at base. (OR)

92 Crathes Castle (Grampian) Built for the Burnett family in the later 16c, with many of the same features as Craigievar; fine contemporary painted ceilings, the top-floor long gallery preserving its original oak-panelled roof; a major tower-house of the developed early modern Scottish tradition, with extensive later gardens. (NTS, OR)

93 Creake Abbey (Norfolk) Remains, chiefly of the church, of a small Augustinian house suppressed in 1506, after which its endowments were transferred to Christ's College (Cambridge); further monastic buildings incorporated in the large farmhouse to the south. (OR)

94 Crichton Castle (Lothian) A late 14c tower-house to which a big keep-gatehouse was added in the first half of the 15c; completing the court, an extraordinary Mannerist north range, with diamond-faceted inner facade over an open pillared loggia, was added in the 1580s by Francis Stewart; fine pioneering staircase, similarly in the Italian style; strikingly wild and isolated setting. (OR) On the castle's approaches, Sir William Crichton's

COLLEGIATE CHURCH of 1449 lacks its nave but is otherwise of the characteristic cruciform plan.

95 Croft Castle (Hereford and Worcester) A big four-square fortress of the late 14c or early 15c, with turret-like round towers at the angles, extensively rebuilt in the 18c. (NT, OR) Handsome pre-Renaissance tomb of Sir Richard (d.1509) and Dame Eleanor Croft in the adjoining PARISH CHURCH. Spectacular setting.

96 Culross Palace (Fife) Built between 1597 and 1611 for the entrepreneurial Sir George Bruce; features include crow-step gables, Renaissance-style pedimented dormers, long gallery, and panelled and painted interiors. (NTS, OR) Another handsome town-house of the same period is THE STUDY, up by the Market Cross, again with dormers and crow-step gables, datable to c.1610. Above the town, the former Cistercian church of CULROSS ABBEY survives (lacking the nave already abandoned in the early 16c, long after lay brothers had ceased to be recruited in any numbers by the community).

97 Dartington Hall (Devon) Built in the 1380s and 1390s for John de Holand, Duke of Exeter; notable especially for the contemporary great hall and kitchen (much restored but authentic in plan) and for the more exceptional survival of a terrace of lodgings in the outer court, provided for members of Holand's household. (OR)

98 Dartmouth Castle (Devon) Built in 1481–93 as England's first major coastal battery, designed specifically for cannon; basement battery (later used as a magazine) with accommodation for the garrison above; early internally-splayed gunports. (OR)

99 Deal Castle (Kent) Largest of Henry VIII's 'Three Castles which keep the Downs', the others being Walmer and Sandown; built in 1539–40 and, though much altered in the 18–19c, still has the overall geometric plan and many original features, including the basement fighting galleries. (OR)

100 Denny Abbey (Cambridge-shire) A complex but important building which began life as a Benedictine priory church, was then adapted as a hospital by the Knights Templar, and finally was rebuilt for Franciscan nuns at the expense of their patron, Mary de St Pol, Countess of Pembroke. The nuns' 14c remodelling of the earlier church as accommodation for themselves and the countess survives, as does their refectory north of the former cloister; their church is known only from foundations. (OR)

101 Dirleton Castle (Lothian) A late 13c drum-tower and curtain-wall castle in the Edwardian style, extensively rebuilt in the late 14c and 15c with a new gatehouse and residential accommodation of some splendour; a further residential range added by the Ruthvens in the 16c, with Renaissance details. (OR)

102 Doddington Hall (Lincoln-shire) Built for Thomas Taylor between 1593 and 1600, probably to a design by Robert Smythson; much 18c remodelling internally, including both great hall and long gallery (top floor), but the original plan is easily reconstructed and the three viewpoint cupolas at roof level are typically late Elizabethan. (OR)

103 Donnington Castle (Berk-shire) Built for Sir Richard Abberbury in the 1380s, with an impressive residential gatehouse fronting the private apartments of the east range; small horseshoe-plan court to the west which has lost all but a few traces of its other domestic ranges; surviving Civil War defences, with earthwork arrow-head bastions (1643–4). (OR)

104 Doune Castle (Central) Built in the late 14c and early 15c for Robert Stewart, Duke of Albany; preserves a notably complete set of domestic accommodation, including both a private and a public hall, with the original kitchen arrangements and individual lodgings. (OR)

105 Drum Castle (Grampian) Big rectangular tower-house of c.1300, being one of the earliest of its class, with first-floor hall and chambers above; adjoining mansion of 1619,

special features of which are the stepped gables, Renaissance pedimented dormers, a straight stone stair, and vaulted basement corridor. (NTS, OR)

106 Dunglass Church (Lothian) Mid 15c collegiate church, founded by Sir Alexander Hume; originally rectangular but soon given a crossing tower and transepts to complete the familiar collegiate cruciform plan. (OR)

107 Dunstanburgh Castle (Northumberland) Big headland castle originally built for Thomas, Earl of Lancaster, in the early 14c with the characteristically massive double-drum gatehouse of the Edwardian style; in the 1380s, the gatehouse was converted into a residential tower-house for John of Gaunt; beautiful but remote location. (NT, OR)

108 Dunster Castle (Somerset) A much transformed but interesting and well-sited castle of which the earliest feature is a 13c gatehouse, superseded in the early 15c by Sir Hugh Luttrell's gatehouse of the 1420s; important interiors of the 1680s, including fine plaster ceilings and a noble grand stair; a nice set of late 17c stables, still with their original stalls. (NT, OR)

109 Earlshall Castle (Fife) Mid 16c tower-house in the Z-plan style, with two towers connected by a residential hall-and-chamber range; fine early 17c top-floor gallery with magnificent contemporary painted ceiling. (OR)

110 Easton-on-the-Hill: Priest's House (Northamptonshire) A small rectangular two-storeyed building, probably of the late 15c; two large chambers connected by a stair in the southeast angle. (NT, OA)

111 Edinburgh Castle (Lothian) A big royal fortress so rebuilt and transformed as to contain little but the foundations of David II's original Windsor-inspired chivalric remodelling of the 1360s. (OR)

112 Edinburgh: Gladstone's Land (Lothian) Fine lofty town-house built for Thomas Gledstanes in 1617–20; six storeys with ground-floor arcade onto the street (Lawnmarket); fine restored great (or

Painted) chamber, with contemporary painted ceiling and frieze. (NTS, OR)

113 Edzell Castle (Tayside) Early 16c tower-house to which extensive domestic quarters were added in the last quarter of the 16c to make a mansion of courtyard plan; remarkable Renaissance (1604) walled garden with banqueting house and bath house attached. (OR)

114 Eltham Palace (London) Impressive moated palace site of which the principal survival is Edward IV's great hall, with its majestic hammerbeam roof; the moat bridge dates, like the hall, to the 1470s. (OR)

115 Evesham: Round House (Hereford and Worcester) Large-scale late 15c town-house, jettied on two stages, on island site of its own. (NO) ABBEY: few surviving remains of this important Benedictine house, the most significant being Abbot Lichfield's grand early 16c church tower (open access, in a park).

116 Fairford Church (Gloucestershire) Rebuilt extensively for John Thame (d.1500) in a single programme continued by his son, Sir Edmund (d.1534); very fine early 16c glass, probably intended originally for Westminster Abbey, and good contemporary woodwork, including roofs, screens and stalls.

117 Falkland Palace (Fife) Later much rebuilt, but features important Renaissance ranges and a French-style gatehouse built in the late 1530s for James V; also James V's Royal Tennis Court (1539). (NTS, OR)

118 Felbrigg Hall (Norfolk) Built for Thomas Windham in 1621–4 and extended in the 1670s in the Dutch Palladian style, the two fronts (south and west) presenting a striking contrast; interiors much transformed at various later dates, but the great hall (to the west of the porch and screens passage) preserves its original plan and scale and there is a notable 'palatial' plaster ceiling, dated 1687, in the drawing room (cf Dunster Castle), with similar work in the cabinet. (NT, OR)

119 Forde Abbey (Dorset) A former Cistercian house at which the last abbot, Thomas Charde, spent lavishly on an exceptionally splendid rebuilding of the cloister and of his own adjoining lodgings; much of this early 16c work survives, including Abbot Charde's unfinished great hall; in the 1650s, remodelled by Edmund Prideaux with the insertion of a grand staircase (cf Ham House) and saloon; Prideaux also refurnished the 12c chapter-house as a private chapel. (OR)

120 Fore Priory (Co. Westmeath) A dependent (or alien) priory of the Benedictines of Evreux, fortified in the 15c with a tower-house at each end of the church; substantial remains both of these and of the earlier claustral ranges to the south. (OR)

121 Fotheringhay Church (Northamptonshire) The surviving nave of a big Yorkist collegiate church, founded in the early 15c; the choir and 15c college buildings have long since been demolished, but the surviving fragment is still impressive, not least for the great west tower and its crowning octagonal lantern. To the east, there is the motte, with ramparts and other remains, of FOTHERINGHAY CASTLE (open access).

122 Fountains Abbey (North Yorkshire) A great Cistercian abbey most beautifully set in a typical riverside location, founded in 1132 among the first of the English white monk houses; substantial remains of the original 12c buildings, with 13c and later extensions, including Abbot Huby's big early 16c tower. Next to the entrance, FOUNTAINS HALL is an important early 17c mansion, built in c.1611 for Sir Stephen Proctor. (NT, OR)

123 Furness Abbey (Cumbria) A rich former Savigniac house which became Cistercian after the orders joined forces in 1147; much rebuilding took place here in the 15c, including the addition of a huge west tower which may have inspired Huby's tower at Fountains. (OR)

124 Fyvie Castle (Grampian) An earlier castle here was rebuilt on a grand scale for Alexander Seton, Chancellor of Scotland (from 1604) and Earl of Dunfermline; subsequently much transformed both inside and out, but the upperworks of the famous south facade (three towers across) are Seton's, as is the remarkable great stair – a turnpike (wheel) stair, grander than any other in Scotland. (NTS, OR)

125 Gainsborough Old Hall (Lincolnshire) Preserves a timber-framed hall on a very grand scale, built for Sir Thomas Burgh in the 1470s; also the contemporary brick-built kitchen, comparable to the kitchen at Haddon Hall as one of the more remarkable late medieval survivals in its class; notice also the late 15c polygonal strong tower, provided by Sir Thomas at the eastern (solar) end of his mansion. (OR)

126 Gawthorpe Hall (Lancashire) Extensively rebuilt by Sir Charles Barry in 1850–2, but preserves important features of its original building date (1600–1605), including the pioneering siting of the great hall at the side and back of the house, with the parlour (now drawing room) to the left of a central front door; the drawing room ceiling and panelling are both original, as is the ceiling of the top-floor long gallery (NT, OR)

127 Gilling Castle (North Yorkshire) The lavish great chamber (1570s) of the original Fairfax house is preserved intact here within an early 18c classical mansion of style and splendour; high-quality panelling, a painted heraldic frieze, ornate plaster ceiling, and heraldic glass. (OR)

Gladstone's Land, Edinburgh See **Edinburgh.**

128 Glastonbury Abbey (Somerset) Extensive remains of one of the wealthiest of the English Benedictine houses and its related buildings (the *George & Pilgrims* Inn, the Tribunal, the tithe barn etc); fine late 14c abbot's kitchen, with other indications of continued building activity throughout the Late Middle Ages. (OR)

129 Goodrich Castle (Hereford and Worcester) Built in the late 13c and early 14c for the Valence earls of Pembroke; important for its sophisticated barbican-protected approaches and for its lavish provision of individual lodgings, in addition to public apartments like the great hall and the chamber and other private quarters of the earl. (OR)

130 Grantham House (Lincolnshire) Much disguised by 18c rebuildings but keeps its central floored-over late 15c hall, since transformed into a fine 18c drawing room. (NT, OR)

131 Great Chalfield Manor (Wiltshire) The surviving private range – central hall with chamber blocks at each end – of Thomas Tropnell's late 15c courtyard mansion; considerable reconstructions have taken place here, but both the hall and great chamber retain their original plans, especially noteworthy being the fine oriel windows lighting each of the first-floor chambers. (NT, OR) The adjoining PARISH CHURCH preserves Tropnell's chantry chapel, with a good stone screen and wall-paintings of c.1480.

132 Great Chart: Yardhurst (Kent) Well-preserved mid 15c Wealden house, with the original wooden tracery in some of its windows. (NO) At the PARISH CHURCH, note especially the chantry of Bishop Goldwell (1477) in the south chancel chapel, with a fine donor window peppered with the bishop's personal rebus (a golden well).

133 Great Coxwell (Oxfordshire) Important 13c stone-built barn with original internal timbering (NT, OR); formerly one of the barns of the Cistercians of Beaulieu (Hampshire), whose other even larger barn, nearer the abbey at St Leonard's Grange, is now roofless but still very impressive.

134 Greenwich: the Queen's House (London) Designed by Inigo Jones for Anne of Denmark (d.1619), James I's queen; externally, a fine example of Inigo Jones' severest Palladian manner; internally, some lavish carved and painted ceilings of the 1630s, with Jones'

celebrated spiral Tulip Stairs, and a chequered marble floor by Nicholas Stone. (OR)

135 Grey's Court (Oxfordshire) A pleasant domesticated 16c manor-house within the walled precinct of a mid 14c fortified residence built for the first Lord de Grey; original features include the four-storeyed 'main' tower, with smaller corner towers and sections of the linking curtain. (NT, OR)

136 Grundisburgh: Bast's (Suffolk) Tall early 16c village house (private but clearly seen from the road), jettied on two stages and built for a London salter, Thomas Wall, who also built a fine chantry chapel for himself at the neighbouring PARISH CHURCH.

137 Guisborough Priory (Cleveland) Remains of one of the more important Augustinian houses, in particular of the priory church which preserves its lofty late 13c east end. (OR) Immediately to the north, in the PARISH CHURCH, the Brus Cenotaph is an important monument of the early 16c, with lively knight figures against the tomb-chest.

138 Gullege (East Grinstead, East Sussex) A late medieval timber-framed farmhouse modernized in the 16c with brick chimney-stacks and a floored-over hall, then acquiring a stone show-front in the early 17c; private and not visible from the road.

139 Haddon Hall (Derbyshire) One of the major monuments of late medieval and early modern England, important features being the chapel, great hall, kitchen, and defences of the late 14c manor-house; also the early 16c parlour, solar, and earl's bedroom, with contemporary fittings, and the remarkably complete early 17c long gallery, panelled in the Northern Renaissance taste; not to be missed. (OR)

140 Hailes Abbey (Gloucestershire) A Cistercian abbey of comparatively late foundation (1246) which became a pilgrimage centre following its acquisition of the Holy Blood relic; continuing prosperity, associated with a 15c revival

of the cult, made possible the rebuilding of the refectory, abbot's lodging and cloister. (NT, OR) In the neighbouring PARISH CHURCH, well worth a visit, are fine wall-paintings of c.1300.

141 Ham House (London) Built in c.1610 for Sir Thomas Vavasour and modified extensively soon after by William Murray (1637–9), most notably by the insertion of a great staircase; fine 1670s interiors in the Restoration palatial style, with much of their original furniture. (NT, OR)

Hamilton House, Preston See **Preston**.

142 Hampton Court (London) Cardinal Wolsey's early 16c brick palace, given to Henry VIII in the late 1520s and subsequently extended by the king and his successors; surviving remains of Henry VIII's interiors include the great hall and the chapel roofs, both of characteristic florid magnificence. (OR)

143 Hardwick Hall (Derbyshire) Designed and built by Robert Smythson for Bess of Hardwick in 1591–7; noteworthy features include multi-windowed facades, viewpoint turrets, and good contemporary interiors; especially important is the innovative siting of the great hall across the building; also the size of the stairs and landings, the decorations and placing of the high great chamber, and the overwhelming scale of the long gallery; many fine contemporary chimney-pieces and other fittings. At a short distance are the ruins of the first HALL, built for Bess of Hardwick to a much less innovatory design. (NT, OR)

144 Harrietsham: Old Bell Farm (Kent) Fine example of an early 16c Wealden farmhouse, with central hall preserving screens passage arrangements, crown-post roof, and original full-height bay (now glazed at ground-floor level only); next to the road. (NO)

145 Hatfield House (Hertfordshire) Built in 1608–12 for Robert Cecil, Earl of Salisbury, Chief Minister of James I, on a site adjoining the former palace of Cardinal Morton (d.1500); the Old

Palace retains its great hall, with a fine late 15c timber roof; a great hall again remains a prominent feature of Cecil's house, most of its furnishings being authentic Jacobean; the grand staircase and long gallery are also of Cecil's time, as are a number of fine chimney-pieces. (OR) The adjoining HAT-FIELD CHURCH includes the Salisbury chapel (1618), built to hold Robert Cecil's stately classical tomb, but notable also for the William Curle floor-monument by William Stone, with its recumbent effigy of pioneering realism.

146 Hengrave Hall (Suffolk) Built for Sir Thomas Kytson, 1525–38; although much rebuilt in later years, Hengrave preserves its southern show-front, with a spectacular trefoiled bay over the main door. (OA)

147 Hermitage Castle (Borders) Exceptionally large tower-house, dating to c.1400, of the earls of Douglas, including a complete set of public rooms and many private lodgings; early 19c corbelled parapets and crow-step gables, but otherwise original and finely set in dramatic moorland isolation. (OR)

148 Herstmonceux Castle (East Sussex) Large-scale brick castle of the 1440s, built for Sir Roger Fiennes; interiors much rebuilt and transformed, but they include a staircase imported here from William Cecil's Theobalds, itself the model for the great stair at Hatfield House; on the exterior, notice the gunports and prominent machicolations of the main gate-house. (OR)

149 Hill Hall (Theydon Mount, Essex) Rebuilt in the French Renaissance style for Sir Thomas Smith in the late 1560s; features include external attached columns and other classical motifs, with important tapestry-style wall-paintings internally. (OR)

150 Hinchingbrooke House (Cambridgeshire) Former Augustinian nunnery rebuilt and extended from the 1540s as a country mansion; fine original bay windows of the mid 16c and early 17c;

gatehouse of c.1500 re-used from Ramsey Abbey (see below). (OO)

151 Holyroodhouse (Edinburgh, Lothian) Wealthy Augustinian abbey, the guest-house of which was developed by the kings of Scotland as a residence; an especially important programme of works was undertaken here after the Restoration for Charles II, resulting in fine French/classical courtyard facades and lavish palatial interiors. (OR)

152 Huntly Castle (Grampian) A 12c motte and bailey equipped in the 15c with a tower-house in the bailey and with an unfinished rectangular domestic range, later rebuilt and extended; especially notable for its French-inspired work of the early 17c, including the grand heraldic frontispiece on the northeast stair turret and the inscriptions and parade of oriels on the south front. (OR)

153 Hurst Castle (Hampshire) Built for Henry VIII in 1539–44 as one of his coast-defence artillery castles; a twelve-sided central tower with an outer defence of three semi-circular bastions linked by angled curtains; many alterations carried out in successive 19c refortifications. (OR)

154 Hylton Castle (Tyne and Wear) A major tower-house of c.1400, afterwards much altered and extended but stripped back recently to something more like its original condition, although without either roofs or floors; sophisticated internal arrangements, with boldly machicolated parapets and turrets at roof level; sad council-estate isolation. (OR)

155 Ightham Mote (Kent) Moated manor-house of the 14–15c, with major additions of the 1520s, including the big chapel in the north range; fine 14c hall and contemporary chapel in the east range, with impressive gatehouse in the west front, rebuilt in the mid 15c; delightful setting. (NT, OR)

156 Isleham Church (Cambridgeshire) Big early 14c parish church extensively rebuilt in the late 15c with the help of the Peyton family; good nave roof, dated 1495 with

characteristic *in memoriam* inscription, and many Peyton monuments. Just to the west, an intact aisleless 12c church is all that remains of ISLEHAM PRIORY, a former alien priory of St Jacut-de-la-Mer (Brittany), suppressed in 1414, after which its property came to Pembroke College (Cambridge).

157 Jordan's Castle (Co. Down) Very complete 15c tower-house, with two full-height turrets on its north face, one of them carrying the newel stair, the other a tier of garderobes; first-floor hall with two storeys of chambers above. (OR)

158 Kanturk Castle (Co. Cork) Handsome 'strong-house' of c.1600 with a defendable ground floor, prominent towers at the angles, and corbels at roof level, provided to support a machicolated parapet; four storeys, the upper three carrying comfortable accommodation. (NT, OR)

159 Kellie Castle (Fife) 15c tower-houses with a linking building of the late 16c; remodelled extensively in the late 1660s and 1670s, following the Restoration, when the great hall was converted into a handsome saloon, painted panelling was installed in the chamber (withdrawing room), and the second-floor Vine Room was equipped with its splendid Holyroodhouse-style ceiling. (NTS, OR)

160 Kells Priory (Co. Kilkenny) The most remarkable example in the British Isles of a fortified monastic house, formerly a priory of Augustinian canons; the 15c defences, which are largely intact, include an extensive towered curtain surrounding the big outer court, with tower-houses also adjoining the priory church. (OR)

161 Kenilworth Castle (Warwickshire) One of England's greater medieval fortresses; late 12c rectangular keep and domestic ranges of the 14c and 16c, including John of Gaunt's great hall in the west range and the Earl of Leicester's gatehouse and southeast residential block ('Leicester's Building'). (OR) The remains of the ABBEY lie immediately to the south of the PARISH

CHURCH, which it once dwarfed and overshadowed.

162 Kilclief Castle (Co. Down) 15c tower-house thought to be datable to 1413–41; big machicolated arch linking the projecting full-height turrets of the east front; vaulted ground floor with hall above, and chambers on two further levels. (OR)

King's College Chapel, Cambridge See **Cambridge**.

King John's Hunting Lodge, Axbridge See **Axbridge**.

163 King's Lynn: St George's Guildhall (Norfolk) 15c hall of one of Lynn's principal late medieval guilds, since much modified and rebuilt. (NT, OR) The hall of the even more important TRINITY GUILD (15c with a late 16c extension) similarly survives next to St Margaret's Church.

164 Kinneil House (Central) A mid 16c tower-house much transformed in the late 17c, with adjoining palace range of the 1550s in which fine tapestry-style wall-paintings have survived; overpainting in the 1620s has obscured the 1550s work in the Arbour Room, but complete panels have been preserved in the Parable Room, which is the earliest intact scheme of its class. (OR)

165 Kirby Hall (Northamptonshire) Built for Sir Humphrey Stafford (d.1575) and Sir Christopher Hatton (d.1591), probably to the designs of Thomas Thorpe; traditional courtyard plan, with great hall, but innovatory French Renaissance and Italian-style elevations, and a big ground-floor loggia in the north range. (OR)

166 Kirby Muxloe Castle (Leicestershire) Brick castle, with provision for artillery, left incomplete on the execution of its builder, William Lord Hastings, in 1483; rectangular plan, moated, with square corner towers and with a big (unfinished) gatehouse on its west front. (OR)

167 Knockmoy Abbey (Co. Galway) One of several Irish Cistercian houses in which the church, during the 15c, was much reduced in size, with both the nave and the transepts walled off; attractive isolated location. (OR)

168 Knole (Kent) Archbishop Thomas Bourchier's 15c country palace, extended by Henry VIII in the 1540s, and remodelled by Thomas Sackville in the first decade of the 17c; major features include Bourchier's great hall (transformed by Sackville), Henry VIII's extensive additional lodgings in the fronting Green Court, and important early 17c interiors, especially the ballroom, cartoon gallery, and great staircase. (NT, OR)

169 Kyme, South (Lincolnshire) Four-storeyed 14c tower-house, built for Sir Gilbert de Umfraville, originally part of a larger building but now standing in a field on its own; private but clearly visible from the road.

170 Lacock Abbey (Wiltshire) Former Augustinian nunnery, founded in 1232; preserves its 13c vaulted chapter-house and all but the west alley of the handsome 15c cloister; converted into a private house for William Sharington after 1539, resulting in the demolition of the church and rebuilding of the south range over the cloister alley and former sacristy; viewpoint tower with Italianate banqueting chambers in the Somerset House style of c.1550. (NT, OR) In the PARISH CHURCH, Sharington's wall-tomb is a Renaissance monument of high quality (1553).

171 Lancaster Church (Lancashire) A dependent priory of the Norman abbey of Séez, its church continuing in parochial use after the suppression of the alien priories in 1414 and the transfer of Lancaster's estates to Syon Abbey.

172 Lavenham Guildhall (Suffolk) Fine early 16c timber-framed town-house, built for the Corpus Christi Guild but much altered internally since that date; on the exterior, preserves a contemporary carved corner-post and fine projecting porch. (NT, OR) Facing the same market-place, the LITTLE HOUSE is a good example of 15c burgess housing, among many such in this unspoilt little town, of which the PARISH CHURCH, rebuilt almost entirely in the Late Middle Ages, is one of the grandest in Suffolk.

173 Layer Marney Tower (Essex) Brick and terracotta prodigy tower, built as the gatehouse of a mansion left incomplete on the death in 1523 of its originator, Henry Lord Marney (OR); important Early Renaissance ornament both on the tower and on the contemporary Marney monuments (also of terracotta) in the adjoining PARISH CHURCH.

174 Levens Hall (Cumbria) Late medieval tower-house incorporated in a late 16c mansion; some fine plasterwork and panelling of the 1590s especially in the drawing room (former great parlour) and adjoining little drawing room, but also elsewhere, making this one of the more complete examples of late Elizabethan decorative taste. (OR)

175 Lincluden College (Dumfries and Galloway) A former Benedictine nunnery, founded in c.1164, suppressed in favour of the college established here in c.1400 by Archibald the Grim, third Earl of Douglas; richly carved stonework in collegiate choir, with early 15c wall-tomb and surviving pulpitum. (OR)

176 Lindisfarne Castle (Northumberland) Small artillery fort of 1549–50, with some original features but extensively rebuilt in 1903 to designs by Edwin Lutyens. (NT, OR)

177 Lingfield Church (Surrey) Rebuilt after Sir Reginald Cobham's founding of a college here in 1431, his fine monument still standing in the middle of the choir; 15c choir-stalls and screens; also good Cobham brasses.

178 Linlithgow Palace (Lothian) Exceptionally complete 15c palace, with great hall, chapel, and royal apartments; early 17c north range; fine turnpikes (newel stairs), heraldic wall panels, chimney-pieces, and many other original features. (OR)

179 Little Moreton Hall (Cheshire) 15c hall and chamber block, with major extensions in the 1560s (east wing) and 1570s (south wing); a memorable example of Cheshire timber-framing, with features which include the great bay windows (1559) of the hall and withdrawing room, and the fine top-floor long gallery in the south wing. (NT, OR)

180 Londonderry City Walls Built in 1613–18 for the Corporation of London's Irish Society; stone-faced earth ramparts, originally with four gates and with angle-bastions for artillery defence; a fine survival of a complete urban defensive system in the contemporary Italian manner.

181 Longford Castle (Wiltshire) Considerably extended and rebuilt in the 1870s, but preserves the triangular plan, with drum towers at the angles, of Sir Thomas Gorges' 1580s pseudo-medieval mansion; interiors transformed but include the long gallery of Gorges' original plan. (OO)

182 Longleat House (Wiltshire) A major house of the Tudor Renaissance on which its builder, Sir John Thynne, was busy for a great many years, principally between 1567 and 1580; much altered internally, but has a pioneering regular plan and important Renaissance exteriors, finished at the top with classical balustrades and viewpoint turrets. (OR)

183 Long Melford Church (Suffolk) Extensively rebuilt, on Clopton and other money, in the 15c and early 16c; fine contemporary roofs; good donor glass; the Clopton Chapel and John Clopton's Lady Chapel (1496) are both excellent examples of chantry chapels.

184 Loseley Park (Surrey) Built for Sir William More in 1561–9, perhaps as a remodelling of an earlier house; panelling in the great hall said to come from Henry VIII's Nonsuch Palace and certainly has Nonsuch associations, as has the great chalk chimney-piece in the drawing room, both being important examples of Anglo-French-Flemish design. (OR)

185 Lower Brockhampton House (Hereford and Worcester) Moated manor-house, with late 14c hall and solar nicely intact, and with a very pretty late 15c gatehouse bridg-ing the moat; isolated and entirely delightful setting. (NT, OR)

186 Lowick Church (Northamptonshire) Handsomely rebuilt in the 15c, largely at the expense of the Greene family whose tomb-church it remained for generations; especially fine west tower of c.1470 with octagonal bell chamber; good family monuments and, in the north aisle windows, sixteen figures from an earlier high-quality Tree of Jesse (c.1320).

187 Ludlow: Corner Shop (Shropshire) A big 15c timber-framed town-house, jettied at two levels; now in use as a shop, but recently carefully restored.

188 Lulworth Castle (East Lulworth, Dorset) Built for Thomas Howard in the early 17c as a Spenserian sham 'castle', intended rather as a lodge than a main residence; square central block with big circular angle towers. (NO)

189 Lyme Park (Cheshire) A house with a long history already before its substantial rebuilding in the late 16c; rebuilt again on a grand scale in the early 18c, but preserves a bizarre classical frontispiece of the 1570s, and the long gallery and great chamber (now drawing room) of that period. (NT, OR)

190 Lytes Cary (Somerset) A late medieval manor-house transformed into a comfortable residence in the 16c when the south wing and other ranges (since demolished) were added; some fine interiors, especially the great parlour and great chamber, of the 1530s; also a good mid 15c hall and 14c chapel refurnished in 1631. (NT, OR)

191 Lyveden New Bield (Northamptonshire) Started in 1594 but left incomplete on the death of its builder, Sir Thomas Tresham, in 1605; built with maximum Catholic symbolism to a cruciform plan, and intended simply as a garden house. (NT, OR)

192 Mallow Castle (Co. Cork) Built as a strong-house in the late 16c for Sir Thomas Norreys, with polygonal corner turrets and many musket-holes as a prominent feature of the facades. (OR)

193 Malton Priory (North York-shire) A former Gilbertine house of which the most substantial surviving fragment is the western portion of the nave, kept in service as the parish church of Old Malton; originally fine but mutilated west facade of c.1200.

194 Martock: Treasurer's House (Somerset) Once the rectory of the Treasurer of Wells, preserving its hall (c.1300), solar block (13c), and kitchen (15c). (NT, OA) Opposite, the PARISH CHURCH was splendidly rebuilt in c.1500, having an exceptionally handsome nave roof of that period.

195 Maxstoke Castle (Warwickshire) Moated castle of the 1340s, built for William de Clinton, Earl of Huntingdon; much transformed internally but has kept its 14c gatehouse, angle towers and linking curtain, all of a size and dignity appropriate to the rank of the newly-created earl. (NO) There are substantial remains also of William de Clinton's PRIORY, an Augustinian community upgraded from a collegiate chantry, including the gatehouses, crossing tower, and circuit wall.

196 Melbury House (Melbury Sampford, Dorset) An innovatory mansion built in the 1530s for Giles Strangways, of which one of the few surviving original features is the tower and its crowning hexagonal viewpoint chamber, among the pioneers of the style. (NO)

197 Melford Hall (Suffolk) Much transformed by later rebuildings, but retains six prominent turrets (in the Nonsuch style) from Sir William Cordell's mid 16c mansion, the whole in fashionable brick; Cordell's great hall, traditionally placed to the right of the door, preserves its scale but not its original decorations. (NT, OR)

198 Michelham Priory (East Sussex) An Augustinian priory fortified against the French in c.1400, with a broad moat and handsome stone gatehouse; parts of the prior's lodgings (west range) and refectory (south range) are incorporated in the present house; attractive water-bound setting. (OR)

199 Middle Littleton Barn (Hereford and Worcester) Great stone barn of Evesham Abbey, with restored but authentic roof, datable to *c*.1300 and still in use. (NT, OR)

200 Milton Abbey (Dorset) The former church (lacking its nave) of a Benedictine abbey, as rebuilt but never completed after the fire of 1309; also Abbot Middleton's personal hall of 1498, with fine timber roof and a remarkable carved screen at its lower end, separating off the screens passage. (OR)

201 Mimms Church, South (Hertfordshire) Important for the 16c Frowyck Chapel and north aisle, with canopied monuments of 1527 and 1540, illustrating the transition here from the medieval to the Renaissance styles.

202 Minster in Sheppey Church (Kent) In its northern part, the former church of an Augustinian (originally Benedictine) nunnery; much of the priory church survives, as does the gatehouse, but little else.

203 Minster Lovell Hall (Oxfordshire) Built as a quadrangular manor-house, with domestic range on the north, for William Lord Lovell in the 1430s; single strong tower at the southwest corner, next to the river. (OR) Just to the northwest, the PARISH CHURCH was formerly a dependency of the Norman abbey of Ivry, substantially rebuilt by Lord Lovell.

204 Monasteranenagh Abbey (Co. Limerick) One of the Irish Cistercian houses at which a contraction of the church occurred in the 15c, the transepts being sealed off and only two bays of the nave kept with the choir and presbytery; the only other substantial remains of the abbey are those of the big chapter-house in the east range. (OR)

205 Monea Castle (Co. Fermanagh) A plantation castle built in 1618–19 for Malcolm Hamilton; tall rectangular residential range, with twin towers at the west end protecting the entrance, strongly reminiscent of Scottish work of the same period; substantial remains of the square stone-walled bawn, with

its gate next to the northwest flanker; pleasant isolated setting. (OR)

206 Montacute House (Somerset) Built for Sir Edward Phelips in the 1590s, with much external display of pinnacles, chimneys and heroic statuary; features include a top-floor gallery running the entire length of the building and good contemporary interiors, especially in the hall and the first-floor great chamber; ideal setting. (NT, OR)

207 Moseley Old Hall (Staffordshire) Built in *c*.1600 but much altered externally in the 1870s when the walls of this originally timber-framed building were refaced in brick; fine brick chimney-stacks of the original building period; top-floor recusant chapel. (NT, OR)

208 Mottisfont Abbey (Hampshire) A small Augustinian priory – not an abbey, though now known as such – suppressed with the other lesser houses in 1536, soon after which William Lord Sandys began the conversion of its church into a house; much altered in the mid 18c, at which time most of Lord Sandys' work was removed and the medieval church fabric again concealed in the new building; pleasant riverside situation. (NT, OR)

209 Mount Grace Priory (North Yorkshire) A former Carthusian community, founded in 1398, of which the buildings are exceptionally complete; usual small church and spacious individual cells, each with its garden and food-hatch next to the door. (NT, OR)

210 Moyne Friary (Co. Mayo) An Observant Franciscan friary founded in *c*.1460 and preserving an exceptionally complete set of buildings, all of similar date and impressive size; note especially the southward extensions of the friary church and the exposed undefended estuarine setting. (OR)

211 Muchelney Priest's House (Somerset) A rare example of a complete stone vicarage of the early 14c, updated in the 15c with new windows; central hall with chamber blocks at each end. (NT, OA) Across the green, the PARISH CHURCH is a 15c rebuilding, immediately

north of the former abbey church, the most substantial remains of MUCHELNEY ABBEY being the *c*.1500 abbot's lodgings, incorporating some bays of the cloister. Together, a group of considerable importance.

212 Much Wenlock Priory (Shropshire) One of England's major Cluniac houses, built with style and ostentation in the 12c and retaining some fragments, in the chapter-house and lavatorium, of that grandeur. (OR) To southeast of the cloister, the former infirmary (12c) and prior's lodgings (*c*.1500) are both important buildings, but are private.

213 Musselburgh: Pinkie House (Lothian) A 16c tower-house extended into a mansion by Alexander Seton in the early 17c, with some fine contemporary interiors, especially notable being Seton's gallery ceiling. (OO)

214 Nantwich: Churche's Mansion (Cheshire) A generous timber-framed town-house of 1577, with central ceiled-over hall and chamber blocks at each end; some contemporary panelling and a surviving timber newel stair; lovingly cared for and now in use as a restaurant. (OR)

215 Neath Abbey (West Glamorgan) Big Cistercian house with substantial surviving remains, including those of Abbot Leyshon Thomas' fine new house of the early 16c, later incorporated in Sir John Herbert's late 16c mansion. (OR)

216 Netley Abbey (Hampshire) A Cistercian abbey of mid 13c foundation, never rich and suppressed with the lesser houses in 1536; converted at that time into a mansion for Sir William Paulet, with the church re-used as Paulet's hall and kitchen and the former refectory demolished to make way for his gatehouse. (OR)

217 Newbury Church (Berkshire) Big early 16c urban church, rebuilt largely at the expense (or at least on the initiative) of John Smallwood, known as 'Jack of Newbury', a wealthy clothier; Smallwood's brass is preserved here still, as are his initials on the contemporary nave roof.

218 Newent (Gloucestershire) Some remains, at the Old Court, of the former priory cell of the Norman abbey at Cormeilles, next to the church. (NO)

219 Nonsuch Palace (Surrey) Only the site of Henry VIII's palace has been preserved, in Nonsuch Park adjoining Cherry Orchard Farm; the site was excavated in 1959–60.

220 Norwich Blackfriars (Norfolk) Rare survival of a great Dominican friary church, together with the south range of the cloister, all recently extensively restored. Not far away, STRANGERS' HALL is a big multi-period town-house of courtyard plan, its mid 15c hall rebuilt in the 1530s for Nicholas Sotherton in the grand manorial style. (OR)

221 Nostell Priory (West Yorkshire) Built for Sir Rowland Winn in the 1730s near the remains of the former Augustinian priory, which have since entirely disappeared. (OR)

222 Nunney Castle (Somerset) A tower-house in the French style, with towers at the angles and a surrounding moat, built for Sir John de la Mare in the 1370s; improbable but attractive situation in the middle of the village. (OR)

Old Bell Farm, Harrietsham See **Harrietsham**.

Ormond Castle, Tipperary See **Carrick-on-Suir**.

223 Otham: Stoneacre (Kent) Much altered during the restoration and extensions of the 1920s, but still has the 15c hall, now back to its full height on the removal of a 16c floor. (NT, OR) In the same village, SYNYARDS (private) is a fine example, easy to study from the street, of a scarcely altered 16c Wealden house.

224 Ottery St Mary Church (Devon) A former 'alien' church of Rouen Cathedral, bought by Bishop Grandisson of Exeter in 1335 and refounded as a collegiate chantry; some fine Decorated monuments and other work of the 14c, with the Dorset Aisle (c.1520) preserving a remarkable fan vault.

225 Oxburgh Hall (Norfolk) Extensively rebuilt in the 19c, with interiors mostly of that period, but keeps the handsome northern show front of the 1480s with its noble central gatehouse and complex brickwork; note the vestigial nature of the 'defences' here, of which the moat is the principal element. (NT, OR) At the neighbouring, largely ruined, OXBOROUGH CHURCH, the surviving Bedingfeld chantry chapel preserves two fine terracotta monuments, both of the 1520s, with much Renaissance ornament. A remarkable and most satisfying group.

226 Pamber Church (Hampshire) Important fragment of a former alien priory church, with choir (early 13c) and crossing (late 12c), but lacking transepts, side chapels and nave; a dependency of the Norman Cerisy-la-Forêt until suppressed with the other alien priories in 1414, after which it came to Queen's College (Oxford) by way of Henry VI's Eton.

227 Paston Church (Norfolk) A thatched 14c church, nicely set; notable chiefly for its two contrasting Nicholas Stone monuments to Dame Katherine Paston (d.1628), in comfortable but traditional reclining effigy, and Sir Edmund Paston (d.1632), whose urn, Tuscan columns, and pediment are in the most austere classical taste. Just west of the church, PASTON BARN (private) is late 16c, but probably incorporates earlier work.

Paycocke's House, Coggeshall See **Coggeshall**.

228 Pendennis Castle (Cornwall) Built in two major stages, the first being Henry VIII's artillery tower (circular with multangular surrounding curtain) of the early 1540s, the second being a refortification in the Italian manner in 1598, with low-lying ramparts well-equipped with flankers. (OR)

229 Penrith Castle (Cumbria) A big four-square castle of the late 1390s, badly knocked about but preserving evidence of residential accommodation and strong towers; machicolated parapets in the French style have left prominent brackets on the south and west walls. (OR)

230 Penshurst Place (Kent) Built initially for Sir John de Pulteney in the 1340s, and one of the most important surviving domestic buildings of that period, notable especially for its giant great hall, still equipped with its original roof; important also is the handsome late 16c long gallery, with its Renaissance panelling intact. (OR)

231 Peterborough Cathedral (Cambridgeshire) Of the abbot's lodgings of this former major Benedictine abbey, only the great 15c gatehouse survives intact to give some idea of the scale of a once princely residence.

Pinkie House, Musselburgh See **Musselburgh**.

232 Pitmedden Garden (Grampian) Fine formal walled garden of the Restoration period, established by Sir Alexander Seton in 1675 and designed in the contemporary French style. (NTS, OR)

233 Polesworth Church (Warwickshire) A former Benedictine nunnery church which preserves original features but is itself no more than a fragment; the nuns' gatehouse has also survived.

234 Portland Castle (Dorset) Built in c.1540 as one of the elements of Henry VIII's coastal defence programme; seaward-facing half-moon battery, with a residential tower to the rear. (OR)

235 Portumna Castle (Co. Galway) A sizable strong-house, rectangular in plan with towers at the angles, built for Richard Burke, Earl of Clanrickarde, in the early 17c; burnt in 1826 and never repaired, but still an impressive shell with many original Renaissance features, including doorcases and gables. (OR)

236 Powderham Castle (Devon) So much transformed in the 18c, and again in the 19c, that there is little left here of the major fortress of the late medieval Courtenay earls of Devon. (OR)

237 Powis Castle (Powys) Surviving drum towers of an ambitious c.1300 rebuilding, but chiefly notable now for its post-medieval interiors, especially the long gallery (1592–3) and the staircase and state bedchamber of the late 1660s and 1670s. Noble setting. (NT, OR)

238 Preston: Hamilton House (Lothian) A big merchant's house of the late 1620s, with crow-step gables, dormers and turrets. (NTS, OA) Rising behind it, PRESTON TOWER is a 15c tower-house of conventional plan to which, at parapet level, a two-storeyed Renaissance pavilion was added in the 1620s. Across the road, NORTHFIELD HOUSE (1611) has many good contemporary features, both inside and out.

Priory Cottages, Steventon See **Steventon**.

Queen's House, Greenwich See **Greenwich**.

239 Raby Castle (Co. Durham) Spectacular but largely 19c fortress of the Nevill earls of Westmorland, of which the best remaining late 14c feature is the big kitchen, complete with simple vault and original louvre; lavish 19c interiors and splendid park setting. (OR)

240 Raglan Castle (Gwent) Built for William Herbert, Earl of Pembroke, in the 1460s, with boldly machicolated towers in the French manner, gunports, and a strong-tower, or keep, separated off from the rest of the castle by its own moat; an impressive assemblage, strikingly placed. (OR)

241 Ramsey Abbey Gatehouse (Cambridgeshire) A fragment only of the great gatehouse of c.1500, most of which was removed after the Suppression to Hinchingbrooke House. (NT, OR) Just to the north-east, across the green, the PARISH CHURCH incorporates a late 12c hospital with hall (nave) and chapel (chancel); this exceedingly rare survival should not be missed.

242 Ravenscraig Castle (Fife) A pioneering coastal artillery fort, begun in 1460; a central rectangular gatehouse block, with terminal tower-houses rounded towards the water, built for James II's queen, Mary of Gueldres (d.1463). (OR)

243 Raynham Hall (Norfolk) Among the few country houses attributable to Inigo Jones, and

even so not certainly by the king's Surveyor; built of brick in the Netherlands manner, with gables also showing that influence, and datable to the early 1620s; interior remodelled in 1720–30; private, but plainly visible from the road.

Red Lion, Southampton See **Southampton**.

244 Roche Abbey (South Yorkshire) A Cistercian house founded in 1147 and suppressed among the greater houses in 1538, when its last days featured a site auction; fine range of surviving walls, although mainly at foundation level, and a pleasant remote site, characteristic of the Order, delightfully watered by bubbling streams. (OR)

245 Rosserk Friary (Co. Mayo) A well-preserved Franciscan (probably Observant) friary, with a fine complete set of late 15c buildings, in a remote estuarine setting. (OR)

246 Ross Errilly Friary (Co. Galway) A big rural Franciscan house, founded in c.1351, with buildings mainly of the late 15c, still in very fair condition; notice the big southward extension, by double transepts, of the church. (OR)

247 Rosslyn Chapel (Lothian) The choir only of an unfinished collegiate church, originally intended to be cruciform; founded by William Sinclair, Earl of Orkney, in 1450, and outstanding for the unprecedented elaboration of its decorative stonework, especially complex in the area of the eastern terminal chapels. (OR)

248 Rothesay Castle (Strathclyde) A 13c stone castle of unusual circular plan, with towers on the curtain; supplied in the early 16c with a bold projecting forework; residential accommodation on its upper floors. (OR)

249 Rufford Old Hall (Lancashire) Built in the 15c, probably for Sir Thomas Hesketh (d.1458); of his date, a fine surviving timber-built great hall, with richly carved movable screen at the lower (service) end, and canopy and bay at the upper; both service and solar ranges have since been lost. (NT, OR)

250 Ruperra Castle (Mid Gla-

morgan) Built in the 1620s as a sham 'castle' in the Spenserian vein for Sir Thomas Morgan; square with circular corner towers (cf Lulworth Castle). (NO)

251 Rushton Triangular Lodge (Northamptonshire) Built for Sir Thomas Tresham in the 1590s to a triangular plan (cf the cross of Lyveden New Bield and the triangle of Longford Castle) signifying the Trinity; much esoteric Catholic symbolism on its facade. (OR)

252 St Albans: Church of St Michael (Hertfordshire) Basically Anglo-Saxon in fabric, re-using Roman brick from the neighbouring Verulamium in its window arches, but with considerable later rebuilding, including a late 19c tower and west end; notable especially for the wall monument to Sir Francis Bacon (d.1626), in life-like effigy, as if taking a nap in his chair.

St George's Guildhall, King's Lynn See **King's Lynn**.

St Mary's Abbey, York See **York**.

253 St Mawes Castle (Cornwall) Facing Pendennis Castle across Carrick Roads at the mouth of the Fal estuary, and built like Pendennis in the early 1540s as part of Henry VIII's coastal defence programme; central tower with semi-circular bastions in a fine pattern of interlocking circles; external commemorative inscriptions praising the king and Prince Edward, his heir. (OR)

254 St Michael's Mount (Cornwall) Strikingly situated former alien priory of the Norman Benedictines of Mont St Michel, granted, following its suppression in 1414, to the Bridgettine nuns of Syon; only the priory church and refectory, much transformed, have survived successive later rebuildings, particularly extensive in the 1870s. (NT, OR)

255 St Osyth's Priory (Essex) A formerly rich Augustinian priory of which important surviving features include the great late 15c residential gatehouse, Abbot Vintoner's early 16c hall and oriel, and some high-quality 13c vaulting in the present chapel; Lord D'Arcy's tall viewpoint tower of the 1550s is among the more extravagant examples of its class. (OR)

St Radegund's Priory, Cambridge See **Cambridge**.

256 Saltwood Castle (Kent) Former castle of the archbishops of Canterbury, of which the most remarkable survival is now the great residential gatehouse completed for Archbishop Courtenay (d.1396) in the late 14c; other medieval buildings include two halls, mural towers and much of the original stone curtain. (OA)

257 Samlesbury Hall (Lancashire) Timber-framed manor-house of mixed date, with spacious 15c hall later equipped with a big polygonal bay and richly carved movable screen, both tampered with but basically early 16c. (OR)

258 Scotney Castle (Kent) Built for Roger Ashburnham, in the late 1370s, in the French style with elaborate water defences, barbican-protected approaches, and machicolated angle-towers (only one of which survives); very pretty, well-gardened situation. (NT, OR)

259 Selby Abbey (North Yorkshire) Now the parish church but formerly the monastic church of a rich Benedictine community, with high-quality 12c work in the nave and an especially handsome early 14c choir and presbytery; all beautifully maintained, though the roofs are modern throughout.

260 Seton Church (Lothian) The surviving choir, crossing and transepts of a big former collegiate church, rebuilt in the late 15c and early 16c as the family chantry of the Seton lords; handsome vaulted presbytery, but nave lost; substantial remains, to the southwest, of the 15c prebendaries' lodgings. (OR)

261 Sheriff Hutton (North Yorkshire) Big rectangular castle with corner towers, similar in plan to Bolton Castle, built by the Nevills, John and Ralph, in the late 14c and early 15c; in considerable decay and not open to the public, but

clearly visible from the adjoining footpath.

262 Sissinghurst Castle (Kent) Late 15c entrance range with central gatehouse of the 1530s; viewpoint tower of the 1560s, originally the inner gatehouse of Sir Richard Baker's now vanished Elizabethan courtyard mansion; ravishing modern garden setting. (NT, OR)

263 Sizergh Castle (Cumbria) Major mid 14c tower-house, extended in the 15c and again in the 1560s; some good Elizabethan interiors with fine chimney-pieces and plasterwork; however, the best panelling (from the Inlaid Chamber) is now in the Victoria and Albert Museum. (NT, OR)

264 Smallhythe Place (Kent) Early 16c farmhouse in which the hall, although still central with chamber blocks at each end, was floored over from the start, having its own big brick chimney-stack. (NT, OR) Just up the road to the north, the PRIEST'S HOUSE is a neat little timber-framed building of much the same date, with an interesting brick CHURCH (1516–17) just beyond it, its gables finished with crow-steps in the Flemish manner.

265 Snowshill Manor (Gloucestershire) A Cotswold house much altered over the years, with good features of later periods; of the earlier, the most important survival is clear evidence of the flooring over of the hall (originally open to the roof) in *c*.1600, with the insertion of new fireplaces at that date. (NT, OR)

266 Soar, Old (Plaxtol, Kent) The solar block of a manor-house of *c*.1290; big first-floor chamber, preserving its original roof, with adjoining chapel and garderobe, both at the same level; vaulted basement store; a brick farmhouse of the 18c now occupies the site of the former hall. (NT, OR)

267 Southampton: Red Lion (Hampshire) A fine example of a 15c town-house (now in use as a pub), running back from the street, with an open central hall and chamber blocks at each end; early 16c chimney-stack inserted at the east end of the hall, also serving the

chamber beyond; good heraldic fireplaces of that date.

268 Speke Hall (Merseyside) Much restored at various dates, but an important example of 16c timber-framing with many fine features, including good interiors (panelling and plasterwork) of the 1560s and early 17c; note especially the mid 16c great wainscot in the hall with its handsome Renaissance detail, the stucco ornament of the great parlour ceiling, the lavish ornamental effects of the external timber-work, and the early 17c moat-bridge and garden gate, both very much in the prevailing Northern Renaissance taste. (NT, OR)

Spon Street, Coventry See **Coventry**.

269 Springhill (Co. Londonderry) Orderly and symmetrically-planned late 17c manor-house, subsequently much rebuilt but retaining the fronting service wings, in the French style, of Scottish models like the contemporary updating of Traquair House (Borders). (NT, OR)

270 Staindrop Church (Co. Durham) The collegiate chantry of the Nevill earls of Westmorland, visible from their castle at Raby; raised to collegiate status in the early 15c and preserving a full set of late medieval choir-stalls; also high-quality family monuments of the 14–16c.

271 Steventon: Priory Cottages (Oxfordshire) Buildings associated with a former priory cell of the Norman Benedictines of Bec Abbey, although neither the surviving hall nor solar belong to that period of monastic use; pretty timber-framing of the 14–16c. (NT, OR)

272 Stirling Castle (Central) A major royal fortress with important features, especially of the 16c, including the magnificent great hall (*c*.1500) and Renaissance palace (*c*.1540), with the French Spur (1550s) as an example of advanced artillery engineering; note also the earthworks of a fine formal garden (the 'King's Knot') on the plain below, dating to the 1620s and clearly visible from the palace defences. (OR)

273 Stoke-sub-Hamdon: Beauchamp Chantry (Somerset) A collegiate chantry which preserves, most exceptionally, the domestic buildings of the chaplains, including their late medieval hall and other domestic quarters, courtyard (with big arched entrance from the street), and barns; a group of high importance and great charm. (NT, OR) The pleasant PARISH CHURCH has several good features, including a fine 15c panelled nave roof.

Stoneacre, Otham See **Otham**.

274 Sudeley Castle (Gloucestershire) Rebuilt in the mid 15c for Ralph Boteler, Treasurer of England (1443–6) and a former war captain, the main outline of the inner court being Boteler's, as is the great barn and chapel; remodelled for Richard of Gloucester (later Richard III), who added the now ruined presence chamber on the east side of the inner court; the Elizabethan outer court, in the style of a college quadrangle, was built for Edmund Brydges, second Lord Chandos. (OR)

275 Sutton Place (Surrey) One of the major pioneering brick and terracotta houses of Henry VIII's courtiers, built in the late 1520s for Sir Richard Weston; a courtyard mansion which has lost its entrance range but preserves Weston's central hall, with solar and service wings; much moulded terracotta ornament in the Renaissance style; lavishly maintained. (OA)

276 Swaffham Church (Norfolk) Rebuilt almost completely in the second half of the 15c at the expense of the wealthier parishioners, led by their rector, John Botright (d.1474); over-restored and refurnished, but keeps its magnificent double-hammerbeam nave roof; the Guild of St John Baptist was one of the parish fraternities associated with the rebuilding, others being the Guilds of Corpus Christi and the Holy Trinity.

277 Swavesey Church (Cambridgeshire) A handsome parish church of the 14–15c, with good 15c benches and other furnishings; in the field to the north, the remains (earthworks only) of the former PRIORY, a dependency of St Serge

(Angers) assigned on its suppression in the early 15c to the support of the Carthusians of Coventry.

278 Syon House (London) The present house, of the 16–18c, replaces a Bridgettine nunnery founded in 1415 and moved to its Syon site in 1431; some slight remains, including vaulted undercrofts, of the nuns' claustral ranges. (OR)

279 Tanfield, West (North Yorkshire) The so-called 'Marmion Tower' is the 15c gatehouse (rewindowed in the later 16c) of the former castle west of the parish church; nothing else survives of the castle, the gatehouse being easily studied from the road. (NO) In the CHURCH, the crenellated iron hearse of Sir John Marmion's late 14c tomb-chest, complete with candle prickets, is a rare survival.

280 Tantallon Castle (Lothian) Big coastal castle of the Douglas earls, on a promontory site fortified in the 1370s with a great curtain wall linking three tower-houses, the central and largest of which also served as a gatehouse; refortified in the mid 16c against artillery, the surviving earthworks including a triangular ravelin. (OR)

281 Tattershall Castle (Lincolnshire) Major brick tower-house of the second quarter of the 15c, built for Ralph Lord Cromwell (d.1456), Treasurer of England (1433–43). (NT, OR). Apart from the moats, scarcely anything else remains of Cromwell's castle here, though his COLLEGIATE CHURCH, built by his executors after his death, remains in use by the parish, subdivided still by the great stone screen which separated the chaplains' choir from the parochial nave; a highly important and strikingly handsome group.

282 Tenby: Tudor Merchant's House (Dyfed) A small but comfortable 15c stone town-house, with a hall on the ground floor and two levels of chambers above. (NT, OR)

283 Tewkesbury: 34–50 Church Street (Gloucestershire) A speculative development of shops and living quarters, originally twenty-four units; c.1450. (NO)

284 Thame Abbey (Oxfordshire) A Cistercian abbey, suppressed in 1539, remains of which have been preserved at the largely 18c Thame Park (private), the most important being Abbot King's lodgings in the tower he built for himself in the 1530s; fine Renaissance interiors of that date, with intact panelling and carved friezes, especially complete in the abbot's parlour. (NO)

285 Thaxted Church (Essex) Exceptionally handsome and largely 15c parish church, with many good features including a fine set of contemporary roofs; the church owed much of its present glory to the cutlers of Thaxted, whose GUILDHALL (just down the hill) is also of the 15c, being jettied on two stages above an open ground floor.

285 Theobalds (Hertfordshire) Nothing now remains of William Cecil's huge mansion, though the site is known and the great staircase survives at Herstmonceux Castle (East Sussex).

287 Thirsk Church (North Yorkshire) Rebuilt, with an especially lavish exterior, in the 15c, probably beginning with Robert Thirsk's endowment here of a chantry in 1419; over-restored internally, though the nave roof is genuine late 15c.

288 Thorington Hall (Suffolk) A substantial and comfortable house of the Great Rebuilding period, mainly of c.1600 with 18c additions; fine original brick chimney-stacks. (NT, OA)

289 Thornbury Castle (Avon) The incomplete fortress-palace of Edward Stafford, Duke of Buckingham, executed in 1521; the imposing west front was only half built when Stafford died, but his lodgings in the south range, although much restored in the 1850s, preserve their spectacular polygonal bays; impressive also is the size of the great outer court, round which Stafford's servants and the gentlemen of his affinity were to have had their quarters; private, but open as a restaurant.

290 Thornton Abbey (Humberside) The most remarkable surviving feature of this rich Augustinian abbey is the great fortified gatehouse of 1382, as much a gesture as a fortification, peppered everywhere with arrow-loops; the high quality of the c.1300 blind tracery on the fragmentary chapter-house walls is some indication of the wealth of what has since been lost in the monastic buildings at the other (eastern) end of the great court. (OR)

291 Threave Castle (Dumfries and Galloway) A very substantial rectangular tower-house, built for Archibald the Grim in the 1370s and 1380s, in which the big vaulted kitchen, with basement below, supports a great hall and chambers above; refortified in the mid 15c with a low surrounding curtain wall and angle towers, pierced for guns; beautiful isolated location. (OR)

292 Titchfield Abbey (Hampshire) A Premonstratensian house suppressed in 1537 and then immediately converted into a mansion for its new owner, Thomas Wriothesley; the impressive 16c gatehouse, cutting through the body of the canons' former church, is Wriothesley's work, as are other fragments in the claustral ranges north of the church. (OR)

293 Tiverton Castle (Devon) A big eastern gatehouse and some towers remain of this former Courtenay castle, once a major stronghold of the late medieval earls of Devon. (OR) Immediately to the south, the handsome 15c PARISH CHURCH is notable especially for the lavish chantry chapel of John Greenway (1517), next to the south porch rebuilt by Greenway at the same time.

294 Tolquhon Castle (Grampian) 15c tower-house converted into a courtyard mansion by William Forbes in 1584–9, complete with a new gatehouse (protected by gun-ports), a long gallery and other apartments at first-floor level, over a kitchen, service-rooms and stores. (OR) In the kirkyard at TARVES, William Forbes' monument is a splendid Renaissance piece, with much classical detail reflecting the scholarly interests of the laird.

295 Tong Church (Shropshire) Big and important collegiate church, rebuilt entirely after the founding of the college in 1410, with a fine set of 15–16c monuments, principally to the Vernons; also a full complement of choir-stalls and, in the Vernon Chapel of c.1515, a good example of a chantry chapel, nearing the end of the chantry tradition.

296 Traquair House (Borders) A major tower-house of mixed periods, chiefly important for the delightful c.1530 mural in the 'Museum Room' and for the low post-Restoration service wings, added in 1660–80 to create a formal forecourt in the French style, as at the contemporary Springhill (Co. Londonderry). (OR)

Treasurer's House, Martock See **Martock**.

297 Trerice (Cornwall) Splendidly intact c.1570 stone show-front, with Renaissance details on the gables; the great hall, still traditionally sited to one side of the entrance and breaking the symmetry of the facade with its huge window, preserves its original ceiling and chimney-piece, as does the drawing room (former great chamber). (NT, OR)

Tudor Merchant's House, Tenby See **Tenby**.

298 Tully Castle (Co. Fermanagh) Regularly-planned plantation castle, built in the 1610s for the Scottish planter, Sir John Hume; rectangular fort-like bawn, with square towers at the angles; on the north wall, a residential range, having a kitchen on the ground floor, with hall and chamber above; fine views over the water. (OR)

299 Turton Tower (Lancashire) 15c tower-house entirely remodelled in c.1596 when the tower itself was heightened and new floors inserted to create three substantial chambers, the top serving as a viewpoint; when the tower was raised, the earlier 16c northeast range was also rebuilt, this being the date too of the fine staircase; considerable Victorian reworking throughout. (OR)

300 Ulverscroft Priory (Leicestershire) The church tower and other fragmentary remains of a small

Augustinian house, isolated and poor, once defended by a substantial moat and ditch; a farmhouse (private) now occupies the southeast angle of the former cloister. (NO)

301 Upnor Castle (Kent) A coastal defence battery, designed to command the Medway and built by Sir Richard Lee in 1559–67; provided in 1599–1601 with landward defences (curtain wall and gatehouse) but principally intended as a platform for artillery against ships. (OR)

302 Valle Crucis Abbey (Clwyd) Cistercian abbey founded in 1201 and much modified internally before its suppression in 1538, these changes including the abandonment of the nave and the transformation of the east claustral range, over the chapter-house, into fine lodgings for the abbot. (OR)

303 Vyne, The (Hampshire) Built in the 1520s for William Lord Sandys, a prominent courtier who was also the rebuilder of Mottisfont; important features of that date include the pioneering long gallery, complete with original panelling, and the large chapel with its contemporary furnishings and high-quality Flemish-style glass; externally much altered and disguised by a major 18c rebuilding, but still preserves John Webb's classical portico of the 1660s. (NT, OR)

304 Walmer Castle (Kent) Built in 1539–40 as one of Henry VIII's major coastal defence works, with a big central artillery tower protected by four semicircular bastions; much altered in the 18c, but well-kept and preserving many original features, comparable to the fighting arrangements of the neighbouring Henrician fort at Deal. (OR)

305 Walsingham Friary (Norfolk) Founded in 1347 and, by English standards, an exceptionally complete set of Franciscan buildings; the big range with tall surviving gables was probably the guest-house, west of the cloister, with the remains of the church to the north and another small cloister to the south; private, but easily seen from the road.

306 Wardour Castle, Old (Wiltshire) A large and complex tower-house of polygonal plan with an open central court, built for John Lord Lovel in the 1390s and clearly much influenced by French castles of identical date; refurbished by Robert Smythson, the noted architect, in the late 16c, at which time Wardour acquired its handsome surviving Renaissance details, especially prominent on the entrance front. (OR)

307 Wark Castle (Northumberland) Scanty remains of a once important royal fortress, dating back originally to the early 12c and refortified by Henry VIII for artillery.

308 Warkworth Castle (Northumberland) A major fortress of the Percy earls of Northumberland; multi-period defences, but notable especially for its great late 14c tower-house, at the north end of the enclosure, and contemporary heraldic panels. (OR)

309 Warwick Castle (Warwickshire) Domestic range extensively rebuilt in the 19c, but the castle has kept its fine late 14c eastern show-front, with central gatehouse (barbican-protected) and tall corner towers (Caesar's Tower and Guy's Tower), each holding a tier of individual lodgings. (OR) At the PARISH CHURCH, the remarkable BEAUCHAMP CHAPEL, built in the 1440s and 1450s at great cost, holds the monument of Richard Beauchamp, comparable in quality to the finest Burgundian tombs of the same period.

310 Watton Priory (Humberside) Formerly a Gilbertine double house of nuns and canons, of which only earthworks remain, with a surviving 15c prior's lodging (private), the best feature of which is a fine oriel. (NO)

311 Westminster Abbey (London) The specially favoured building project of Henry III, of which the nave was finally completed in the 15c; equipped with a great chantry chapel by Henry VII, whose tomb (by Pietro Torrigiani)

is a major monument of the northern Early Renaissance. Across the road, WESTMINSTER HALL, although much rebuilt, preserves a late 14c hammerbeam roof of great distinction.

312 Westwood Manor (Wiltshire) A late 15c manor-house, modified extensively in the 16c and early 17c, when the hall was floored over and some good decorative plasterwork installed; a modest house, but of great charm and nicely set. (NT, OR)

313 Whitby Abbey (North Yorkshire) Once among the greater Benedictine houses, but now preserving little more than the skeleton of its church, of which the most notable survival is the high-quality 13c presbytery. (OR)

314 Whitehall: Banqueting House (London) A pioneering hall in the Palladian manner, designed and built in 1619–22 by Inigo Jones for James I's palace at Whitehall; important painted ceiling by Rubens. (OR)

315 Wilderhope Manor (Shropshire) Built in the 1580s for Francis Smallman, and still very traditional in plan, with central hall and flanking chamber blocks, even retaining its original screens passage arrangements; the hall, though, is of one storey only, with a big chamber above and with substantial oak newel stairs; unspoilt isolated setting. (NT, OR)

316 Wilton House (Wiltshire) The major country house of the Herbert earls of Pembroke, partly destroyed by fire in 1647 and rebuilt soon afterwards by John Webb with lavish palatial interiors (the Double Cube Room etc) usually attributed to Inigo Jones. (OR)

317 Winchcombe Abbey (Gloucestershire) Very little remains of this formerly great Benedictine house (NO), though the handsome PARISH CHURCH, immediately to the west of the abbey site, owed its 1460s rebuilding at least partly to the generosity of the abbot.

318 Windsor Castle (Berkshire) Substantially rebuilt in the 19c, but preserves the plan of Edward III's major fortress and some fragments

of his original buildings, including the shell of his great tower; the ST GEORGE'S CHAPEL is an early Tudor rebuilding, still Gothic in flavour but with furnishings which belong rather to the Renaissance. (OR)

319 Wingfield Castle (Suffolk) Built for Michael de la Pole in the late 14c, to which period belongs the southern show-front, with tall central gatehouse and polygonal corner towers, all surrounded by a water-filled moat. To the east, the PARISH CHURCH, collegiate from 1362, has fine monuments and a nice set of stalls, while at WINGFIELD COLLEGE, immediately to the south of the church, buildings (including a hall) of the 14–16c have been preserved. Altogether, a group of high importance. (OO)

320 Wingfield Manor, South (Derbyshire) The impressive remains of Ralph Lord Cromwell's double-courtyard mansion, built in 1439–56, including the great hall and High Tower. (OR)

321 Wolfeton House (Dorset) Battered fragment of a much larger house, but has features of great importance, including the 'festive' work (early 16c) on the south facade and the purely classical great staircase of the late 16c, much in advance of its time. (OR)

322 Wollaton Hall (Nottinghamshire) Much restored externally and internally purged of ornament, but still in substance the fantastic prodigy house of Sir Francis Willoughby, built between 1580 and 1588; designed by Robert Smythson in a mixture of French and Flemish styles; note the retention of the great hall, although in the centre of the building and with a big prospect chamber overlying it. (OR)

323 Wootton Wawen Church (Warwickshire) A former Anglo-Saxon minster church which became the nucleus of a dependent priory of the Norman Conches Abbey, the patronage subsequently coming (after the 15c suppression of the priory) to King's College, Cambridge.

324 Worcester: The Greyfriars (Hereford and Worcester) Handsome late 15c timber-framed building with later additions, thought to have been the guest-house of the Franciscan friary suppressed in 1538. (NT, OR)

325 Worksop Church (Nottinghamshire) A former Augustinian priory church on a big scale, especially notable for its 13c Lady Chapel; also surviving is the substantial 14c priory gatehouse, being one of the larger examples of its kind.

326 Wymington Church (Bedfordshire) A minor but pretty late 14c parish church, rebuilt by John Curtyes (d.1391), a wool-merchant and Mayor of the Staple of Calais, whose tomb (between chancel and south chapel) is still prominent there.

327 Wymondham Church (Norfolk) A great former Benedictine church, taken over by the parish in 1538 but already earlier the occasion for competitive building, as the townsmen embellished their parochial nave and built their enormous west tower; fine 15c roofs and (south of the high altar) a handsome terracotta monument of c.1525, with much Early Renaissance ornament.

328 Yarmouth Castle (Isle of Wight) One of the smaller forts of Henry VIII's coastal defence programme, but finished in 1547, later than the others, and incorporating a single arrow-head bastion on the southeast angle, very much in the Italian tradition. (OR)

329 York: St Mary's Abbey (North Yorkshire) The fragmentary remains, chiefly of the church and enclosure walls, of an important Benedictine house, dissolved in 1539 and formerly one of the richest in the kingdom. (OR)

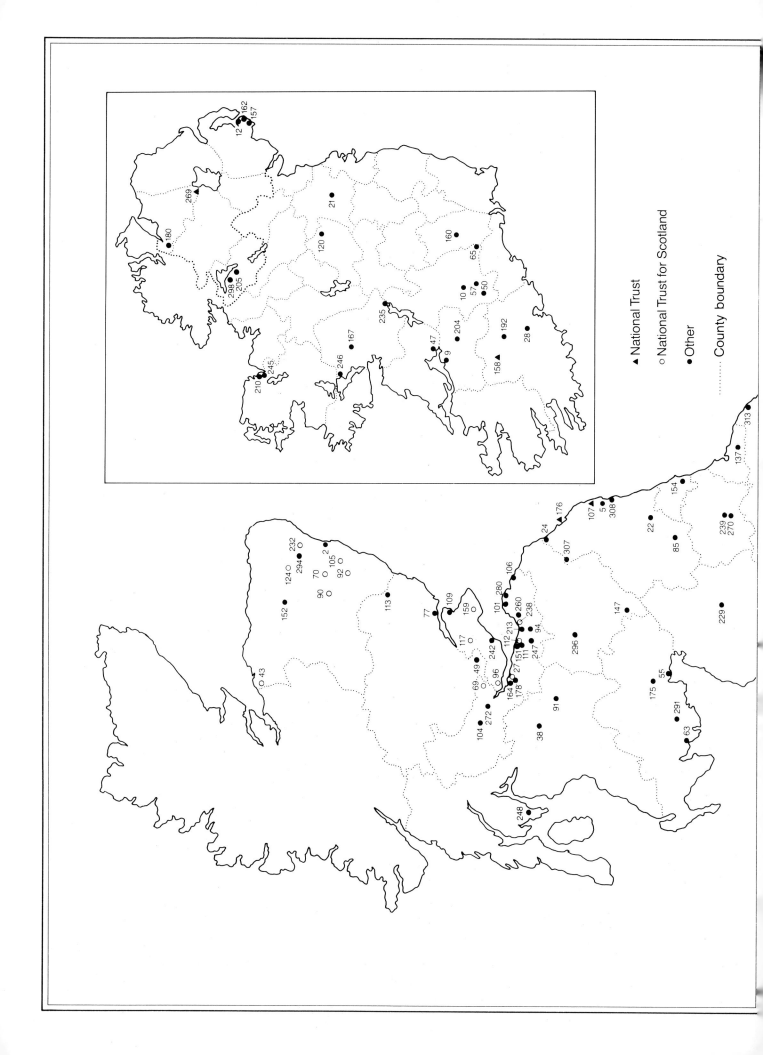

National Trust

National Trust for Scotland

Other

County boundary

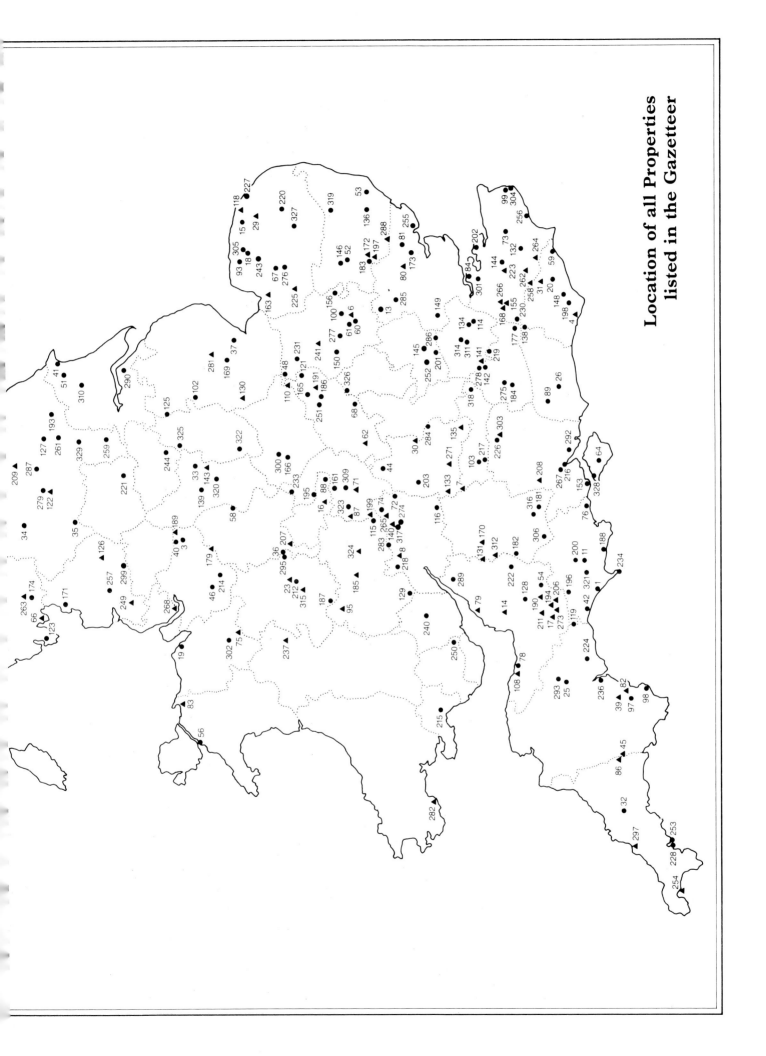

Location of all Properties
listed in the Gazetteer

Glossary

Alien priory a religious house, usually small and often no more than a cell or estate centre, owing allegiance to a monastery outside Britain.

Aisle the division of a church which, behind an arcade, adds space to the chancel or nave.

Augustan from Augustus Caesar (d.14); descriptive of a period of particular classical refinement in literature and the arts, often applied (as Augustan Age) to the reign of Queen Anne (1702–14).

Augustinians communities of priests, known individually as canons, who lived a monastic (regular) life, adopting the Rule of St Augustine; also known as Austin canons.

Austin friars congregations of hermits brought together in 1256 under the Rule of St Augustine; also known as the Hermit Friars of St Augustine.

Baluster a short pillar or post, usually in a series supporting a rail, together comprising a balustrade.

Barbican the outwork, sometimes itself a gate, protecting the entrance of a castle.

Barrel vault a vault, usually plain and of semicircular section.

Bartisan a turret corbelled out at roof level from the top of a tower.

Bastion a projection from the line of a rampart or wall, intended to provide covering fire; hence 'angle-bastion', 'arrow-head bastion', 'demi-bastion' etc.

Bawn the walled enclosure, often of regular plan, attached to a tower-house.

Belvedere a viewpoint chamber, on the top of a building or a natural eminence.

Benedictines monks observing the Rule of St Benedict; also known as 'black monks' from the colour of their habits.

Blind arcade a line of arches against a blank wall, put there for decorative effect.

Boss a raised and carved projection, usually round or shield-shaped, at the intersection of vaulting ribs.

Bridgettines a reforming order of nuns, founded by Bridget of Sweden in the mid fourteenth century and introduced to England at Syon Abbey on the invitation of Henry V.

Canon in the form 'regular canon', a priest living in a community bound by a common Rule, usually that of St Augustine.

Canopy a cover (suspended or projecting) over a dais or rood – as in 'canopy of honour' – or a choir-stall.

Caponier a covered and loopholed passage, crossing the base of a dry moat at right angles and commanding it with fire in both directions.

Carmelites originally the twelfth-century Order of Our Lady of Mount Carmel, reorganized in the thirteenth century as friars (the 'white friars').

Carthusians founded by St Bruno in 1084 as a contemplative order of monks, bound to silence.

Caryatid a carved human figure used as a substitute for a column.

Celestines a reformed branch of the Benedictine Order, founded in the mid thirteenth century.

Chancel the eastern division of a church, usually reserved to the clergy.

Chantry the endowment of a priest, or college of priests (as in 'collegiate chantry'), to sing masses for the soul of the founder.

Choir the division of a church, between nave and presbytery, fitted with stalls (hence 'choir-stalls') for the monks.

Cistercians reformed Benedictines, also known as 'white monks', first established at Cîteaux in 1098 and greatly expanded as an order under the leadership of the twelfth-century St Bernard.

Clerestory a line of windows, towards the top of a wall and usually over an arcade, helping to light a church interior.

Cloister an open space, surrounded by a roofed passage, provided at a monastery for exercise and study.

Cluniacs monks of the great 'family' of Cluny Abbey (Burgundy), founded in 909 and later the nucleus of a far-flung order.

Coffered ornamented, as in a ceiling, with sunken decorative panels.

Compline the last of the daily monastic hours, celebrated at sunset or around six.

Conventuals Franciscan friars who observed a mitigated Rule, as distinct from the more fundamental Observants.

Corbel a projection or bracket, often decoratively carved, supporting a beam or other structure.

Cornice a projecting ornamental moulding, used to finish off the top of a wall.

Coved given a concave section, as in a ceiling or individual moulding.

Crenellations battlements.

Crossing the space, in a cruciform church, where nave, transepts and chancel intersect.

Crown-post the central post, joining tie-beam with collar-beam, in a timber crown-post roof.

Crow-stepped stepped like a stair, as in a 'crow-stepped' gable.

Curtain a fortified free-standing enclosure wall between corner or interval towers.

Cusped furnished with projecting points between arcs in a typical Gothic ornament.

Dado the lower portion of a wall or screen, as distinguished by a moulding at waist height.

Dominicans an order of preaching friars, also known as the 'black friars', founded by St Dominic in the early thirteenth century.

Embrasure a splayed opening, usually a gunport of some kind.

Entablature the upper part (architrave, frieze, and cornice) of a classical order, next above the columns and their capitals.

Escutcheon a shield carrying armorial bearings.

Fan vault a vault of inverted concave-sided semi-cones, each of them ribbed like a fan.

Fenestrate equip with windows.

Flanker an embrasure commanding the face of a rampart from a recess in the flank of a bastion.

Flushwork knapped flint and dressed stone used together to form a decorative pattern.

Flying arch a single linking arch, as between the turrets of a tower-house.

Forework a forward defence, by rampart or wall, of a castle, usually giving extra protection to the main entrance.

Franciscans an order of friars, founded by St Francis in 1209, and vowed to corporate poverty; also known as Friars Minor or 'grey friars'.

Friar a priest and member of one of the Mendicant orders, usually with a special training in preaching.

Frieze a decorative band towards the top of a wall, under the cornice.

Garderobe a privy or lavatory.

Gilbertines a double order of nuns and canons, founded in the early 1130s by Gilbert of Sempringham and originally much influenced by the Cistercians.

Glacis a sloping bank, usually steep and designed to be swept by crossfire.

Groundplat a plan.

Hammerbeam the projecting horizontal bracket which supports the arched braces and struts of a late medieval 'hammerbeam' roof.

Hearse an iron frame protecting and holding candles over an effigy.

Humanist a scholar of the Renaissance period who interested himself in the humanities (the study of Greek and Roman antiquities).

Jamb the side of a window or door.

Jetty the overhang, supported on projecting floor joists, of the upper storey of a timber building.

Lavatorium a basin or trough for hand-washing, next to the refectory entrance of a monastic house.

Light a part of a window divided from its other parts by mullions.

Loggia a colonnade, roofed but open on one side.

Machicolation(s) a projecting parapet with holes in the floor through which missiles could be dropped on an attacker.

Mannerism the name given to a style, familiar through much of the sixteenth century both in architecture and the arts, characterized by exaggeration for effect.

Mazer a bowl or drinking-cup, sometimes of pottery but often of silver or of wood silver-bound.

Mendicants friars who, having taken the vow of poverty, live by begging.

Minorite a Franciscan friar.

Mullion the vertical division, in stone or timber, between the elements (lights) of a window.

Murder-hole a hole, usually one of a series, in the roof of a gate passage, through which missiles might be rained on an intruder.

Nave that part of the church intended for the congregation, west of the chancel arch or crossing.

Newel in a circular stair, the central pillar round which the steps ascend; hence also 'newel stair'.

Obit a commemorative mass celebrated on the anniversary of the decease of the founder.

Observants Franciscan friars of the stricter observance, advocating a return to the primitive Rule of St Francis.

Openwork pierced work, as in display battlements or a carved balustrade.

Oratory a small chapel or place of private prayer.

Oriel a window projecting on brackets from the facade of a building.

Orillons the spurs of an arrow-head bastion.

Pediment a triangular gable, also used as an ornamental finish over a window or a door.

Pele a tower, as in pele-tower (tower-house).

Perpendicular a late medieval architectural style, peculiar to England and characterized by vertical tracery.

Piano nobile the main reception-room floor of a palace or big house, usually set over a basement and given special prominence in the facade.

Pilaster a column, decorative in purpose and projecting only a little from the wall; hence 'engaged pilaster'.

Pinnacle an ornamental cone or pyramid finishing off the top of a buttress or gable.

Pit-prison a prison chamber below floor level, usually accessible only by trap-door from above.

Plinth the projecting base of a column or wall.

Portcullis a heavy grating, descending vertically from above, intended to seal off a gate-passage.

Possessioner an endowed religious community supported by lands and other properties; hence 'possessioner houses'.

Postern a side or rear entrance, secondary to the main gate.

Prebendary a priest supported by a fixed stipend or pension (prebend).

Premonstratensians an order of canons, also known as 'white canons', founded by St Norbert in 1120 and observing the Rule of St Augustine, modified towards greater strictness.

Presbytery the eastern and most sacred part of a church, beyond the choir, holding the high altar.

Presence chamber the chamber in which a king or great lord receives his petitioners or guests.

Pulpitum the screen in a monastic church separating the choir from the nave.

Quatrefoil an ornamental arrangement of four lobes separated by cusps, usually contained within a circle.

Ravelin in artillery defences, a triangular outwork projecting forward from the main rampart.

Rebus a personal device, often a picture representing the elements of a surname.

Refectory the hall or other common chamber where monks took their meals together.

Rib a raised band – structural, decorative, or both – projecting from a vault or ceiling.

Savigniacs an order of monks (originally hermits) founded in 1105 by Vitalis of Mortain and absorbed by the Cistercians in 1147.

Screens passage the cross-passage at the lower end of the hall, beyond which are the doors to pantry, buttery and kitchen.

Solar a private chamber, reserved to the lord and his family.

Soul-mass a mass for the soul(s) of the dead.

Speres the vertical piers and panels to each side of, and framing, a movable screen at the lower end of a hall.

Strapwork flat interlaced bands, resembling straps, common in Northern Renaissance decorative schemes.

String course a horizontal external projecting moulding, often added for decorative effect.

Stucco plaster, as in a ceiling or frieze.

Sumptuary regulating expenditure: hence 'sumptuary laws'.

Tempera a paint or distemper, favoured in wall-painting because of its quick-drying properties.

Templars a military order (the Poor Knights of Christ and the Temple of Solomon) founded early in the twelfth century for the succour of pilgrims to the Holy Land; suppressed in 1312.

Terracotta unglazed pottery fired in moulds to reproduce decorative motifs.

Tertiary a member of the third (lay) order, observing a modified rule but remaining in secular life, as in 'Franciscan Tertiary'.

Tomb-chest a stone table-like coffin on which an effigy is laid.

Tracery ornamental work in the upper part of a window or of a similar space like a screen or a blind arcade.

Transepts the short arms of a cruciform church, north and south of the crossing.

Trefoil three lobes separated by cusps.

Trompe l'oeil painting intended to create an illusion, thus 'deceiving the eye'.

Tuscan the simplest of the classical orders, characterized by a plain base and unfluted column.

Undercroft a basement or ground-floor chamber, often employed as a store and supporting residential accommodation above.

Wainscot wooden panelling.

Wall-head the top of a wall, under the roof, gable or parapet.

Wall-passage a passage accommodated in the thickness of a wall.

Warming-house the common chamber, in a religious house, where the monks or nuns might warm themselves by the fire.

Wealden house a timber-framed house of a distinctive late medieval type first recognized in the Kentish Weald; rectangular, with a central hall and with chamber blocks only slightly projecting at first-floor level at each end, all under a common roof.

Weeper a carved mourning figure, often shown hooded against a tomb-chest.

Window-head the upper part of a window.

A Note on Sources

Throughout this book, both in its writing and during the original fieldwork, I have referred constantly to Nikolaus Pevsner's invaluable county guides in *The Buildings of England* series. In addition, I have used whatever guides I could obtain to individual monuments, many of which are neither described nor illustrated in comparable detail anywhere else. A fuller development of the principal arguments in this book can be found, with precise references, in earlier works of my own, including *The English Medieval Town* (1976), *Medieval England* (1978), *The Parish Churches of Medieval England* (1981), *The Castle in Medieval England and Wales* (1982), *The Abbeys and Priories of Medieval England* (1984), and *Medieval Britain from the Air* (1984).

In addition, I have made particular use of the following, to which the reader might wish to refer:

AIRS, MALCOLM, *The Making of the English Country House 1500–1640*, 1975.

ARMSTRONG, C.A.J., *England, France and Burgundy in the Fifteenth Century*, 1983 ('The piety of Cicely, Duchess of York: a study in late medieval culture').

CLARK-MAXWELL, W. G., 'The outfit for the profession of an Austin canoness at Lacock, Wilts., in the year 1395, and other memoranda', *Archaeological Journal*, 69 (1912), pp. 117–24.

COLVIN, H. M. (ed.), *The History of the King's Works, Volume IV, 1485–1660 (Part II)*, 1982.

DICKENS, A. G. (ed.), *Tudor Treatises*, Yorkshire Archaeological Society Record Series 125, 1959 (for Michael Sherbrook on the suppression of Roche Abbey).

DRURY, P. J., '"A fayre house, built by Sir Thomas Smith"; the development of Hill Hall, Essex, 1557–81', *Journal of the British Archaeological Association*, 136 (1983), pp. 98–123.

DYER, CHRISTOPHER, 'English diet in the Late Middle Ages', in *Social Relations and Ideas. Essays in Honour of R. H. Hilton* (eds T. H. Aston, P. R. Coss, Christopher Dyer and Joan Thirsk), 1983, pp. 191–216.

GIROUARD, MARK, *Robert Smythson and the Elizabethan Country House*, 1983 (revised edition, first published 1966).

HARE, J. N., 'The demesne lessees of fifteenth-century Wiltshire', *Agricultural History Review*, 29 (1981), pp. 1–15.

HEAL, FELICITY, 'The idea of hospitality in early modern England', *Past & Present*, 102 (1984), pp. 66–93.

HICKS, M. A., 'The Beauchamp Trust, 1439–87', *Bulletin of the Institute of Historical Research*, 54 (1981), pp. 135–49.

ISHAM, GYLES, 'Sir Thomas Tresham and his buildings', *Reports and Papers of the Northamptonshire Antiquarian Society*, 65:2 (1966), pp. 3–35.

JAMES, MERVYN, 'Ritual, drama and social body in the late medieval English town', *Past & Present*, 98 (1983), pp. 3–29.

JONES, S. R. and SMITH, J. T., 'The Wealden houses of Warwickshire and their significance', *Transactions and Proceedings of the Birmingham Archaeological Society*, 79 (1960–1), pp. 24–35.

KEEN, MAURICE, *Chivalry*, 1984.

MCROBERTS, DAVID, *The Heraldic Ceiling of St Machar's Cathedral, Aberdeen*, Friends of St Machar's Cathedral, Occasional Papers No. 2, 1981.

MARKS, RICHARD, 'The glazing of Fotheringhay Church and College', *Journal of the British Archaeological Association*, 131 (1978), pp. 79–109.

MARKS, RICHARD, 'The glazing of the collegiate church of the Holy Trinity, Tattershall (Lincs.): a study of late fifteenth-century glass-painting workshops', *Archaeologia*, 106 (1979), pp. 133–56.

Medieval Archaeology, 8 (1964), p. 242, 9 (1965), p. 179, and 10 (1966), pp. 177–80 (for Sopwell and Sir Richard Lee).

MORGAN, MARJORIE, 'Inventories of three small alien priories', *Journal of the British Archaeological Association*, 3 (1939), pp. 141–9.

MYERS, A. R. (ed.), *English Historical Documents, Volume IV, 1327–1485*, 1969, pp. 1146–50 (for the Peterborough inventory).

RIGOLD, S. E., 'Yardhurst, Daniel's Water', *Archaeological Journal*, 126 (1969), pp. 267–9.

SIMPSON, RICHARD, 'Sir Thomas Smith and the wall paintings at Hill Hall, Essex: scholarly theory and design in the sixteenth century', *Journal of the British Archaeological Association*, 130 (1977), pp. 1–20.

STARKEY, DAVID, 'Ightham Mote: politics and architecture in Early Tudor England', *Archaeologia*, 107 (1982), pp. 153–61.

STONE, LAWRENCE, *Family and Fortune. Studies in Aristocratic Finance in the Sixteenth and Seventeenth Centuries*, 1973 ('The building of Hatfield House 1607–1612').

SUMMERSON, JOHN, *Architecture in Britain 1530 to 1830*, 1953.

SUMMERSON, JOHN, 'The building of Theobalds, 1564–1585', *Archaeologia*, 97 (1959), pp. 107–26.

SUMMERSON, JOHN, *Inigo Jones*, 1966.

SUTTON PLACE, *The Renaissance at Sutton Place* (catalogue of an exhibition to mark the 450th anniversary of the visit of King Henry VIII to Sutton Place), Sutton Place Heritage Trust, 1983.

TANNER, N. P., *Popular Religion in Norwich with Special Reference to the Evidence of Wills*, Oxford D. Phil. thesis, 1973.

THOMSON, J. A. F., 'Piety and charity in late medieval London', *Journal of Ecclesiastical History*, 16 (1965), pp. 178–95.

VALE, M. G. A., *Piety, Charity and Literacy among the Yorkshire Gentry, 1370–1480*, Borthwick Papers 50, 1976.

WALCOTT, MACKENZIE E. C., 'Inventories of (I) St Mary's Hospital, or Maison Dieu, Dover; (II) The Benedictine Priory of St Martin New Work, Dover, for Monks; (III) The Benedictine Priory of SS Mary and Sexburga, in the Island of Sheppey, for Nuns', *Archaeologia Cantiana*, 7 (1868), pp. 272–306.

WAYMENT, HILARY, *The Stained Glass of the Church of St Mary, Fairford, Gloucestershire*, Society of Antiquaries of London, Occasional Paper (New Series) V, 1984.

WOOD-LEGH, K. L. (ed.), *A Small Household of the XVth Century, being the Account Book of Munden's Chantry, Bridport*, 1956.

Index